England under Edward I and Edward II, 1259–1327

A History of Medieval Britain

General Editor
Marjorie Chibnall

Advisory Editor
G. W. S. Barrow

This series covers the history of medieval Britain from the Roman withdrawal in the fourth century to 1529. The books combine the results of the latest scholarship and research with clear, accessible writing.

Published

Anglo-Norman England, 1066–1166
Marjorie Chibnall

Angevin England, 1154–1258
Richard Mortimer

England under Edward I and Edward II, 1259–1327
Sandra Raban

The Closing of the Middle Ages? England, 1471–1529
Richard Britnell

In preparation

The Age of Settlement, c.400–c.700
Philip Dixon

The Emergence of the English Nation, c.650–c.920
Richard Abels

Late Anglo-Saxon England, c.920–1066
Bruce R. O'Brien

Plantagenet England, 1329–1399
R. B. Dobson

Lancastrian England, 1399–1471
Simon Walker

Medieval Wales, 1050 to the Death of Owen Glyn Dwr
Ifor W. Rowlands

Scotland, 400–1100
David Dumville

Later Medieval Scotland
Norman A. T. MacDougall

England under Edward I and Edward II, 1259–1327

Sandra Raban

BLACKWELL
Publishers

First published 2000

2 4 6 8 10 9 7 5 3 1

Blackwell Publishers Ltd
108 Cowley Road
Oxford OX4 1JF
UK

Blackwell Publishers Inc.
350 Main Street
Malden, Massachusetts 02148
USA

British Library Cataloguing in Publication Data

A CIP catalogue record for this book is available from the British Library.

Library of Congress Cataloging-in-Publication Data

Raban Sandra,
    England under Edward I and Edward II/ Sandra Raban
    p. cm — (A history of medieval Britain)
    Includes bibliographical references and index.
    ISBN 0–631–20357–5 (acid-free paper) — ISBN 0–631–22320–7
    (pbk. : acid-free paper)
        1. Great Britain—History—Edward I, 1272–1307. 2. Great
    Britain—History—Edward II, 1307–1327. I. Title. II. Series.
    DA229.R33 2000
    942.03′5′092—dc21
    [B]   00-023643

Typeset in Sabon 10 on 12pt
by Kolam Information Services Pvt Ltd. Pondicherry, India
Printed in Great Britain by T.J International Ltd, Padstow, Cornwall.

This book is printed on acid-free paper

For Tony

Contents

List of Plates

List of Maps

Preface

This book has been a welcome opportunity to set out for a wider audience the understanding of late thirteenth- and early fourteenth-century England that I have gained over many years of teaching and research. It owes a lot to my pupils. Some have gone on to their own distinguished academic careers. Others were not primarily historians, but were preparing to become teachers. From them I learned how to look at the period with a beginner's eye and to communicate the interest and excitement of a very different age. Through them also, I have been influenced by the shift in history teaching away from simply imparting knowledge, which as the following pages amply demonstrate is distinctly insubstantial, towards an understanding of the nature and methodology of the discipline. Although the worst excesses of this change of emphasis have been mocked, the overall gain in subtlety of understanding about the past and ourselves cannot be underestimated.

My greatest academic debt is to Marjorie Chibnall, General Editor of the series. I was supremely fortunate to have her as my principal mentor both when I was an undergraduate and as a doctoral student. Her example of the highest scholarly standards, combined with shrewd humanity, has been an enduring inspiration to me. She has read two drafts of the text and her comments have, as ever, been most valuable. I am also greatly indebted to Paul Brand, who has read the chapters on government and politics. On this occasion, as previously, he has saved me from many solecisms. Wendy Childs and Jeremy Goldberg have also given me significant help. I thank them all. The remaining errors are mine alone.

I began this work while I was Senior Tutor at Trinity Hall and I am grateful to the College for granting the study leave which has enabled me to finish it. I have appreciated the interest and support of my colleagues and I hope that they will enjoy the result. Special thanks are due to Karen Attar for her help with the proofs and the staff of

Blackwell Publishers for their kindness and efficiency. Last, but certainly not least, I owe a tremendous debt to my husband for his unswerving support and encouragement.

S. R.

Introduction

The period between 1259 and 1327 was one of striking contrasts. For many of the peasantry, it was a time of scarcely relieved misery as pressure on land in many regions became acute and famine haunted their lives. Even the weather conspired against them as, for two or three decades, it grew colder and wetter. As in all pre-industrial societies, the need of the poorest to survive at all costs constituted an invitation to the wealthy to abuse their power and control over land, although it is debatable how far they either chose or were able to do so. These, like so many others, are questions to which we bring our own intellectual and political baggage and where understanding depends on sensitivity to the values of a society significantly different from our own.

England itself was a scene of contrasts. One might even question how far it could be conceived as an entity. Certainly it was a single realm under the crown, but even the most cursory glance at royal itineraries reveals that the north-west was largely ignored and that the north-east might have suffered the same fate but for the exigencies of war with Scotland.[1] In governmental terms, England often meant the heartland of the south-east. As late as the seventeenth century, royal authority became steadily less effective the further it stretched from the centre. In the Middle Ages, the Marcher lords and the bishop of Durham in his palatinate enjoyed virtual autonomy.

In economic and demographic terms too, central and south-eastern England was distinctively different from the more thinly settled, upland region north of the Humber/Severn line. The fourteenth-century historian Ranulf Higden, writing in Chester, commented on 'the richer soil the larger number of people, the better cities and the more suitable harbours' of the south.[2] The comparative poverty of the north became

---

[1] Hindle, *Medieval Roads*, 36–9.
[2] Taylor, *The Universal Chronicle*, 169.

even more marked as constant Scottish raids after 1297 destroyed crops and pillaged chattels. Even within regions, there were major geographical differences which could in turn affect lifestyle and culture. The isolated lives of marshland fishermen and fowlers were very different from those who had to co-operate to work the open fields. Between neighbouring settlements a difference in something as simple as inheritance customs could affect family structure and patterns of migration.

Although it has been said that limitations on internal trade could lead to starvation in one area while relative plenty existed a short distance away, this localism existed alongside a startling degree of inter-regional dependence. This is not surprising where geographically specific commodities such as the tin of Cornwall or the lead of the Peak District and Mendips are concerned. More striking is the recent suggestion that agriculture over a wide area was geared to the London food market.[3] It has long been evident that landlords with property spread over several counties operated on an integrated basis, capitalizing on different local conditions both for their own consumption and in production for the market. Nor was it only landlords who took a wider view. Tenants, far from spending their entire lives within the narrow confines of their birthplace, sometimes travelled quite long distances on seignorial business, while their siblings were often forced to leave in search of a living. There were many too whose military service or maritime occupation took them even further afield.

At royal and aristocratic level, networks extended across the Channel into France, Spain and the Low Countries. Court culture was more French than English. Mercantile activity stretched southwards as far as Italy and Spain and northwards to Scandinavia. Indeed, to a country flirting uneasily with European integration in the present day, the countless links between medieval England and the rest of Europe are a matter for thought. And, of course, England was part of that quintessentially medieval entity – Christendom. The affiliations of religious houses knew no national boundaries; an English Cistercian monastery might have a parent house in Burgundy and a daughter house in Norway. In countless ways English churchmen were linked to the Continent, while for the laity, pilgrimage provided the stimulus and opportunity for rich and poor to venture far afield. Over all this presided the Pope, whose authority, in theory at least, reached out from Rome or Avignon to the remotest parish.

---

[3] Campbell, 'Measuring the Commercialisation', 137–8; D. Keene, 'Medieval London and its Region', *London Journal*, xiv (1989), 99–111.

The paradoxes do not stop there. By the later thirteenth century, England had become literate as a society, despite the fact that most people could not read or write. Government depended on the written word, and record keeping both by the crown and many of its leading subjects had reached an impressive level of sophistication. To this day, one can with ease take a reference from a seignorial copy of a court case and find it among the public records. Year on year records of royal correspondence, revenue and court proceedings had become routine. Such expertise was not confined to government circles. Lords habitually copied, indexed and cross-referenced their title deeds and any other documents important to them. They kept court records and accounts; some had even discovered the benefits of profit and loss calculations. Even the humblest members of society had their role in the proliferation of the written record, although they had to participate at second hand.

The growth of literacy had profound implications both for them and for us. It made possible a judicial and governmental machine which operated so effectively that the rule of law prevailed for much of the time and which permitted the collection both of taxes and an unparalleled amount of information. An ordered realm fostered the growth of small market towns free from fear of spoliation and the need for costly fortifications. The ready supply of literate officials facilitated the direct interest taken by many lords in the exploitation of their land, a distinctive feature of estate management in the thirteenth and fourteenth centuries and an interlude between the *rentier* policies more commonly found at other periods.

For the church, whose learning had once been synonymous with literacy, the spread of a more restricted and pragmatic literacy presaged a less promising future. For the moment, those who wrote for their living were still by definition clerks in holy orders, but just as clerical skills were spilling over into lay society, so clerical authority too would eventually be challenged. In the meantime, society as a whole remained profoundly pious and largely unquestioning. Key ecclesiastical structures established by the eleventh century – the parish and the diocese, alongside numerous religious houses – stood firm. Here the contrast lay between superficial strength and tensions which were the first harbingers of change. The territorial acquisitiveness of churchmen was called increasingly into question, and bishops became noted more for their administrative abilities than their saintliness.

For the historian, the profusion of written evidence makes the thirteenth and fourteenth centuries a most exciting time to study. So comprehensive indeed are the surviving records of the English countryside at this time, that nineteenth- and twentieth-century Russian scholars,

curious about their more recent experience of serfdom, turned to England as an older but better-documented society. The names of Vinograd-
off, Postan and Kosminsky loom large alongside those of English
historians. There is nevertheless a contrast between the extraordinary
wealth of the available evidence and its extreme paucity on certain
topics; medieval England is refracted through the eyes of those who
have left records, and they were far from typical. Without the archives
of the crown and the largest religious houses, highly privileged and
located largely in the south-east, the harvest would be much more
meagre.

Despite the mass of surviving information, we also know very little
about the individuals who provided it. From time to time a personality
shines forth from the dry text. Such was Joan of Acre, who defied her
father Edward I by marrying 'a certain knight elegant in appearance but
poor in substance', arguing that since it was 'not ignominious or shame-
ful for a great and powerful earl to marry a poor and weak woman; in
the opposite case it is neither reprehensible nor difficult for a countess to
promote a vigorous young man'; or the bellicose Earl Warenne, who
supposedly brandished his ancient and rusty sword in the face of commissioners asking by whose warrant he held his lands.[4] Significantly,
both were royal or aristocratic figures. For the most part, the sort of
intimate personal records that begin to appear a century later are lacking. Above all, the thoughts and feelings of ordinary men and women
are almost entirely beyond reach.

It is also important to bear in mind that, even at its most copious, the
surviving evidence is full of pitfalls for an overly trusting scholar.
Attempts to cull insights through the application of statistical methods
tend to provoke the criticism that the raw data is insufficiently robust to
support reliable conclusions. Narrative accounts can be equally deceptive. Many chronicles were written long after the event. Even when
contemporary, what purport to be observations full of circumstantial
detail often turn out not to be original at all, but to echo the phrasing of
earlier writers or scripture. Skilled interpretation is required to decode
the author's meaning. Conversely, texts identified correctly as forgeries
by earlier scholars are now often thought to embody authentic tradition
and are no longer dismissed as useless. Official records are not as free of
ambiguity as they appear either. A knowledge of procedure is often
required to understand what is really going on.

Politically the period opens with civil war and ends with the
deposition and murder of the king. The decades in between witnessed
baronial unrest and numerous military campaigns. To call it a time of

---

[4] *Women of the English Nobility and Gentry*, 43; Clanchy, *From Memory*, 36.

crisis is no exaggeration. But there were also conspicuous achievements. Wales was brought decisively under English rule and, if this was not true of Scotland, there were at least some notable victories to balance the defeats. It was a key time in the evolution of Parliament even though the danger of reading too much into these early years has to be resisted. It was also a formative period in the development of the Common Law.

The period between 1259 and 1327 was not only a landmark in constitutional terms. It was also the high tide of a society about to change forever under the onslaught of recurrent plague. Whether the tide had already begun to recede before the first outbreak of Black Death in 1348–9 remains debatable. Both politically and economically, England was subjected to a severe buffeting in the second decade of the fourteenth century. The Great Famine of 1315–18, followed by cattle disease, and heavy war taxation accompanied by the incursion of the Scots into northern England, certainly took their toll. Whether this was sufficient to deal a mortal blow to faltering landlord economies and to prevent the population recovering to its former peak is unclear. The evidence is ambiguous and scholars are not at present agreed as to its meaning. The fragmented and localized nature of the records means that it may take further years of patient exploration before a convincing picture emerges. In this respect, the current volume is a report of work in progress.

Each generation writes the history that it needs. Economic considerations loom large in current thinking, while for many people politics and the constitution are at best taken for granted or at worst regarded with cynicism. Least fashionable of all in today's secular society is the church. It is not surprising therefore that much of the most exciting work in the past half century has focused on society and the economy. This accordingly forms the starting point and the context for what follows. However, to neglect the most powerful element in society and especially its religious dimension would be to take a wilfully myopic view of the past. To understand a society perhaps one tenth the size of our own, we need to appreciate the close and complex interrelationships between ruler and ruled, church and laity, town and country, and the extent to which they are often filtered through our own preconceptions. This book is an attempt to view England, from the mid-thirteenth century until the deposition of Edward II, within the wider context of English history, to show what we think we know and where we are as yet uncertain. It is necessarily both provisional and personal. Its structure, beginning with the land and its people, only then turning to the political nation, reflects a 'bottom up' rather than 'top down' approach appropriate to a society where most people lived out their lives untouched by national events.

1
The Land

England has been famously called 'an old country' in 1086; almost every place name today can be found already in Domesday Book.[1] This fact, interesting though it is, masks a much more complex picture. It is unlikely that these place names represented villages as we know them. Modern nucleated settlements seem to have evolved later, perhaps as late as the late twelfth century. Nor was Domesday England fully occupied. Large tracts of woodland had not yet been brought under the plough and marshland lay undrained. This situation gradually changed in succeeding centuries until, around the mid-thirteenth century, the limits of colonization had been reached in most places. Yet even this seemingly straightforward picture of progressive settlement is misleading. Archaeologists, profiting from road building and aerial photographs taken during recent summer droughts, now suggest that thirteenth-century England had not only been colonized, but re-colonized; that much of the land laboriously brought into use in the post-Conquest period had already been cultivated in late Iron Age and Roman Britain, before reverting to the wild. The reasons for this are not entirely clear, but probably owe something to the plague and social disruption which seem to have afflicted England in the twilight days of the Roman Empire.[2]

Although the process of colonization is complicated, it nevertheless seems reasonably clear that by the mid-thirteenth century England was fully settled. One of the most interesting developments in recent scholarship has been the way in which landscape historians in the wake of W. G. Hoskins, and palaeobotanists such as Oliver Rackham, have taught us how to interpret the physical remains we see around us. Who would have guessed, for example, that oxlips are a sign of ancient woodland or that ivy is a feature of those belonging to a more recent date? For the

[1] Lennard, *Rural England*, 1.
[2] Taylor, *Village and Farmstead*, 111, 125–8.

trained eye, there are ample signs that by the second half of the thirteenth century the hunt for land had become increasingly desperate.
Lynchets (terracing) show west-country farmers attempting to cultivate
ever higher on the moors while others were driven down to the beaches.
In the later thirteenth century, settlements were established on Dartmoor
for the first time since the Iron Age, while far away to the north similar
attempts were made to wrest a living from the inhospitable fells.[3] Even
in more fertile midland England, a low evening sun can reveal traces of
ridge and furrow which mark land brought under the plough at this
period, never to be cultivated again.

Within the broad division between the upland, pastoral areas of the
north and the gentler, more arable countryside to the south and east,
sub-regions each have their own distinctive landscape. No one could
confuse the Kentish Weald with Romney Marsh or the Vale of York with
the Yorkshire Dales. This physical identity is not simply a matter of
land, but also buildings. Northamptonshire, for example, is liberally
endowed with limestone and ironstone, so it is no accident that this
county has some of England's finest church spires and some of the most
distinctive looking striped buildings. The situation in Norfolk is very
different. Flint was the preferred substitute for stone, just as in Suffolk
and Cambridgeshire timber frames and wattle and daub characterize all
but the most important buildings. Despite the fact that modern materials
and building styles have done much to erode individual architectural
identity and modern farming methods have altered the appearance and
use of the countryside, the enduring differences between one place and
another indicate how much more intensely localized medieval England
must once have been. Within the broader regional contrasts of the open
fields of the Midlands, the enclosed fields of Kent or the summer
pastures of the Pennines and Fens, were communities which might lie
physically close to each other, but were yet divided in terms of local
topography, custom and even dialect. Ribbon development and modern
communications make it hard for us to imagine settlements isolated
from each other in the landscape, linked by little more than winding
paths through woodland or scrub where in remoter regions wolves
might still be encountered, or where, as in the Fens and along the
River Severn, malaria was endemic.

The amount of travel and communication was greater than this picture might suggest. A census conducted by the prior of Spalding in
1268–9 shows that many sons and daughters of peasants in the fenland
village of Weston had left their own community for Spalding or nearby

---

[3] Hoskins, *Making of the English Landscape*, 103–4; Rackham, *History of the Country-side*, 106–8.

villages, while a number were as far afield as Norfolk, Suffolk or even London and overseas. Among the four sons of Edric son of Robert, two remained in the village, one as the prior's reeve, a third had become a canon of Markby, while the fourth was a carpenter in London.[4] This mobility implies a good deal of traffic both within the locality and beyond on the part of quite unassuming people. So does the dense network of weekly markets and annual fairs which had been licensed by the king before 1300. The obligation to transport the lord's goods to such centres or between his properties often appears among villein labour services. Even more often, smallholders must have carried their own seasonal surpluses to market just as they do to this day in many parts of rural France. At the other end of the social scale, magnates expected to obtain specialist goods from foreign merchants at the great regional fairs. Bishop Robert Grosseteste, writing a generation before Edward I came to the throne, advised the newly widowed countess of Lincoln to 'buy your wine, wax and wardrobe at the fair of St Botulf (Boston), what you consume in Lindsey, Norfolk or in the vale of Belvoir; when in the country of Caversham and of Southampton buy at Winchester; when in Somerset at Bristol. Your robes purchase at St Ives.'[5]

That there was a major road network of sorts to service all this activity can be seen from the maps drawn by Matthew Paris, the prolific historian of the great monastery of St Albans in the mid-thirteenth century, or the later Gough map of 1360. These roads, the king's highway, were mostly broader tracks, edged by order of the second Statute of Winchester (1285) with verges 200 feet wide to frustrate those lurking 'with evil intent'. Mature trees alone were spared destruction, subject to the proviso that all undergrowth was removed.[6] Only roads surviving from Roman times were engineered in any modern sense, forming until the advent of motorways the core of our own road system. In the absence of proper drainage, both roads and fields must have been a quagmire for much of the year, so it is not surprising that medieval England witnessed a far higher proportion of waterborne traffic than is now the case. Coastal trade reached deep inland in shallow draught vessels, impeded only by weirs constructed to power mills or to create fisheries. The street plans of towns such as St Ives in Cambridgeshire or Great Yarmouth, still oriented towards the river or sea, illustrate the dominance of waterway over highway, just as the remains of quays for unloading in Cambridge bear witness to its past as a port, even though the river now sees nothing more commercial than punts for hire.

[4] BL, Add. MS 35296, fos. 221v–3v.
[5] *Walter of Henley*, 399.
[6] *Statutes of the Realm*, i, 97.

A great deal of imagination is needed to visualize the medieval countryside, so far reaching have been the changes of the Industrial Revolution followed by even more sweeping changes in the twentieth century. Perhaps the most dramatic difference between thirteenth-century England and the present day, and the most difficult to comprehend, is the contrast in the scale of settlement, particularly in towns and cities.

The extent of medieval settlement is inseparable from the size of the population, and evidence for this presents intractable problems of interpretation. No census was attempted on a countrywide basis in the Middle Ages to match the prior of Spalding's individual effort with unfree tenants and their families on his manors around Spalding. The closest equivalent to a national census are records from the first poll tax of 1377, but since they omitted those under fourteen years of age and are vitiated by an unknown degree of evasion, they cannot yield a safe estimate of total population. Nor, moreover, can one do much more than guess about the effects of the Black Death of 1348–9 and the lesser, but still severe, visitation of the 'Grey Death' in 1361–2 and further recurrences in 1369 and 1374. The nearest we can get to a comprehensive picture of medieval English population comes from Domesday Book, compiled in 1086. It embraces most of England as far north as Yorkshire, Lancashire and Cheshire, but is otherwise problematic for demographic purposes. It records tenants, but gives no details about their households. The presence of women has to be assumed because few are explicitly mentioned. It is not clear whether or not slaves had families and, if there were landless men living outside tenant households, they too are ignored. In order to estimate the total population, assumptions about all these groups are required. Much ink has been spilt as to the likely size of an eleventh-century family, let alone the number of non-family members who might be included in the household. There is nothing even of this flawed nature to hint at the size of the population c.1300. Nevertheless, although frustrating and uncertain, the evidence from these two great pools of data can tell us something. Domesday Book provides invaluable information about the distribution of population across the country not only in 1086, but so far as later more piecemeal evidence suggests, for the rest of the Middle Ages. It is not unexpected that Cornwall and the upland districts of northern England were thinly peopled, but this offers a measure of reassurance that the relatively dense population revealed in East Anglia really existed.[7] Most valuable of all, however, is the sense of scale offered by both sources. Although neither can yield an accurate absolute figure, both suggest a total population of between one and a half and three million. Even on

[7] See map 1.

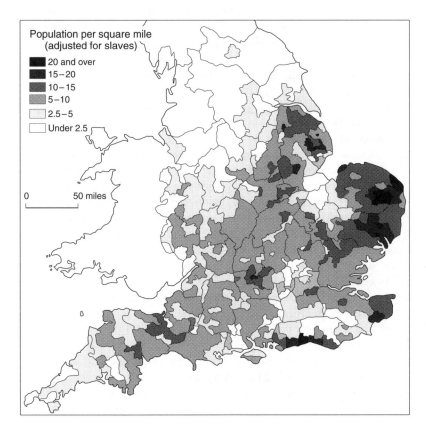

MAP 1 The population of England in Domesday Book (1086)

the wildest assumptions of underestimate, and it seems likely that current estimates may be revised upwards in due course, it is clear that medieval England sustained a tiny population by modern standards.

The questions exercising historians for most of this century are to what heights this tiny population had risen in the intervening period, whether it had reached its ceiling by 1300 and whether, under the weight of its own numbers, it had begun to fall before the Black Death. In the absence of countrywide data, conclusions have necessarily been drawn from a multiplicity of local studies, many of which rely on indirect evidence. These, taken together with Domesday Book and the 1377 poll tax returns, have led to an estimate of a maximum population of some six million in 1300. Although much of the data is susceptible of more than one interpretation, there are indications that even at this level, so modest in comparison with the current English population of forty-nine million, some parts of the country were suffering severe land hunger in the second half of the thirteenth century.

One of the few means of making a direct comparison between populations at the end of the eleventh and thirteenth centuries is by juxtaposing Domesday Book with records surviving from the hundred roll inquiry of 1279–80.[8] Although only a few midland counties are represented in the latter undertaking, and the data is much too unsystematic for statistical analysis, its structure is sufficiently similar for effective use. Haddon, in the old country of Huntingdonshire, is an agreeably straightforward example. Today there is little more than a farm close by an attractive country church set in gently rolling fields. In 1086, it was a flourishing if small community belonging to the abbot of Thorney, comprising eighteen tenants in villeinage probably scattered around the parish with their households. A church and a priest were already there. More important in terms of future population growth, the woodland which would once have covered the landscape had been almost completely cleared, leaving only one acre of underwood and very little room for later expansion. Despite this, by 1279 Haddon supported a considerably larger population. There were now twenty-three villeins, nine of whom had tenements which had been split into half the size of the more usual one virgate (twenty-four acre) holding.[9] Two free tenants had appeared during the intervening period, although one had disappeared again in the recent past. Much more significant for demographic purposes was the appearance of sixteen cottars, many of whom had half an acre of land or less. Thus, excluding the priest, the eighteen households of 1086 had risen to forty by 1279. This increase had only proved possible by fragmenting existing holdings, since there were no untapped reserves of land on which to call.[10] The names of some of these smallholders suggest that they earned their living as blacksmiths, carters or shepherds and may not therefore have been dependent for subsistence on their exiguous tenements. Nevertheless, it is likely that the demand for land in this village exceeded supply, even if crisis point had not yet been reached.

Although one always needs to be cautious about the variable inclusion or exclusion of smallholders in the records, evidence from elsewhere echoes a decline in the size of peasant tenements and indicates that land was becoming more expensive and difficult to obtain. Since custom tended to restrict the extent to which rents could be increased in

[8] See chapter 6.
[9] Virgates varied, but the inquiry recorded the size of those in Haddon.
[10] *RH*, ii, 644.

response to demand, the best index of higher land values is the increasing level of entry fines paid when new tenants entered their holdings. Whereas a mark (two-thirds of £1) or even half a mark was common earlier in the century, by its end those living in fully colonized areas such as the Vale of Taunton might find themselves having to pay anything from £10 to a massive and exceptional £80. Even in less hard-pressed parts of the country such as the east Midlands, tenants of Ramsey Abbey, who rarely paid more than £1 c.1250, were paying more than £3 after 1300.[11]

Perhaps the most dramatic evidence of land hunger was the way in which marriage patterns in Taunton were distorted by the need for young males to gain access to land. In normal circumstances, widows were not regarded as prime marriage partners, as a later study from Cambridgeshire shows, but in this community peasant custom gave second husbands a life interest in widows' dower land after their death. Consequently a pattern emerged, characterized as a marriage fugue by Sir Michael Postan, whereby young men married widows, who often predeceased them, resulting in second marriages to much younger partners.[12] One should not exaggerate the importance of this. Not all widows were old, and it was common for older men to marry younger women. Unlike today, marriage was not feasible until a man had the means to support a family and, even where land was more plentiful, this might take years to achieve. Accustomed as we are to the partnership of contemporaries chosen for love, it is easy to misconstrue a society in which the choice of a spouse was a matter of economic significance and family interest and where limited life expectancy made remarriage commonplace. We perhaps also overlook how unusual and recent our own social practices with respect to marriage are. Within living memory, in many parts of Europe and even England itself, it was common to see husbands with younger wives especially in the upper reaches of society. Moreover the idealized picture of a family comprising children living with their natural parents existed for a very short span of time between the mortality of Victorian and Edwardian times and the divorce of our own.

The institution of marriage may now be under some pressure in England, but in other cultures and in the thirteenth and fourteenth centuries it was central to society and the key to demographic change. Ready availability of land meant that it was easier to marry, and marry earlier, resulting in more families and a longer childbearing span with a

---

[11] Titow, *English Rural Society*, 73–6.
[12] Postan, *Medieval Economy and Society*, 33, and orally; J. Ravensdale, 'Population changes and the transfer of customary land on a Cambridgeshire manor in the fourteenth century', in Smith, *Land, Kinship and Life Cycle*, 202–22.

consequential growth in population. Conversely, shortage of land meant that for many people marriage was postponed or even excluded altogether. By this means, communities could unconsciously gear their numbers to available resources. Malthus, writing in the eighteenth century, had identified such a mechanism, and something of the sort probably lies behind the demographic plateau detected at High Easter and Great Waltham in Essex in the second half of the thirteenth century.[13]

Whereas evidence of this sort led Postan and his immediate followers to paint a rather bleak picture of the later thirteenth-century countryside, more recent scholarship has tended to question the extent to which the population had outgrown its resources by this date. Signs of acute stress were mostly confined to anciently settled arable parts of the country, such as the southern estates of the bishop of Winchester. Cornwall, by contrast, with a more diversified economy encompassing the extraction of surface deposits of tin, boat building and fishing, was less dependent on agriculture. Similarly, the inhabitants of marshland could exploit the ample reserves of fish and fowl as well as the reed beds and lush summer pasture; their arable requirements were minimal. Life in the pastoral uplands must always have moved to different rhythms. Limited from the start by the inhospitable nature of the terrain, these areas probably also avoided the overcrowding experienced by more favoured communities to the south.

That conditions should vary from region to region is not surprising. It has taken longer to appreciate that any question of over-population might involve more than a simple equation between man and the land. Marxist historians have been quick to point out that high rents charged by exploitative feudal landlords would reduce further the capacity of the land to support increased numbers, although there is some debate as to how far custom constrained any such inclinations. An even more important factor was the part played by commercial activity. If theories now under consideration become the new orthodoxy, it seems likely that in the later thirteenth century England had the means to increase its productivity in response to rising demand to a greater extent than was once thought.

Most estimates of medieval English population have drawn on landlords' estate records because these are the most comprehensive sources available. Urban records scarcely exist before 1300 and are not really suitable for demographic purposes. Until recently this has occasioned a curious collective amnesia among historians as to the potential role of towns in absorbing and supporting the surplus rural population. It is unfortunate that we know even less about the size of towns and the

[13] Poos, 'The rural population of Essex', 522.

proportion of the population who lived in them than about the population as a whole. Nevertheless on the positive side, it is becoming clear that town dwellers generated sufficient demand for agricultural produce to stimulate productivity to levels which were once thought unattainable by such a society.

It was long argued that the bounds of medieval agricultural technology were limited essentially to what could be achieved by the use of natural fertilizers and good husbandry. Knowledge of both was demonstrably widespread. Great attention was paid to the collection and spreading of manure and dressing the soil with marl (clay with a lime content and fertilizing properties). These activities can be found on widely scattered estates such as those of Isabella de Forz, one of the most formidable women of her day, or the intensively cultivated plots of smaller farmers such as those around Norwich.[14] Walter of Henley, writing towards the end of the thirteenth century, offered a wealth of detailed practical advice about estate management and agricultural methods. To continue with manure by way of illustration:

c 68   Your dounged (dunged) landes youe may not plowe to deepe, for doung dothe waste dounwarde.
c 69   [Now I will tell you] what advantage cometh by doung meddled (mixed) with earthe. If the doung weare (quite by itselfe) it would endure twoe or three yeares according as the land is coalde or whoate (hot). But the doung myngled with land (earthe) wille endure twice so long howbeit it wille not be so sharpe, or ranke, as the other....[15]

And so he went on, devoting altogether nine chapters to this important topic. Most of the information on which medieval landlords drew was sound, although there seems to have been some ignorance about the beneficial effects of planting legumes. This meant that the land was often fallowed to the greater benefit of weeds in the year following beans or peas, a particular irony when food was scarce.[16]

One should not underestimate the skills of medieval farmers simply because they lacked the technology and resources available to their modern successors, especially as some of these so-called advances are proving to be distinctly double-edged. The use of chemical fertilizers and plant breeding has resulted in an explosion in yields. Medieval grain yields of something like 3.5:1 look puny beside modern yields of

[14] Mate, 'Profit and productivity', 331; Campbell, 'Agricultural progress', 28–41.
[15] *Walter of Henley*, 326–9.
[16] Mate, 'Medieval agrarian practices', 27; D. L. Farmer, 'Grain yields on Westminster Abbey manors, 1271–1410', *Canadian Journal of History*, xviii (1983), 346.

200–300:1, but there were no fears about the malign effects of nitrates, pesticides and genetic engineering.[17] Antibiotics may have increased the survival rate of animals, but they also had unfortunate implications for human health. Moreover, it has been argued that good medieval practice could achieve rates comparable to those of the Agricultural Revolution or even modern hill farmers without such equivocal help.[18] There was clearly some interest in maximizing agricultural productivity in the later thirteenth century and the expertise was available to obtain good results. The ceiling in productivity depended on the extent to which such expertise was employed.

Supplies of manure were finite and marling was an expensive undertaking, involving as it did the digging of the clay, its transport and application. It has also been suggested that generations of over-cropping had resulted in soil exhaustion by the early fourteenth century. This, like so many other hypotheses, has proved difficult to substantiate. Experiments at Rothamsted Research Station indicate that while yields might fall in the absence of fertilizers, they would eventually level out, albeit at less than a quarter of the original yields.[19] Such data as we have comes inevitably from the estates of the wealthy, who probably rented out their least productive acres, concentrating resources on the best land, thereby obscuring any fall in average yields. Desperation may have driven peasants into exhausting their land. Alternatively, they may have managed to cosset this, their most precious possession, with proportionately greater supplies of manure and the one commodity they had in abundance, labour. We do not know.

However, learning from our academic cousins, the historical geographers with their theoretical models, we can now explain how market demand might have spurred medieval farmers into using their skills in such a way that more was wrung from the soil than would otherwise have been the case. Land use itself was altered, with beneficial effects on productivity, when it became economic to exploit marginal land, such as the Norfolk breckland, as demand drove prices to a high enough level. Thus, what was once seen as a symptom of land hunger, might now be interpreted as an enterprising response to the market. Crops appear to have been geared to the market in a highly specific way, particularly in the London hinterland, where oats, for example, were grown on a commercial scale to feed the animals bearing men and goods to and from the capital. The Feeding the City project and work on regional

[17] Jordan, *The Great Famine*, 25.

[18] M. J. Stephenson, 'Sheep farming in England, 1100–1500: a study in agricultural productivity', unpublished Cambridge PhD thesis (1987), 37, 46.

[19] Postan, *Medieval Economy and Society*, 70.

centres such as Norwich, are steadily illuminating the close and productive relationship between town and countryside.[20]

How far should these new insights modify the notion that England
was in some demographic difficulty by the later thirteenth century?
Over-population is a matter of definition. By present standards, the
countryside was virtually empty. The issue is not one of physical overcrowding, but whether there was sufficient food to support life on a day
to day basis. Here the voice of contemporaries may help to gauge
whether or not famine stalked the land. Among the grievances of the
Petition of the Barons in 1258 reference was made to the 'many men
coming, on account of the present famine, from different parts of the
land, and making their way through the different counties, die of hunger
and want'.[21] Other sources bear witness that it had been an appalling
year. Matthew Paris notes the famine and recounts how Richard, the
king's brother, had arranged for some fifty large ships to import emer-
gency supplies of grain. That there were further disaster years in the
later thirteenth century can be inferred from other chroniclers' graphic
accounts of storms, followed by flooding of biblical proportions, or
extremes of heat and cold. However, they make surprisingly little reference to hardship, let alone starvation. Perhaps the authors were too
insulated from the harsher realities of life, closeted safely within the
walls of religious houses. For them it was random catastrophes such as
the collapse of London Bridge in the bitter winter of 1281, or the high
prices caused by scarcity that seemed most noteworthy.[22] It could be
argued that any under-developed society, reliant on agriculture, would
be vulnerable to intermittent harvest failure. If so, it is not to the
extremes of harvest failure that we should look to assess the precariousness of life by the later thirteenth century, but to sources which show
what happened in response to the more limited harvest fluctuations.
Thus, evidence from the estates of the bishop of Winchester suggesting
extreme harvest sensitivity is of greater significance than what happened
in times of serious famine. Heriot payments, death duties owed by
unfree tenants to their lord, indicate that the poorest tenants might die
even in years of moderate harvest failure. If this were the case, then the
effects on the landless can only be imagined.[23]

[20] Bailey, 'The concept of the margin', 1–15; Campbell, 'Measuring the commercialisation', in Britnell and Campbell, *A Commercialising Economy*, 136–9; J. A. Galloway, D.
Keene and M. Murphy, 'Fuelling the city: production and distribution of firewood and fuel
in London's region, 1290–1400', *EcHR*, xlix (1996), 447.
[21] *Documents of the Baronial Movement*, 84–5.
[22] *Chron Majora*, v, 673; *Gervase of Canterbury*, ii, 272; *Annales Monastici*, iii, 280,
287, 338, 370, 391.
[23] Postan and Titow, 'Heriots and prices', 172–3.

Whether England as a whole was poised on the verge of crisis by the end of the thirteenth century is a matter of judgement. In places it seems unlikely and in the past we have probably underestimated the capacity of society at this date to respond to the demands of demographic growth. However, although revisionism is a fashionable academic pastime, we should not go to the opposite extreme. Despite being more commercially oriented than was once thought, the integrated market of today was worlds away. In 1258, the Dunstable annalist tells us that while famine had driven the price of a quarter of wheat up to twenty shillings in Northampton, in Bedford it cost seventeen shillings, while in Dunstable itself, it could be purchased for a mark.[24] It was possible to starve to death through ignorance that food was available close by as well as for lack of the means to buy it. In areas where land was known to be under population pressure, the evidence suggests overwhelmingly that life had become very uncertain.

If there is room for debate about conditions in the late thirteenth century, there can be no doubting the scale and seriousness of the famine which struck the whole of northern Europe in the second decade of the fourteenth century.[25] On this occasion, chroniclers were shaken out of their detachment to describe the sufferings of ordinary people following a series of disasters beginning with the harvest failure of 1315. In that year and the following, torrential rain drenched much of the country ruining all but the hardiest crops. The chronicle associated with John de Trokelowe, another monk of St Albans, is unusually explicit in recounting the effects of eating rotten food: high fever and '*pestis gutturuosa*.'[26] He also told harrowing tales of parents furtively eating their children alive. Stories of cannibalism are echoed in other chronicles, but the debt of these writers to biblical models makes it unwise to take them literally. They were more probably employing metaphor in their effort to convey the unprecedented horror of the crisis.[27]

As if things were not bad enough, harvest failure in 1315 and 1316, and again in 1321, was matched by devastating epidemics among both the human and animal population. Murrain, as animal disease was generically known at the time, raged among sheep in the same years, only to be succeeded between 1319 and 1321 by an even more catastrophic cattle epidemic, probably rinderpest. The study of genetics is beginning to explain the apparently random behaviour of disease. The

---

[24] *Annales Monastici*, iii, 208.

[25] The following account of the Great Famine draws on Kershaw, 'The Great Famine', 88ff; and Jordan, *The Great Famine*, pt 1.

[26] *Trokelowe*, 92–5.

[27] J. Marvin, 'Cannibalism as an aspect of famine in two English chronicles', in M. Carlin and J. T. Rosenthal (eds), *Food and Eating in Medieval Europe*, London, 1998, 73–86.

scab afflicting sheep flocks from the 1270s seems to have been a new if not wholly unprecedented phenomenon.[28] The death of plough oxen hit harder than anything else, since their replacement was not a matter which could be achieved in a single season. Without the resources to buy in new stock fetching premium prices, the rebuilding of a herd could take years. In the meantime, the land lay untilled.

Horrors recounted by the chroniclers are given substance by sober figures recording reduced yields and livestock mortality in the account rolls of great estates. Nothing of this sort exists to show the impact on peasant farmers, but an unusually large number of holdings changed hands at this date, as if tenants were forced to sell up in order to survive at all. Manor court rolls show a high incidence of food theft in communities that were so small and tightly knit, that, in normal circumstances, theft was a far less common occurrence than in our own. It is also to court rolls that we look to form some notion of the death rate. Heriot payments on the Winchester manors suggest that about seventeen per cent of tenants died. Court rolls for Halesowen in Worcestershire point to a similar figure, with perhaps fifteen per cent of the resident males dying.[29] No doubt some of these victims, especially among the very young and the elderly, would have died anyway. High infant mortality and an average life expectancy which may not have exceeded the mid-thirties, made death a familiar visitor. It is also clear that the gravity of the crisis varied from place to place. Whereas the situation in larger towns was so bad that bodies were said to litter the streets, the west country seems to have escaped lightly. Landlords in east Kent and coastal Sussex, seem to have recovered swiftly from the worst of the crisis.[30] Those lucky enough to bring in a good harvest or escape the murrain no doubt grew rich on the proceeds. Likewise, those with money to lend found customers beating a path to their door and bargains to be had with the profits. On balance, however, the years between 1315 and 1322 must have been among the grimmest on record and, but for the almost unimaginable catastrophe of the Black Death, might loom larger in common knowledge.

Human agency in the form of the Scottish wars took a further toll through taxation, purveyance and, most seriously of all for those counties affected, the devastation caused by Scottish raids. These were not new problems. So far as taxation was concerned, the situation had been worse towards the end of Edward I's reign, when there were levies in

[28] S. Jones, *The Language of the Genes*, London, 1993, ch. 11: Stephenson, 'Wool yields', 381; Kershaw, 'The Great Famine', 108–11.

[29] Postan and Titow, 'Heriots and prices', 169; Razi, *Life*, 39–40.

[30] Mate, 'Agrarian economy', 88–9.

each of the four years between 1294 and 1297. By comparison, those of the famine period were fewer and lower. Nevertheless, they were the heaviest of Edward II's reign and, occurring in both 1315 and 1316, could not have come at a worse time. Purveyance (also known as prises), the compulsory purchase of victuals and transport for the king's use, had been a fierce bone of contention in the last decade of Edward I's reign. It now greatly intensified the suffering caused by crop failure. Those forced to surrender their goods were rarely paid in cash and often not at all. If they were lucky enough to be given a receipt in the form of a notched wooden tally stick, they found it hard to collect their debts. The damage extended beyond producers, since the removal of supplies led to prices rising still further on the open market. Taxation and purveyance, hard enough in themselves, were rendered worse by the way in which they were collected. Royal officials often creamed off a profit for themselves, making the burden on those who paid even heavier. Estate accounts show how the wealthy often bribed their way out of making a fair contribution, leaving the peasantry to bear the brunt of the exactions. Inevitably, the counties worst hit by purveyance were those closest to the fighting or along good supply routes. The cereal-growing regions of eastern England as far south as Cambridgeshire and Essex were often called upon, and these were areas where arable land was already inadequate to support the population.[31]

Worst hit of all was northern England. Raiding was used by Robert Bruce as a deliberate weapon to force Edward II to the negotiating table. Between the battle of Bannockburn in 1314 and the thirteen-year truce agreed in 1323, there was a series of raids penetrating ever more deeply into the realm. Typically, the Scots swept southwards on the eastern side of the Pennines, seizing cattle and valuables, trampling crops and burning buildings before crossing to the west and making their way back home. By 1316 Yorkshire itself was vulnerable. Estate records are eloquent as to the scale of the destruction. At Bamburgh in Northumberland, the marauders in 1316 even dug up the artificial warren in which rabbits were bred. The richest were again sometimes able to buy their way out of trouble. Durham Cathedral Priory paid tribute and escaped attack until 1322, when it fell victim to the savage onslaught known as 'the burning of the bishopric'. Peasants had little option other than to flee, taking their livestock with them. The last straw for those who had survived the worst of the famine must have been the invasion of autumn 1319, when barns brimming with the first good harvest for years were razed to the ground.[32]

---

[31] Maddicott, 'English peasantry', 6–32; Prestwich, *War, Politics and Finance*, 179.
[32] McNamee, *Wars of the Bruces*, 72–104.

Just as we find it impossible to make an accurate estimate of mortality, so the extent to which the population rallied after all these shocks has proved elusive. Opinions and sources vary. In 1326, tenants at Easingwold, ten miles north of York, were recorded as unable to pay their farm (rent) because thirty-one of them had either been killed in battle or by Scottish raiders. Of those remaining, seventeen were impoverished, seven had fled and a further seventeen been reduced to begging. There was no quick recovery there. Further north things were worse still. What had once been a clearly defined border between England and Scotland, in this period became a permanent tract of wasteland.[33] These were extreme cases. Elsewhere one might anticipate an improvement in living conditions as earlier inheritance was made possible by the death of the elderly and infirm. This in turn would permit earlier marriage, leading to a baby boom and full recovery in the longer term. Some such recovery in the population seems to have taken place at Halesowen and Brigstock in Northamptonshire by the 1330s and 1340s, but it is not evident on the Essex manors of Great Waltham and High Easter, where the number of males over the age of twelve continued to decline. The tax records of 1341 no doubt exaggerate the seriousness of rural distress as local communities sought to minimize their liability, but they reveal a picture of widespread desolation and depopulation which is geographically and politically consistent enough to carry some conviction. In the North Riding of Yorkshire and in Lancashire land was said to be abandoned because of lack of plough beasts and Scottish incursions. In Sussex and Cambridgeshire vast acreages of marshland were under water. More generally, the poverty of the people or the soil were mentioned frequently, along with murrain.[34] The scattered and conflicting nature of the evidence is such that the jury is still out on whether or how far the population as a whole was significantly below the pre-famine level on the eve of the Black Death. Some places probably escaped the crises virtually unscathed. Others, given time, would recover or even benefit from lower numbers. Only the far north is likely to have suffered lasting harm. Whatever the ultimate outcome, it was too soon at the time of Edward III's accession in 1327 for much real recovery to be evident.

The catalogue of disasters striking England after 1250 may not have been just a reflection of the vulnerability of a land-hungry populace in the face of the normal range of weather fluctuations. We are beginning to think that they heralded the first signs of a shift in the weather

[33] Ibid., 11, 115.
[34] Baker, 'Nonarum Inquisitiones', 522–30.

pattern.[35] Climatic history has grown greatly in sophistication in recent decades and gained added importance because of the threat of global warming. To the observations of chroniclers, can now be added results from dendrochronology (dating from tree rings), pollen counts and analysis of the ice cap, each contributing to a greater understanding of long-term change. The cyclical nature of weather patterns has been appreciated for many years. It is a commonplace that the Thames froze on a regular basis in Stuart times, while across the North Sea, skaters often formed the inspiration for early seventeenth-century Dutch painters. It seems likely that, beginning in the mid-thirteenth century and following a period of relatively warm weather, England experienced a period of exceptional storminess perhaps associated with a rapid cooling of the Arctic. In 1309, during an exceptionally hard winter, the Thames froze so solidly that fires could be safely lit on the ice.[36] Violent storms led to inundations of the sea on the south and east coasts, effectively ruining the coastal towns of Winchelsea and Dunwich and causing widespread damage elsewhere. Cooler, wetter conditions also led to the retreat of cultivation from higher ground. Quite small reductions in average temperature could shorten the growing season, with disastrous consequences for grain harvests.

England by the early fourteenth century was not a good place to be unless you were both rich and lucky. Of no other time could Hobbes' famous aphorism that the life of man was 'solitary, poor, nasty, brutish and short' seem more justified, as one thinks of peasants attempting to survive on holdings that were often inadequate and where vagaries of weather or sickness might eliminate the already slim chance of winning through to the next year. Only in the absence of solitariness does this society score. Living conditions were cramped and the support of kin and community vital for survival. Yet for all this, England was a relatively fertile country with a higher ratio of cultivable land than many of its continental neighbours. In terms of resources, chiefly tin and wool, it was considered rich. Nonetheless, taking the available evidence, such as it is with all its imperfections and ambiguities, it seems inescapable that the total environment, if not necessarily the land itself, had deteriorated since the mid-thirteenth century. The cataclysm of the Black Death, when it struck in 1348, assailed a country and people already well accustomed to misfortune.

[35] The following account of the medieval climate draws on Lamb, *Climate History*, 186–7; Bailey, '*Per impetum maris*', 184–208; Parry, *Climatic Change*, 79, 97–8.
[36] Nightingale, *Medieval Mercantile Community*, 124.

2

The People: Rural Society

Early medieval theorists took a severely functional view of society, dividing it into *oratores, bellatores, laboratores*: those who prayed, those who fought and those who worked. By the thirteenth century, this simple categorization needed expanding to encompass the growing body of individuals who lived by commerce or their professional skills. Yet although different from our accustomed nineteenth-century class-based analysis, it remains a useful and less anachronistic broad framework within which to examine the sort of people who inhabited the increasingly troubled country described in the last chapter.

Those who suffered the worst of these difficult conditions were inevitably the labourers – 'those who worked' the poorest members of society. They were by far the most numerous group in medieval England, although it is impossible to put a figure on them. They are also the people about whom we know the least. For the most part they were country dwellers, literally peasants (*paysans*), although the distinction between rural craftsmen and those who earned their living as artisans in towns was often blurred. They also varied widely as to their means and status.

The growing role of the royal courts in the late twelfth and early thirteenth centuries had made it increasingly necessary to distinguish between peasants who were legally free, and therefore within their jurisdiction, and those who were not. This was no easy feat in a country which had developed myriad forms of land tenure and custom, each suited to local circumstances. The complexity of the situation is illustrated by the Oxfordshire returns to the 1279–80 hundredal inquiry. Peasant tenants were described in more than a dozen different ways, some reflecting the size of their holdings, others the terms on which they held them or the nature of their obligations, while the remainder were designated according to their status. Interestingly, the one term never used was the generic 'peasant'. The commonest categories in Oxfordshire, as elsewhere in the midland countries, were those of villeins, freemen and smallholders, most frequently called cottars. On some estates there were echoes of the past, with *servi* descended from pre-Conquest slaves. Sochmen, free or unfree, were another ancient survival recalling their ancestors' subordination to the jurisdiction of a lord. In Bedfordshire and Buckinghamshire, there were signs of the future, where *cyrographii* or *firmarii* heralded the growing importance of leases held for life or terms of years.[1] Some of these labels represented fine shades of distinction or the preferred local designation, others carried significant implications for the individuals concerned.

Essentially free land was held by charter (written title) and alienable during the lifetime of the tenant, whereas unfree holdings were the property of the lord to be disposed according to his wishes, subject only to the constraints imposed by custom. Since freedom could attach either to land or blood, problems might arise where unfree tenants acquired free land or *vice versa*. The abbot of Peterborough, in the late thirteenth century, alert to the danger of unfree peasants who had purchased small parcels of newly colonized free land and who might thereby challenge their servile status, took the decisive step of collecting all their charters and registering their tenure on his court rolls, the appropriate procedure for the transfer of unfree tenements. He was not alone in taking such action and he and other lords were able to do this because in law unfree tenants, together with their families, chattels and land, belonged absolutely to their lord. Hence anything they bought was also the lord's property.[2]

The situation, although starkly defined in law, was far less clear cut in practice. By the later thirteenth century, there were well-established payments which provided unfree peasants with much the same security of tenure and freedom of action as those who were free, albeit at a price. Heritability had become the norm, subject to a heriot payment on death or retirement – the best beast where a tenant was rich enough to have one, otherwise a money payment – and an entry fine paid by the incoming heir. Other payments in effect licensed the peasant's choice of marriage partner for daughters, schooling for children, sale of live-stock or absence from the manor. In each case, the rationale was com-pensation to lords for some diminution in the value of their property; an educated peasant, for example, might be lost to the land, or the children of a peasant woman might belong to another lord should she marry outside the manor. Given the high level of population by the later thirteenth century, such consequences were not unduly injurious to the

---

[1] *RH*, ii, 336a, 344a, 346a, 688ff.
[2] King, *Peterborough Abbey*, ch. 6; Raban, *Mortmain Legislation*, 31–3.

lord. Thus the interests of both parties were accommodated by compromise, although the obligation to pay represented an additional disability for the unfree.

The most onerous burden laid on many unfree peasants was the payment of rent in the form of labour services. However, these were by no means universal or restricted to the unfree. The abbot of Thorney's free peasants in Huntingdonshire were often required to turn out to help in harvesting. This reflected the heavy labour obligations characteristic of this part of the country. At Haddon, their unfree counterparts owed the abbot labour services on some 150 days in the year, often with one or more helper. Only during the period of Christmas festivities coinciding with the dead time in the agricultural cycle was there any break.[3] Moreover, the lord was able to commandeer the labour of his unfree tenants at precisely those seasons when they most needed to work on their own land and, at peak periods, family labour was requisitioned too. In theory at least, lordship bore heavily on the unfree, but labour services too might be commuted for a cash payment at the lord's will. Where such arrangements were not forthcoming, peasants sometimes preferred to absent themselves and pay the consequent fine. The incidence and weight of labour services also varied greatly from region to region and between estates within regions. Indeed, they were largely irrelevant in the upland pastoral areas of the north and west since they chiefly involved the heavy work associated with arable agriculture.

How far peasants were disadvantaged by lack of freedom is a nice judgement, not least because lords often prevented villein tenements from fragmenting under the pressure of land hunger into units too small to support a family, with the result that they were often larger than those of less regulated freeholders. There is also some evidence that lords treated their own unfree tenants preferentially with regard to entry fines.[4]

The extent to which lords exploited their power over unfree tenants has been a matter of some debate, not least because historians have come to the question with their own ideological assumptions. The concept of freedom is itself problematic. It is hard to know how far free status was valued for its own sake as opposed to freedom from specific restraints or obligations. Villeinage does not appear to have carried a stigma comparable to that of belonging to the lowest castes in Hindu society, although there was the famous case of a Worcestershire freeman who, in 1293, drowned himself in the Severn rather than compromise his status by accepting the villein tenement that was being forced upon

---

[3] *RH*, ii, 644.
[4] Hatcher, 'English serfdom', 18.

him.[5] Intermarriage between free and unfree occurred sufficiently often for there to be a specific common law action to clarify the status of resulting descendants. Villeins appear as often as freemen among village jurors. Relatively few unfree peasants sought manumission, although this too was on offer in return for compensatory payment. When they did seek to become free, it was usually because they planned ordination or some other occupation in which servile status was a bar or inconvenience, rather than as a matter of abstract principle. In a society where notions of good lordship carried weight, no doubt much depended on the extent to which lords felt bound by them. What remains unclear is how far the unscrupulous were able to abuse their power, particularly as peasants became ever more hungry and desperate for land.

Seignorial authority, particularly on larger estates, was exercised at a distance through the manorial court. Court rolls which survive in quantity from the 1270s show the extent to which lords were in the hands of the local community. Merton College, Oxford, for example, found it extremely hard to remove unsatisfactory tenants or collect chevage (payment to leave) from absentee villeins. Nor did the college succeed in imposing additional carrying services.[6] It seems clear that custom offered some protection to the tenant, making it difficult for lords to impose outright increases in rents whether for free or unfree land. While a major boon for the peasantry, this was a real problem for lords, since a combination of inflation, particularly at the turn of the twelfth and thirteenth centuries, and higher land values as a result of rising demand, meant that rents established in the distant past were often well below the market rate by the later thirteenth century. That some lords responded with arbitrary increases in labour services we know from challenges in the king's courts and the violent reaction which sometimes occurred if a legal solution was not forthcoming. At Beoley in Worcestershire in 1278, the peasantry were provoked into an assault on the abbot of Halesowen himself and his retinue.[7]

Monastic landlords have often been seen as particularly oppressive in this context, reinforcing their economic muscle with spiritual authority. The Cistercians of Vale Royal in Cheshire were certainly ruthless. They exploited their villein tenants, seizing their goods and evicting them when they sought redress. There were some extenuating circumstances; the monks had been in financial difficulties almost from the date of the abbey's foundation by Edward I in 1270. Originating in an oath taken

---

[5] Hilton, 'Peasant movements', 90.

[6] R. Evans, 'Merton College's control of its tenants at Thorncroft, 1270–1349', in Razi and Smith, *Medieval Society and the Manor Court*, 241–50.

[7] Hilton, 'Peasant movements', 83; *idem, Medieval Society*, 159–61.

when he was in fear of shipwreck, the king's commitment did not prove enduring. All work was halted on his orders in 1290, leaving the buildings half completed and the enterprise underfunded.[8] Although few of the greater ecclesiastical houses behaved so badly, or were so economically crippled, many were conservative in their attitudes and could be both restrictive and provocative in refusing to acknowledge changing circumstances. It is no accident that the gatehouse of the abbey at Bury St Edmunds is more appropriate to a castle than a monastery. The intransigent attitude of the monks to the town which had grown up around the abbey resulted in major revolt in 1327. Before the situation had been brought under control, the abbey had been sacked and looted and the abbot subjected to humiliating personal attack and imprisonment. The erection of the gatehouse was both the price of pardon and a guarantee of protection against future insurrection.[9] Not all wealthy houses were imbued with the assertiveness of Vale Royal or the reactionary instincts of Bury St Edmunds. Some tackled the problems thrown up by economic change with the sort of quiet manoeuvre attempted by the abbot of Ramsey on his manor at Elton in Huntingdonshire. He decided to switch to cheap hired labour and take a cash rent instead of labour services from his villeins in order to benefit from the rising value of land. His reasoning was faultless; unfortunately the richer villeins promptly bribed his reeve not to implement the new policy. The reeve, himself a villein, no doubt preferred to oblige those among whom he lived rather than carry out his lord's wishes and suffer the resulting opprobrium.[10] For a rich ecclesiastical lord, distant from the estate in question, measures which might result in a truculent labour force could be more trouble than they were worth and hard to implement.

Great earls like Gilbert de Clare, who was killed at Bannockburn in 1314, were perhaps more physically intimidating. He managed to impose new services on his villeins at Thornbury in Gloucestershire in the early fourteenth century despite the twin impediments of distance and manorial custom.[11] Smaller, less powerful local lords may have been more intimidating still. We know very little about them, but that little suggests that knightly families sometimes behaved in an even more arbitrary fashion than great lords. Constrained by the need to raise an

[8] VCH Cheshire, iii, 156–9; M. Prestwich, 'The piety of Edward I', in W. M. Ormrod (ed.), England in the Thirteenth Century, Grantham, 1985, 120.

[9] VCH Suffolk, ii, 62–3.

[10] Select Pleas, 95.

[11] P. Franklin, 'Politics in manor court rolls: the tactics, social composition and aims of a pre-1381 peasant movement', in Razi and Smith, Medieval Society and the Manor Court, 171.

adequate income from their scant holdings, they were able to act more effectively by virtue of their residence in the locality. This is certainly the implication behind the high return from life leases which had replaced older forms of tenure on some small Huntingdonshire estates close to Elton.[12]

However, while there are cases of lords abusing their power, the more comprehensive picture afforded by the returns to the 1279–80 hundredal inquiry suggests that for many peasants, free or unfree, the harsh conditions of the later thirteenth century were mitigated by low rents. It is also important to remember that landlord demands were not necessarily the only, or even the most important determinant of peasant well-being. Size of holding also entered the equation; a substantial tenement carrying a heavy rent obligation might support a family more readily than a lightly burdened but tiny freeholding. In the final analysis, all were at the mercy of chance and the elements. Countless family tragedies lie behind the sudden surge in the sale of smallholdings seen during the famine years.[13] Childlessness or the death of a spouse could equally spell disaster, leaving no one to tend the land or care for the elderly. Estate surveys are littered with widows eking out an existence on cottage holdings. These were the women whose predicament in a later, equally cruel age sometimes gave rise to guilt-induced accusations of witchcraft.[14]

Rural poverty was not the monopoly of smallholders. Those with no land at all, who consequently needed to seek some means of subsistence, faced the most uncertain life of all. Where family funds permitted, younger sons might be found an apprenticeship or set to their books in the hope of a career in the church or administration. However, as in less developed countries today, both countryside and town were filled with those who could only find seasonal employment or who lived by their wits. The fortunate might find regular work within the family or as a member of the lord's household or agricultural labour force. Even this was no guarantee of security; during the famine, hard-pressed landlords laid off their servants, leaving them to join the ranks of the desperate and starving. Bolton Priory in the Yorkshire Dales was reduced to halving its labour force, while a chronicler recounted how 'those who were accustomed to supporting themselves and their dependants in a suitable manner travelled along streets and through places as beggars'.[15] Those lucky enough to scrape a living might still find that marriage was

---

[12] Raban, 'Landlord return', 29–30.

[13] See chapter 1.

[14] A. MacFarlane, *Witchcraft in Tudor and Stuart England: A Regional and Comparative Study*, 2nd edn, London, 1999, 163–4.

[15] Kershaw, 'The Great Famine', 93–4.

out of the question unless they secured the means to provide for a family. Many died without ever doing so, but such a prospect was never entirely beyond hope. In a society where life was precarious, many would sooner or later fall heir to a family holding through the death of a parent or sibling. Circumstances for an individual could change substantially during the course of a lifetime. Once on the tenurial ladder, smallholders could gradually build up larger tenements by piecemeal acquisitions perhaps to support a growing family, only to shed them again as their requirements diminished in old age. Without belittling the undoubted misery of the poorest members of society, their plight must be seen in perspective. As in so many other instances, appearances could be deceptive; limited resources often owed as much to youth or age as to membership of any fixed stratum in the economic hierarchy.

If the boundaries between rich and poor peasants were often blurred, so too were those between the more prosperous peasantry and lesser knightly families. Whereas knighthood at the time of the Norman Conquest had entailed fighting, by the thirteenth century those who held land in return for military service contributed towards the cost of soldiers through the payment of scutage rather than necessarily fighting themselves. Consequently, knighthood came to be determined by wealth rather than military capability. This change was accompanied by a growing concern about the shortage of knights both for the defence of the realm and their crucial role in local government. From time to time, the crown attempted to coerce those with land worth £20 a year into assuming knightly status. Freeholders who had accumulated sizeable holdings, perhaps by serving as bailiff or acting in some other capacity for their lord, were among those most likely to prove eligible.

At the other extreme, many lesser knights provided with very small fees in the post-Conquest period, had fallen on hard times in the late twelfth century. Others followed them during the thirteenth century. Contemporaries blamed greedy magnates for preying on those who no longer had the means to support a way of life which had become more elaborate and therefore more expensive. For some, accidents of politics, notably supporting the losing side at the Battle of Evesham in 1265, dealt a final blow. Guilty and innocent alike were hit in the scramble for spoils in the wake of the royal victory. More than a thousand estates changed hands countrywide. Gilbert de Clare and his men alone seized some 164 manors scattered over twenty-five counties. The king succeeded in recovering them, but instead of restoring them to their former tenants, they were granted to a fairly small circle of his followers. It speedily became clear that such a massive transfer of property had implications both for future peace and local government, which depended on knightly participation. The solution was the Dictum of

Kenilworth of 1266, by which the Disinherited as they came to be known, were allowed to buy back their estates from the king's grantees at rates varying from one to seven times their annual value. This enabled many to recover their patrimony, but saddled them with huge and unforeseen debts.[16] Those with money to invest found the next few years a time for rich pickings.

Each knightly failure must have resonated uncomfortably in county society, leading to a rising chorus of alarm. What may not have been appreciated was the underlying rhythm of rise and fall whereby such families built up their fortunes through marriage and service or lost them through debt or failure of the male line. For every knight such as Geoffrey of Southorpe, the Peterborough Abbey knight whose struggle against financial disaster culminated in near destitute retreat to the house of the Carmelite friars at Stamford, there were others such as Geoffrey de Langley who forged a successful career in royal service, amassing estates worth at least £200 per annum in Warwickshire and Gloucestershire by his death in 1274.[17] What at the time looked like rapacity, on closer inspection often seems to have been larger landlords buying back manors from their impoverished knightly tenants either as an act of good lordship or to maintain control over what was happening on their own estates. Fellow knightly families building up their holdings were more genuinely predatory, if only because they were necessarily encroaching on the estates of others rather than recovering possession of their own. For similar reasons, the most genuinely rapacious magnate was probably Queen Eleanor of Castile because, as an outsider with heavy expenses and no English inheritance or patronage network on which to draw, she had more need than most to accumulate land to establish her position. Rishanger's anodyne obituary written forty years after her death: 'Truly she was a devout woman, gentle and merciful, a friend to all Englishmen, and indeed a pillar of the realm' contrasts markedly with the dry contemporary observation that she 'acquired many splendid manors' and the archbishop of Canterbury's more forthright admonition that her acquisition of estates mortgaged to the Jews and the exploitation of her tenants were leading to 'public outcry and gossip'.[18]

It is with thirteenth- and fourteenth-century knights, those who in traditional terms 'fought', that individuals at last begin to emerge into historical visibility. One of the two estate books of the Hotot family,

---

[16] Knowles, 'The resettlement of England', 25–30; Raban, 'The land market and the aristocracy', 254–5.

[17] King, *Peterborough Abbey*, 43–4; Coss, 'Sir Geoffrey de Langley', 167–8.

[18] D. Parsons, *Eleanor of Castile*, 9, 25; Raban, 'The land market and the aristocracy', 257–9.

which held property in Northamptonshire and Bedfordshire, has survived. Scruffily written in part at least by Thomas Hotot (d. c.1278) himself in a mixture of formal book hand and the court hand employed by those who used writing in their day-to-day business, it records mid-thirteenth century land acquisitions and obligations, together with anything else he deemed to be important. A similar compilation of 1322, the creation of Henry de Bray, lord of Harleston also in Northamptonshire and steward to the abbey of St Andrew's, Northampton, is also extant. As well as the inevitable details about property, there is a good deal of incidental material about his family connections and relations with his various lords.[19] These families showed a keen interest in their estates and considerable enterprise in adding to them. It was to men such as these that Walter of Henley addressed his treatise on husbandry.

To judge from the expenses he recorded, Henry de Bray was a vigorous builder. He appears to have entirely reconstructed his house and its precincts in 1289, paying £12 exclusive of the cost of stone and timber beams for a new hall and north chamber.[20] Although Henry de Bray's hall no longer exists, Longthorpe Tower just outside Peterborough provides a rare glimpse of the conditions in which a peasant family prospering into minor knightly status lived. The structure consists of a house probably begun in the late thirteenth century, dominated by a solid two-story tower added c.1300 by Robert of Thorpe. It is hard to imagine what life must have been like in this essentially defensive building. Rooms were less than five metres square within the thick stone walls. Nevertheless, the riot of wall paintings dating from c.1330, which still remain in the Great Chamber, indicate a rich visual environment (see plate 1). Interestingly so, indeed. The sophistication of the imagery, even if not echoed in the workmanship, is surprising in the home of a family so recently counted among freeholders. Like Henry de Bray, Robert of Thorpe made his mark through service, as steward to the abbot of Peterborough, and perhaps this connection accounts for the ambitious subject matter.

The paintings tell us something about the mental world of the occupants. The subjects are varied, ranging from biblical stories to the seven ages of man and the wheel of senses, interspersed with portraits of birds found in the neighbourhood. There is also a good example of the story of *The Three Living and the Three Dead*, although it is too damaged to reproduce. More commonly found on the walls of country churches in England and France in association, in later centuries, with the *Dance of Death* cycle, it shows three young huntsmen sharply confronted by the

---

[19] *Hotot estate book*, 3ff; *Henry de Bray, Passim*.
[20] *Henry de Bray*, xxiv–xxvi.

PLATE 1   A wall painting showing the wheel of senses, *c.*1330, in Longthorpe
Tower, near Peterborough

vanity of riches and the lurking presence of death in the form of three
skeletons. In their varied themes, these paintings evoke life in all its
unpredictability and evanescence. Although a colourful environment, it
was not a comforting one.[21]

The most famous images of medieval English rural life were commissioned by another knightly family: that of Sir Geoffrey Luttrell, whose
handful of estates was spread between Lincolnshire, Leicestershire, Not-
tinghamshire and Yorkshire and who was called upon to serve the king
thirteen times between 1297 and 1322. His psalter, now variously dated
to the 1320s–30s or possibly shortly before his death in 1345, also has
disquieting features. Weirdly conceived monsters appear among everyday scenes and illustrations inspired by chivalry or folklore. Even the
well-known ploughman and other colourful agricultural workers were
not all they seem: in reality peasants would have worn rough, drab
clothing (see plate 2). It has been suggested that this small volume
(35.4 cm x 24.4 cm) with its huge script attempted to portray an orderly
and idyllic world, increasingly at variance with reality. The symbolic
messages are not altogether clear to modern readers, but there can be no

---

[21] King, *Peterborough Abbey*, 51, 132–3; Alexander and Binski, *Age of Chivalry*,
249–50.

PLATE 2   Ploughing, from the margin of the Luttrell Psalter, *c*.1325–45 (*Add. MS 42130, fo. 170*)

doubt that messages were intended and would have been readily intelligible to contemporaries.[22] Nor were they always reassuring. Knightly families were vulnerable to the peasant anger and unrest which were beginning to find a voice in the early fourteenth century. They also lacked the resources enjoyed by greater landlords to insulate them from catastrophe. Although they may not have correctly identified the causes, they were right to sense the precariousness of knightly existence.

If men like Henry de Bray or Robert of Thorpe were vulnerable, they acted as stewards to those better able to weather disaster. Unlike knights who rarely had more than a handful of estates, the greatest lords, lay and ecclesiastical, usually possessed a large number, often widely distributed across the country. Some, such as Gilbert de Clare, also had estates in Ireland and Wales.[23] These estates were largely accumulated through inheritance, marriage, service to the crown, or, in the case of the church, through benefaction over long periods of time. The diversity of their origin explains why they were so widely scattered. A significant proportion were likely to be in the hands of tenants, often descendants of those knights settled on the land in the post-Conquest period. Manors remaining under the control of their lords were either at farm, that is leased for a fixed annual render, managed by local officials, bailiffs, serjeants or reeves under the overall supervision of a steward or, most frequently, a combination of the two. The precise balance between direct

[22] BL Add. MS 42130; Camille, *Mirror*, 184–92, 286, 307 and *passim*. See cover illustration and chapter 5. The later date is suggested by J. Goldberg and R. Emmerson in a forthcoming essay.
[23] Holmes, *Estates of the Higher Nobility*, 35–8.

exploitation and leasing depended on the needs and capabilities of the lord. Monasteries comprising large static communities, where monks were outnumbered many times by their support staff of servants and administrators, needed vast amounts of food on a day-to-day basis. It made good sense for them to retain estates in the immediate neighbour-hood in order to supply regular provisions to the household. More distant manors might either be leased, or exploited to yield cash crops or more specialized produce not available locally. Where a good run of accounts has survived, it is possible to reconstruct the remarkable way in which some of these monastic estates were administered as integrated enterprises.

Crowland Abbey is a case in point, and is described in two old studies which are not now very accessible to readers. A moderately well-endowed pre-Conquest Benedictine house set in the heart of undrained Lincolnshire fen, it owned properties in both the surrounding marshland and on higher ground in the nearby counties of Huntingdonshire, Northamptonshire, Cambridgeshire and Leicestershire. Some were fifty miles or more from the abbey but, despite this, by the end of the thirteenth century there was considerable specialization in production and a centralized accounting system. The upland manors of Northamp-tonshire, better suited to arable agriculture, supplied grain to the abbey, while the fenland granges with their rich grazing operated as cattle farms. Crops and livestock were exchanged as required between manors and via the centre. The abbey is best known, however, for its sheep farming operation known as the *Bidentes Hoylandie*, set up *c*.1276. Selected manors functioned as a single wool-producing enterprise, under separate management and subject to separate accounting. Lambs were reared on the upland estates before being transported down river on rafts to the fen pastures, and fleeces were collected together at Crowland to be sold through King's Lynn.[24]

Lay magnates and, to a large extent, bishops lived a far more peripat-etic existence than those belonging to the enclosed religious orders and also required a higher proportion of their income in cash. The logistics involved in frequent removal and provisioning substantial households on a regular basis under medieval conditions must have been extremely challenging, even where skeleton staff were left in place at each resid-ence. Elizabeth de Burgh, heiress in her own right after the death of her brother Gilbert de Clare and possessed of dower and jointures by virtue of her three marriages, divided the years between the death of her last husband in 1322 and her own death in 1360 among residences in Clare

---

[24] Wretts Smith, 'Organisation of farming at Croyland Abbey', 170ff; Page, '*Bidentes Hoylandie*', 605ff.

(Suffolk), Anglesey (Cambridgeshire), Great Bardfield (Essex), Usk (Gwent) and, in her final years, London. Each move necessitated the transport not only of clothing, but also household goods and furnishings, so every department of the household was assigned carts and pack-horses for the operation. Her will provides a glimpse of some of the items involved and offers a hint of an aristocratic lifestyle. Her bed was hung with green and red striped velvet and had fur-lined coverlets. She also had a set of green chamber hangings with a border pattern of owls, and another with blue cockerels and parrots on a tawny background, altogether an environment richer and more comfortable than that of the knightly Thorpes at Longthorpe Tower. Arrangements for supplying this mobile household were eased by gearing estates closest to each residence towards produce for the table and stable when required. More exotic requirements such as wine, spices, fur and fabrics were obtained from the nearest great fair, often St Ives, or the ports of Colchester, Ipswich and King's Lynn. Specialities such as salmon from Usk or horses from her Irish estates were transported long distances, but most of her more distant manors were managed to bring in roughly three-quarters of her income in cash.[25]

With such complicated administrative arrangements, it becomes clear how opportunities existed for peasants and knights to carve out careers as estate officials, but the initiative remained with the lord. Prior Henry of Eastry (1285–1331) towered above his immediate predecessors at Canterbury Cathedral Priory, rescuing his house from debt and completely re-organising the way in which the estates were run.[26] Management of this calibre was inevitably rare. Moreover, it was not the most obvious quality that a religious house might hope to find in its spiritual leader. The incidence of resourceful managers was even more unpredictable among lay magnates where heredity rather than choice determined leadership. For these lords too, a gift for estate administration was not the quality most highly valued in aristocratic society: military prowess and an honourable reputation counted for more. It may not be a coincidence that one of the lay lords most active and successful in increasing income from her estates was Isabella de Forz, debarred by gender from the pursuits of her male peers. How many of them would have found time to emulate her attendance in person at estate audits?[27]

Although for these great lords, harvest failure did not spell ruin or famine in the way that they might for knights and peasants, they were

[25] Ward, 'Elizabeth de Burgh', 29–41; *idem, English Noblewomen*, 58–64, 82, 88, 108; Holmes, *Estates of the Higher Nobility*, 110–11.
[26] Smith, *Canterbury Cathedral Priory*, 22–3, 53–4.
[27] Mate, 'Profit and productivity', 327–34; Ward, *English Noblewomen*, 110–11.

not immune from all natural hazards. The *Bidentes Hoylandie* organization at Crowland Abbey was wound down between 1307 and 1314, probably because of the growing risk of scab. An estate might easily lose a significant proportion of its stock in a single outbreak. Crowland was rich enough to weather severe blows of this kind with administrative adjustments, but the poorer Augustinians of Bolton Priory were almost destroyed by the disasters of the second decade of the fourteenth century.[28]

Religious houses were at least protected from some of the worst misfortunes afflicting lay magnates. Wealthy lay landlords might suffer harvest failure or loss of livestock, but as with knightly families, a more fundamental disaster was failure of the male line. Elizabeth de Burgh inherited her share of the great earldom of Gloucester and Hertford when it was split between herself and her two sisters after their brother Gilbert's death without male heirs. So common was the extinction of aristocratic lines for this reason in the later thirteenth century that Edward I has been accused of deliberately exploiting it as a means of acquiring land with which to endow his numerous male progeny. Henry de Lacy's surrender of his estates to the crown in 1294 cannot have been unconnected with the death of his two sons in tragic accidents. The elder drowned in a well at the castle his father was building at Denbigh, while his brother fell from a turret at Pontefract castle. Isabella de Forz, countess of Devon and Lady of Wight in her own right and predeceased by her children of both sexes, preferred to keep the king dangling for the best part of twenty years before clinching a deal on the Isle of Wight and three of her mainland manors on her deathbed in 1293. The circumstances surrounding this eleventh-hour transaction are not entirely clear and forgery or undue influence on the part of royal emissaries have been mentioned, but it is doubtful whether such a purchase would have been mooted had there been a son to inherit.[29]

Widows' dower was another heavy burden on landholders of all rank, but especially for those with the obligations, but not necessarily the means that accompanied high status. Although custom varied, particularly among the peasantry, and husbands were free to augment the amount of land custom dictated, a widow could expect to hold for the rest of her life at least a third of the land in her husband's possession at the time of his death. The growing practice of joint tenure among the aristocracy in the later thirteenth century, enabling the surviving partner to hold the entire property for life, and the frequency with which men married women younger than themselves, only exacerbated the

---

[28] Kershaw, *Bolton Priory*, 17. See p. 72.
[29] McNulty, 'Henry de Lacy', 22, 27; McFarlane, *Nobility*, 248–67.

problem. The earls of Warwick were notably afflicted in the second half of the thirteenth century. A third of William de Beauchamp's maternal inheritance was tied up in dower by Ela Longespée for his entire tenure of the earldom (1268–98). His predecessors were even more unfortunate, having to support Philippa, widow of Earl Henry, as well as Ela Longespée.[30] No doubt many peasant heirs experienced frustrations similar in all but scale, frustrations which for the victims must have been worse when the widow in question was a stepmother perhaps only lately appeared on the scene. The problems encountered by many widows in gaining control of their dower land is witness to the tensions it created. However, if churchmen escaped these challenges to the very existence or viability of their estates, they were also denied the classic layman's answer to impoverishment: a good marriage. This explains why some of the larger religious houses resorted to buying estates by the later thirteenth century after the stream of gifts had dried up, thus adding to the chorus of knightly alarm.

Accidents of fate could befall anyone irrespective of wealth or station. Another bond common to all ranks in rural society was dependence on land, not merely to support life, but for status and power at whatever level it was exercised. Although day-to-day agricultural activities were not usually at the forefront of the minds of those who fought or prayed, land – its acquisition and retention – was an overwhelming preoccupation. It is hard for us to appreciate this territorial drive and the dynastic ambitions flowing from it. Lords spent what appear to be huge sums on litigation in defence of their title against rival claimants. Security of tenure was probably the most sensitive point at issue between crown and subjects. At a personal level, choice of marriage partner whether for lord or peasant was largely governed by territorial considerations, the wishes of the individual subordinated to those of the family. Quite simply, land – getting it, keeping it and, for all but the richest, exploiting it – dominated the lives of perhaps ninety per cent of the population. Even the remainder, who lived by trade or craftsmanship, turned to the purchase of land as soon as they were prosperous enough to do so. England in the thirteenth and fourteenth centuries, and for centuries to come, was above all a land based society.

So far, in this account of rural England, scant mention has been made of women. Although in all probability comprising more than half the population and playing an essential role in its activities, information about them, particularly of an informal and personal nature, is even more elusive than for their male counterparts. They are recorded almost

---

[30] E. Mason, 'The resources of the Earldon of Warwick in the thirteenth century', *Midland History*, iii (1975), 73.

exclusively by men, only emerging into documentary daylight when the overshadowing power of father or husband was removed. Until recently, their silent presence was taken for granted, but once again present-day concerns have spilled backwards into the past to dictate the historian's agenda; women's studies have become a growth industry. It is therefore pertinent to enquire how far the experience of women differed from that of men in a society where, on the one hand, all were subordinate in varying degree to a higher authority and, on the other, disaster and death were all too frequent levellers.

In two respects the position of women differed fundamentally from that of men. The first was a matter of culture. Depicted by church teaching as either the embodiment of Eve the temptress or Mary the Virgin mother, they were imprisoned within stereotypes which often worked to their disadvantage. Although there was a strong misogynistic slant to much of the teaching about women, whether theological or gynaecological, it would be a mistake to hold celibate and prejudiced churchmen responsible for all the ills women had to endure. In reality, the situation was more complex. Moreover, the church had conferred one major boon by insisting on a woman's free consent before a marriage could be considered valid. Many of the social constraints to which women were subject in daily life arose from the custom of patrilineal inheritance, which made it vital for a husband to ensure that his wife was in no position to bear another man's child. Paradoxically, the very ability of women to hold land, even if only through default of a male heir, made them more of a commodity in the marriage market than would otherwise have been the case. In the upper reaches of society, the prevailing military ethos and the fact that land was held, notionally at least, in return for military service excluded women from a role in society which their holdings would otherwise have conferred. Thus, for a variety of reasons, women were in a distinctively different social position from that of men and one which was often hostile in the limitations it imposed.

The second respect in which their experience differed fundamentally from that of men was a matter of biology: their unique capacity to bear children. This was not open to all, however, either because of a vocation to the celibate life, the lack of a dowry or what must have been a quiet tragedy for many, barrenness. Relatively little is known about child-bearing in this period. Records focus overwhelmingly on death rather than birth, but for many married women life must have consisted of one pregnancy followed by another, accompanied by very high infant and maternal mortality. Again, one must beware of simplistic judgements. When suitable sources become available from the sixteenth century, childbirth appears surprisingly safe, with the important proviso that the mother was neither unusually young nor old and that there were no complications.[31] Methods of family limitation were known, even though crude by modern standards. They consisted chiefly of *coitus interruptus* or herbal preparations to procure abortion. Early fourteenth-century penitentials suggest that both were quite widely used, but the need to ensure that parents were survived by at least one child must have outweighed other considerations and led to unrestricted conception for most of the time.[32] In a society where people were classified by function, those who bore children might have constituted a fourth group alongside those who worked, fought and prayed, had women not been so invisible. Their contribution was not entirely unappreciated, however, as the substantial sacrifice inflicted by society on the heir through the institution of dower indicates; the key role of wife and mother was acknowledged in the assignment to them, if only for a life term, of a significant proportion of the most valuable commodity the family possessed.

There was inevitably a gulf between the daily life of those at different ends of the social spectrum, notwithstanding the cultural environment common to all women. Much sentimental nonsense has been talked about the more egalitarian relationship enjoyed by peasant women as they worked alongside their husbands on the family holding. The freedom to share in unremitting toil was no doubt something peasant women would have surrendered given the chance. However, the lives of many peasant wives deviated as much from their theoretical subservience as the position of unfree peasants differed from its strict definition in law. Although women were effectively debarred from the official life of the community either as jurors or members of tithings (the mechanism for law enforcement), court records reveal them as playing an active, often independent role in other ways. Many paid their own merchet (marriage) fines, thus effectively controlling their own choice of husband and, moreover, financing it from their own resources. They were also to be found engaged in their own enterprises, most commonly ale brewing. One should not overestimate these opportunities, however. Conditions for the peasantry in the late thirteenth and early fourteenth century were such as to pressurize women into whatever by-employment they could find in order to supplement the family income. Time for this had to be found alongside shared agricultural work and the more gender-specific duties of housewife and mother.

Life at the other social extreme was more leisured, but aristocratic and knightly women were far from the sort of ornaments, useless for all but

[31] Schofield, 'Did mothers really die?', 250–7.
[32] Leyser, *Medieval Women*, 130–1.

breeding, conjured up by Victorians in the light of their own experience. Women of highest rank often had their own households to oversee, as well as those of their husbands in their absence. The fact that many were named as executors in their husbands' wills also argues that they were regarded as capable and trustworthy in important matters of business. Some, like Queen Eleanor of Provence or her daughter-in-law, Queen Eleanor of Castile, emerge as strong and ruthless personalities who played a major part in their husbands' activities. The twelve Eleanor crosses, where Eleanor of Castile's body rested on its journey from Lincoln to Westminster, and the three lavish tombs for her heart, entrails and body respectively, are a telling witness to Edward I's grief at her loss, even if they also doubled as royal propaganda (see plate 3).[33]

At best these women functioned as valued partners. It has often been observed, however, that widowhood offered the only opportunity for women to operate as individuals, free from subordination to the authority of father or spouse. As Jeremy Goldberg has observed, much nonsense has been talked about this too. For peasant women, widowhood often meant penury, even though the chances of remarriage at this date were greater than after the Black Death, when young men could obtain land by other means.[34] It is also noticeable that the most assertive wealthy widows, women such as Isabella de Forz or Elizabeth de Burgh, were often heiresses in their own right. Arguably, those accustomed to a sense of their own importance from an early age were better able to take on the challenge of responsibilities more usually dealt with by men. For high-ranking widows too, therefore, remarriage may often have been welcome. They also had the third and time-honoured option of taking the veil.

The range of people and activity comprised within English rural society was enormous, more so perhaps than in countries like Italy where the aristocracy was city based. For much of the time, English magnates could be found living on one or other of their rural estates. It was a hierarchical society; those who fought and prayed were sustained as lords by those who worked. In return they provided the peasantry with land and protection. But, although this reciprocal bond is central to our notion of what distinguishes the Middle Ages from other periods, it is evident that the things common to all ranks were in many ways more fundamental than those which separated them, as their attitudes to land

---

[33] Howell, *Eleanor of Provence, passim*; J. C. Parsons, *Eleanor of Castile, passim*; N. Coldstream, 'The commissioning and design of the Eleanor Crosses', in D. Parsons, *Eleanor of Castile*, 55–67.
[34] *Women in England*, 19.

PLATE 3   The Eleanor Cross at Hardingstone, near Northampton, 1291–4

and women demonstrate. One should not underestimate, either, the communal or kinship links which cut across those of lordship.[35] Less well recorded, they were not necessarily less strong.

[35] See chapter 5.

3

The People: Towns and Traders

Although for the purposes of this book it is convenient to separate the people of late thirteenth-and early fourteenth-century England into town and country dwellers, in many ways it does violence to reality. Urban and rural life were bound indissolubly together. Towns were surrounded by fields cultivated by their inhabitants, and craftsmen were at work in the countryside. Family links and commercial needs generated a constant traffic from one to the other. Yet for all their interdependence, contemporaries themselves saw distinctions between them. In law and custom particularly, towns with borough status differed significantly from their rural surroundings. Their inhabitants were commonly subject to separate law courts and urban life was governed to a much greater degree through communal organization rather than lordship. Although trade was no longer confined to towns by law as it had been in Anglo-Saxon times, major transactions still tended to take place in towns, not least because they were safer. Larger towns were often physically as well as legally cut off from the countryside, confined within walls, their gates closed at night. Remains of substantial walls at York and Norwich indicate their commanding isolation in the rural landscape.

Unlike northern Italy or the Low Countries, where the agricultural hinterland revolved around great cities, English urban society was characterized by small towns serving the needs of a rurally based society. This is reflected in the relatively low proportion of the population thought to have lived in them, perhaps ten to fifteen per cent.[1] Only London seems to have been large enough to match the great cities of the continent. The remainder comprised regional commercial and administrative centres, often county towns, together with a network of some 500 small market towns barely distinguishable from larger villages. The

[1] For varying estimates of the proportion of the population living in towns see Britnell, *Commercialisation*, 115; Miller and Hatcher, *Medieval England: Towns*, 278.

smallest had perhaps as few as 2,000 inhabitants. Only York, Winchester, Norwich and Bristol are thought to have exceeded 10,000. Even London, though possibly as large as contemporary Florence, was small by our standards. On the largest current estimate of a population of c. 100,000, it was smaller than present-day Oxford or Cheltenham and a great deal more compact, concentrated as it was within the area of the modern City. Nearby Westminster was a separate and very different community, largely owned by Westminster Abbey.

While we can feel reasonably secure in making qualitative judgements about the nature of English urbanization and the predominance of agricultural activity in medieval society, historians are on much more treacherous ground when it comes to the sort of numbers just cited. The element of doubt in the accepted guesstimates is most graphically illustrated by the range of recent figures for the population of London c.1300, which differ by more than sixty-five per cent.[2] Problems in calculating the size of rural communities from court rolls and other seignorial records are as nothing compared with those of towns. This is not surprising given the different way in which town and country were governed. By this date, most towns were administered by merchants organized into gilds, whose records were far less liable to survive into the twentieth century than those of magnates or the great religious houses. It was not until the later fourteenth century that towns began to seek incorporation, thereby gaining an institutional identity of their own, together with the continuity of government likely to promote good record keeping. Even where evidence survives about the owners of urban property, it is by no means easy to estimate how many individuals lived in the premises, whether as family, apprentices or servants. Towns were also likely to have a larger, unrecorded underclass living on the streets or in makeshift dwellings.

This was particularly true as towns, like the countryside, had to adjust to a high and increasingly vulnerable population. A drift towards towns by the landless in the hope of subsistence is certain, though impossible to measure. This migration was sometimes recorded in their place of origin. Court rolls reveal countless modest chevage payments registering permission to reside away from the manor. In addition to those who were said to be in London, Stamford and Lynn, the Spalding censuses describe a small but significant group of young people who had abandoned their villages and whose whereabouts was unknown. They were recorded as 'vagabundus'. Evidence from towns themselves shows that migrants came chiefly from surrounding villages. Ninety per cent of those settling in Stratford-upon-Avon came from the immediate

[2] See, p. 51.

hinterland. In the early fourteenth century, people flocked into Bristol by land and water from Worcestershire, Shropshire, Herefordshire, Somerset and the Cotswolds.[3] Major towns such as York, Norwich and, above all, London drew migrants from further afield. Many, like those among the London pepperers, no doubt came in search of a living and stayed to prosper as traders.[4] Although written evidence is sparse, urban historians are more fortunate with archaeological remains. Rescue digs conducted in the course of the almost universal redevelopment of modern city centres have revolutionized our understanding of medieval towns, especially those of the Anglo-Saxon period. Findings from the thirteenth and fourteenth centuries have been less dramatic, but they demonstrate increasingly dense occupation of sites within towns, as well as a growth of suburban dwellings where incomers struggled to find room to live. Plots which originally had a single building along the street frontage were replaced by structures on all four sides, creating tightly packed courts. Records of Halesowen in Worcestershire provide a rare glimpse of the way in which some of these less prosperous townspeople might scrape a living by hawking food and drink.[5] Others, their fate little different from that of their modern counterparts in the shanty towns of the developing world, have left few traces either on the fabric of towns or in their archives, unless they happened to fall foul of the law.

Earlier in the twentieth century much of the scholarly work on urban England was bedevilled by a confusion between towns as economic entities and places with borough status. This was understandable. The distinction was often blurred; towns were not necessarily boroughs, nor were settlements granted a borough charter guaranteed to prosper commercially. The towns that grew up to service the needs of the abbeys of Bury St Edmunds and St Albans were famously refused borough privileges by their monastic lords. Conversely, the earl of Cornwall, who created a borough out of the fen-edge hamlet of Holme in Huntingdonshire, in the hope that it might grow into a trading centre, had only succeeded in attracting a handful of burgesses by 1279.[6]

The fully fledged boroughs of the thirteenth century evolved gradually from the boroughs and burgesses of Domesday Book and earlier. They are relatively easy to identify because their privileges were enshrined in charters which were kept safe and often copied into the archives of royal or seignorial grantors. Most charters had been acquired during the course of the twelfth century and were usually modelled on pre-existing

[3] See chapter 1; BL, Add. MS 35296, fo. 209ff; Penn, 'Origins of Bristol migrants', 126–9.

[4] Nightingale, *Medieval Mercantile Community*, 101–2.

[5] Hilton, 'Lords, burgesses and hucksters', 10–11.

[6] *RH*, ii, 652b.

grants, often that of Breteuil in Normandy or the largest borough in the vicinity. The charters of Gateshead, Durham and Alnwick were based on that of Newcastle upon Tyne, and that of Salisbury on Winchester.[7] There had been a burst of borough foundation by entrepreneurial lords earlier in the thirteenth century. This attempt to boost the value of land on their manors and to bring in a healthy income from tolls had largely come to an end by 1230 as the countryside was filled to saturation point with aspirant commercial centres. Holme was a victim of this situation. Within easy distance of the county town of Huntingdon and the abbot of Thorney's thriving town of Yaxley, there was little prospect of economic success. Earlier lords had sometimes gone to the length of creating completely new settlements, but by the later thirteenth century such plantations usually arose from special circumstances such as the king's military needs or, in the case of New Winchelsea chartered in 1283, the inundation of the older settlement by the sea.

The degree of planning in these plantations was quite remarkable and far from the usual stereotype of medieval towns with their narrow streets and haphazard development. When in 1296 Edward I needed to rebuild Berwick-upon-Tweed after the destruction wreaked by the war with Scotland, he summoned experts who knew how to 'devise, order and array a new town'. Once a site had been identified, the new town was carefully laid out. At New Winchelsea, men were appointed to 'plan and give directions for streets and lanes and assign places suitable for a market and for two churches'. Elsewhere, accounts record the purchase of rope so that the plots could be accurately measured. In north Wales, the king directed his officials to draft in carpenters, diggers and other craftsmen. In less militarily sensitive areas, building was left to the new burgesses.[8]

Without traders towns were doomed to failure. The provisions of borough charters were designed to attract them by setting out or confirming privileges intended to facilitate a more commercial way of life than existed in the countryside. The continental axiom that 'town air makes free' applied equally to England; any serf resident within a borough for a year and a day was commonly enfranchised. Those who possessed burgage tenements enjoyed powers of disposition not open to rural landholders, however important. Each could buy and sell freely and, in the words of the late twelfth-century charter of Burford in Oxfordshire, 'choose as his heir his son, or daughter, or wife or anyone else without licence of his lord'.[9] The right of burgesses to regulate their own affairs and conduct their own courts independent of seignorial

[7] *British Borough Charters*, i, 25; ii, 19.
[8] Ibid., ii, 25; Beresford, *New Towns*, 3–4, 14–19, 82.
[9] *British Borough Charters*, i, 73.

interference was crucial to the well-being of the trading communities, particularly where the collection of taxes was concerned; the rapacity of royal officials had been notorious before these freedoms were achieved. There were equally obvious advantages in exemption from the tolls of other trading centres, even if these were often hotly disputed. Most charters conferred the right to charge myriad levies on traders coming from elsewhere. These inevitably conflicted with equally widespread grants to the merchants of other boroughs giving them exemption from tolls anywhere in the kingdom. By the later thirteenth century, most disputes of this sort had been resolved, but many traders bringing goods to market still faced payment to enter and purchase, as well as more obscure charges such as tronage (for the use of public weights), stallage (the right to set up a stall), or lastage (the right to load). Although these levies played a positive role in encouraging lords to create boroughs, their overall economic effect was negative. Each represented a surcharge on transactions, thereby adding to the cost of goods. Nor did the expense begin at the borough gate; there were tolls to be paid at every step of the route to market, along roads and rivers, at the quayside and over bridges. Despite the high costs, however, there is little doubt that by the later thirteenth century goods of all sorts were actively traded, often over long distances and in considerable quantity.

By the beginning of Edward I's reign, the volume of these transactions sustained a large number of market towns without any pretension to borough status. Yaxley in Huntingdonshire, the principal manor of Thorney Abbey, was one such. By this date, the settlement had shops and a toll booth which also housed six stalls. Names such as Mercator or Marchaunt indicate full-time traders and in 1322 Yaxley was included among well-established centres such as King's Lynn and Huntingdon in orders to send victuals to the north. Already in the thirteenth century the town served a wider catchment area than its immediate locality. Officials of Henry III purchasing wine at Boston fair used Yaxley as an entrepôt before transporting it to the king's Northamptonshire estates, while Owston Abbey in Leicestershire found it worth travelling to Yaxley to buy fish.[10]

Essential to the prosperity of this small town was the privilege of holding a market on Thursdays and an annual fair lasting five days starting on the Saturday before the feast of the Assumption (15 August). A dense network of town and village markets existed throughout the country by this date, so that it was possible to find somewhere to trade

---

[10] *RH*, ii, 641a; *Cal Lib, 1226–40*, 89, 91, 107–8, 135; *1251–60*, 298; *Rot Litt Claus*, i, 39; ii, 121; *Close Rolls, 1231–4*, 72; *Cal Close, 1318–23*, 670; Hilton, *Economic Development*, 137; CUL, Add. MS 3020, fos. 18–25.

within walking distance on any day of the week. They have now been mapped in various ways for a number of counties.[11] In Huntingdonshire, those who went to Yaxley on Thursday might go to St Ives on Monday, Woodston or Ramsey on Wednesday, Alwalton on Friday, or Peterborough on Saturday. Other markets were scarcely further away.[12] Only the crown could grant the right to hold a market, and lords appear to have been keen to secure such a grant for any remotely plausible estate, either to avoid paying tolls to their rivals or to swell their own coffers. How far some of the grants known to us from enrolment in the royal chancery represented genuine commercial activity is an open question. As with attempts to foster town life, there must have been an increasingly high failure rate as ever less-promising locations were promoted. Nevertheless, the enthusiasm of lords to establish markets and the economic impetus provided by a high density of population meant that trading facilities were available not merely in towns, but in a continuum of settlements stretching from London at one extreme to quite small villages at the other.

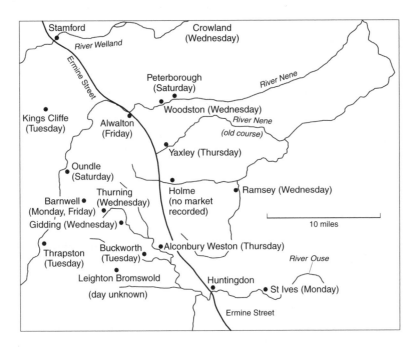

MAP 2 Markets in the vicinity of Yaxley, Huntingdonshire, c.1300

[11] Britnell, 'Proliferation of markets', refers to a number of studies. Examples are Platt, *English Medieval Town*, 24, 26, 76; Beresford, *New Towns*, 288.
[12] See map 2.

By the thirteenth century, market grants were usually associated with permission to hold an annual fair lasting several days, or even weeks for those which were more important. Apart from their social aspect, these gatherings fulfilled an important function in a society where demand for more specialized items was still insufficiently strong to command their availability all the year round. Many of the more expensive goods, chiefly cloth or wine, were sold by foreign merchants who found it convenient to travel from fair to fair, their route so much a matter of routine that goods purchased at one fair might well be paid for at their next destination. The yearly round began with Stamford fair held before Easter, followed by St Ives after Easter, Boston in late June, Winchester in late September and finally Northampton fair in November. Modern fun-fairs are sometimes the last vestige of these medieval fairs, held at the traditional date, but now shorn of their commercial role. Elsewhere, traditional fairs have lasted longer. In Greece, for example, the *pane-gyria* (the annual celebrations of the local saint) still held in rural areas retain a medieval flavour. Alongside feasting, music and dancing, itinerant small traders sell clothes and other cheap goods which may, even today, be the major annual purchase for the few remaining up-country shepherds.

Of the English fairs which stood out as pre-eminent, Winchester, Northampton and Stamford were already important as towns in pre-Conquest England, whereas Boston and St Ives were relative newcomers. Indeed for much of the year St Ives retained the air of the evocatively named village of Slepe on to which it had been grafted by the abbot of Ramsey. Villeins on this and neighbouring estates were required as part of their labour services to collect sticks to make hurdles to demarcate stalls set up for the fair and to keep watch at night against thieves. Among the Ramsey Abbey archives there are records of the summary court proceedings held between 1270 and 1324 to deal with disputes and offences before those involved left the village. Known as pie powder courts, deriving from the Norman French *pieds poudres* (dusty-footed travellers), these hearings bring the fair to life. Inevitably most of the cases dealt with disputes about payment or quality of goods. In 1317, for example, John of Honing sold a last (load) of red herring for nine marks, swearing that all were of the same quality as those in the three kemps (barrels) which he had shown the purchaser. In the event, it was claimed that the good red herring were mixed in with stickleback and other herring that were putrid. There was a similar dispute in 1312 concerning a consignment of liquorice. There were also problems of law and order, chiefly theft and assault, caused by the crowds thronging the village. Prostitutes or those harbouring them were not infrequently brought to court, and in 1287 a householder was fined for sheltering lepers and thereby putting his neighbours at risk.[13] Tradesmen from Yaxley and other neighbouring communities came to sell victuals. Others came to buy and sell from all over England, from Flanders, Brabant and, in smaller numbers, from various parts of France.

It is no accident that the great fairs were located in southern and eastern England. This reflected both the orientation of overseas trade with Flanders, France, Italy and, to a lesser extent, Scandinavia, and the rich eastern hinterland from which wool, England's main export, was drawn. Yet despite their lively contribution to the thirteenth-century economy, the days of the great fairs were numbered. The heyday of these fairs had been in the late twelfth century and first half of the thirteenth century. From the middle of the thirteenth century they were beginning to falter. Northampton and Stamford were the first to be hit; Boston retained its buoyancy longest. Winchester and St Ives were still doing good business in the 1280s, but thereafter there was a decline from which they never recovered.

Prosperity rested fundamentally on the presence of overseas merchants. Once they ceased to come, there was nothing to attract traders from all over England and the fairs dwindled to purely local importance. The character of a fair in any one year had always been volatile; overseas merchants were unpredictable in their attendance and purchasers could not always rely on finding the same commodities from one season to the next. The degree to which success was underpinned by the wool and cloth trades became clear when for a variety of reasons these goods were no longer marketed at fairs. In part this was due to a wider north-European trend away from peripatetic trading. The great fairs of Champagne and Flanders declined at much the same date, but there were specific local factors which exacerbated the situation in England. Changes in the native cloth industry towards a cheaper product meant that there were fewer high-quality cloths to attract specialist purchasers from distant places. Political events in 1270–71, 1294–1303 and again in 1307–22 disrupted relations with Flanders and led to the virtual exclusion of Flemish merchants. The blow was such that, over a period of time, it transformed the market to the great advantage of London. The export of wool was further disturbed by the introduction of the staple (derived from *étaple*, the Old French for market), whereby briefly in the mid-1290s and then on a more permanent basis from 1313 until the end of Edward II's reign, merchants were directed to trade through designated centres on the Continent. Alternatively they could tour the country buying directly from producers and selling cloth at the same time. A Flemish list incorporated by Francesco Balducci Pegolotti into

---

[13] *Select Cases Concerning the Law Merchant*, 14, 91, 102.

the trading manual he compiled *c*.1315, while creative in its rendering of English place-names (and the inclusion of Scotland under England), nevertheless shows a detailed and comprehensive knowledge of the major suppliers on the part of overseas merchants.[14] Imports were increasingly handled by merchants resident in London, especially after 1285, when Edward I forced the city to admit aliens of good repute as citizens.[15] Changes in the pattern of royal purchasing reinforced this development. Whereas perhaps three-quarters of the needs of Henry III's court had been supplied from the great fairs, his successors bought progressively less there. By the end of Edward II's reign, the royal household was supplied mainly by English merchants able to source the majority of their requirements without leaving London. Fairs had become increasingly irrelevant.

Although not entirely immune from the setbacks affecting the rest of the economy in the later Middle Ages, the relentless growth of London over the course of the medieval period is an outstanding feature of English urbanization. Famously described by Bede as 'an emporium of many people coming by land and sea', it was by the late thirteenth century on a different scale from its nearest English rivals, not just in terms of size and economic importance, but also in its social structure.

Given its importance, it might seem surprising that there is no comprehensive study of London at this period. It is less surprising when one appreciates that the size and complexity of the task mirrors the size and complexity of the community itself. Since the 1960s, however, steps have been taken towards making good the omission. Initial work focused on institutional aspects of the city, along with its chequered relations with the crown. The story appears to be largely one of conflict – between powerful merchants and the more entrepreneurial of the craftsmen, between rival groups within these categories, and between assertive citizens and their demanding ruler. Alone among English towns, London was swept up in the continental communal movement of the late twelfth century. The legacy of this ensured more than a century of constitutional manoeuvring between crown and citizens until an acceptable balance between their interests was achieved. Except for thirteen years between 1285 and 1298 when Edward I revoked the city's liberties and placed it under the control of two royal wardens, government was in the hands of a mayor and common council drawn from aldermen representing each ward. The size, wealth and strategic importance of London meant that relations with the crown would always be sensitive, and the city was

[14] Moore, *Fairs of Medieval England*, 77–83, ch. 5; W. Cunningham, *The Growth of English Industry and Commerce*, 5th edn, Cambridge, 1910, 618, 628–41.
[15] Nightingale, 'The growth of London', 94.

inevitably embroiled in wider political events. Citizens were quick to capitalize on this in the crisis of the 1290s and the more frequent crises of Edward II's reign. In 1319, they won concessions that Edward I would never have countenanced, but they also lost when the wheel of political fortune turned once again.

Not all the pressures were external, however. The city's voracious need for supplies, while beneficial as a stimulus to agricultural production, had a deeply unsettling effect on relations between different groups within the city. Ever burgeoning opportunities for trade led to an expansion within both mercantile and manufacturing elements, especially victualling. Critical issues in this period were how far newly emergent traders typified by the fishmongers and skinners could penetrate the aldermannic elite dominated by older associations of drapers, vintners, mercers, goldsmiths and pepperers, and how far all these merchants could exclude craftsmen from any sort of power and status.

Pamela Nightingale's monumental work on the pepperers' fraternity of St Antonin, which later became the Grocers' Company, is the most important recent contribution to London's institutional history, but in tune with changing academic interests, there have also been more specifically economic and demographic studies. In the early 1980s an ambitious project to reconstruct the topographical layout of each London parish was based at the Museum of London. It was the earliest results of this project examining teeming Cheapside that have encouraged historians to revise their estimates of London's population c.1300. Whereas Gwyn Williams, first writing in the early 1960s, felt 40,000 to be a reasonable estimate, Derek Keene argued that if occupants of the 400 or so shops, 2,000 lesser trading outlets, fourteen taverns and countless associated living quarters of London's principal marketing street were replicated throughout the city, 100,000 might be more realistic. Both were agreed on the vast number of drinking dens. On balance, it seems unlikely that densely packed Cheapside was typical of London as a whole, but even a more modest estimate of c.60,000 represents a significant increase on figures advanced only a generation earlier. The impact of the Feeding the City project has already been noted. Other scholars are gradually publishing studies of individual citizens, their interconnections and the tangled relationships between rival groups. The completion and synthesis of all this work is an essential preliminary to a definitive account.[16]

Regional centres, too, have attracted individual studies in recent years. Often country towns, they tended to enjoy prime locations at junctions

[16] Nightingale, *Medieval Mercantile Community*; Williams, *Medieval London*, 19, 21–2; Keene, 'London before the Great Fire', 12–14, 20; Nightingale, 'The growth of London', 95–6.

of river and road communication, enabling them to capture the lion's
share when the volume of trade shrank along with the population. They
were also insured against the vagaries of the economy by their role in
government, enabling inhabitants to earn their living by servicing
castles, law courts and other activities undertaken by royal officials.
Southampton serves as a good example. During the thirteenth century
it throve on the export of cloth, corn and livestock from its hinterland
and imported a vast array of goods. Among foods there was every form
of marine life from sardines to whale and spices ranging from pepper,
saffron, and cinnamon to exotic items unfamiliar to the modern palate
such as zedoary (an aromatic root) and cubeb (a berry). Rice, a standby
of today's cuisine, entered the port at that time as a luxury available
from merchants only at a steep price. Above all, Southampton's prosperity rested on the wine trade with Gascony. Unlike so many towns of the
east Midlands, whose economy depended primarily on the manufacture
of cloth, Southampton was essentially a trading centre.[17]

Like London, larger towns had a distinctively urban social structure
which was evolving to meet the needs of inhabitants biased towards
trade and commerce. Borough charters normally granted a degree of
self-government, although the means of achieving this varied somewhat.
The duties of administering justice and collecting annual farms (fixed
cash payments to the Exchequer) were usually assigned to bailiffs. Like
London, they were also subdivided into wards each in the charge of
aldermen elected from among the more prominent burgesses. Many
boroughs possessed a common seal, but property was held jointly in
the name of trusted individuals until incorporation became the norm.
The office of mayor had appeared in those towns where seignorial
control had been most successfully thrown off, often accompanied by
quite elaborate institutions. By 1300, Oxford, for example, had a council consisting largely of former bailiffs, a king's court presided over by
the bailiff to deal with law and order offences, a hustings court dealing
with cases initiated by writ and a mayor's court which handled debts
and infringements of market and craft regulations.[18]

More interesting in many ways than the dry institutional arrangements were the social and occupational groupings which lay behind
the formal exercise of authority. Even in the seignorially dominated
countryside, there was a strong undercurrent of communal action most
clearly evident in the creation and enforcement of village by-laws. Such
activity necessarily came to play a much more prominent role in larger
communities once the organizing hand of lordship was shaken off and

[17] Platt, *Medieval Southampton*, 69–77, 81–3. See chapter 8.
[18] *VCH Oxfordshire*, iv, 61, 336–8.

immigrants were deprived of the protective support of their family and kin. They quickly discovered the benefits of banding together into associations of one sort or another in order to regulate their affairs, to provide mutual support and to present a united front in external dealings. As might be anticipated, London was more complicated and precocious in these developments but, as with the hierarchy of trading centres, the specialized mercantile gilds there represented one extreme of a continuum which reached down to simple village gilds at the other.

The origins of gilds are lost in the mists of pre-Christian times when they were little more than drinking clubs. Drinking and feasting remained important, but intertwined with other purposes. In many towns the earliest and most important body was the gild merchant representing the entire burgess community. It was natural that leading citizens among them should seek greater freedom on behalf of fellow members and then exercise the newly won powers until, in time, gild officers were transmuted into the fully fledged town officials of the late thirteenth century. By this time, craft gilds too had made their appearance, conspicuous among them those of weavers and fullers, who were excluded from gilds merchant and who were consequently determined to exert their political muscle.

Many craft gilds owed their origins to a religious fraternity through which those following the same calling came together for spiritual and material help in times of need. For instance, the cordwainers' gild of the Blessed Virgin Mary in Lincoln, founded in 1307, made provision for the officials of the gild to attend funeral ceremonies of members, bearing candles to burn at the altar, as well as contributions from gild funds to buy bread for distribution as alms. Members, male or female, falling into poverty were eligible for financial help for up to three years. After that there were to be no further subventions, but if the member was truly destitute at death the gild would pay for burial. Only incidentally might these groups come to exercise a regulatory function and even then their rules were likely to be more an expression of intent than an effective means of control. The girdlers of York were typical when, in 1307, they legislated for quality control by forbidding work done by moonlight and tried to limit competition by restricting master craftsmen to one apprentice who had to serve a minimum term of four years. Their intentions were clear, but the end was beyond their capacity to enforce. In London especially, the insatiable demand for labour made it impossible to exclude competent workers whatever their gild status.

Many gilds remained simple religious fraternities, particularly where the mutual bond rested on something other than occupation. Surviving returns chiefly from eastern England belonging to a governmental inquiry instituted in 1388 reveal numerous parish gilds in town and

country, their membership as varied as their purposes. Many could date
their foundation to the thirteenth or early fourteenth centuries. Others
were so long established that they no longer knew how they had come
into being.

With all this variety, it is hardly surprising that gilds also lack a
comprehensive modern study. Historians have hesitated to grapple
with the intricacies of a subject where any one individual might belong
simultaneously to several gilds and any single gild more often than not
combined a multiplicity of purposes. Earlier historians, less daunted and
less aware, were over-prescriptive in seeing a straightforward chrono-
logical progression from the emergence of gilds merchant to that of craft
gild and a heavily regulated path from apprentice to master craftsman
within craft gilds. Where the existence of parish gilds was acknowledged, their role was largely seen as distinct. Real life was at the same
time more pragmatic and less coherent. London never had a gild merchant. Colchester had neither gild merchant nor craft gilds, although
most larger towns seem to have developed both along broadly similar
lines, as the particular requirements of the community dictated. The gild
of the Blessed Virgin in Boston, founded in 1260, illustrates well how a
parish gild might mesh with the local economy. Its purpose was to
provide mass at dawn and at nine o'clock in the evening so that those
whose business took them out of town at the more conventional hours
of worship might not be prevented from attending.[19] Medieval urban
society, like its modern counterpart, was fabricated from the warp and
woof of relationships forged by membership of bodies which might
equally reinforce or cut across social status and occupation. Moreover,
if later medieval evidence is anything to go by, responsibility for the
annual cycle of festival and feast lay with the gilds. In this respect, as in
the day-to-day regulation of affairs, they became to towns what feudal
lords were to the countryside and hence of the greatest importance.

Although many gilds existed to meet the needs of traders, often dealing in commodities other than those indicated by their gild affiliation,
others demonstrate that in the late thirteenth and early fourteenth
centuries, towns were not occupied merely by buyers and sellers. They
were also home to a variety of manufacture. Of this, cloth was the most
important. Stamford, Lincoln, Northampton and Beverley were
acknowledged producers of fine cloth in the mid-thirteenth century.
Lincoln and Stamford were noted for their 'scarlet' although it is Lincoln
green that has passed into folk myth along with Robin Hood and his

---

[19] Black, *Guilds*, 3–4; *York Memorandum Book*, i, 180–1; Westlake, *Parish Gilds*, 157,
172–3 and *passim*; Rosser, 'Crafts', 8–10; Carus-Wilson, *Medieval Merchant Venturers*,
223–7; Britnell, *Growth and Decline*, 36, 160.

equally mythical band of merry men. Other towns, large and small, were also active cloth producers, Leicester being a particularly well-documented example. A generation ago, historians identified a crisis in the cloth industry in the later thirteenth century, together with a shift in production from towns to the countryside in order to escape ever more suffocating gild restrictions. Once again, an earlier picture is now thought to have been too clear cut. Too little allowance was made for clothmaking in the countryside from the earliest times, whether for domestic consumption on large estates or within the peasant household. Moreover, the symbiotic relationship between town and country was as strong in this sphere of activity as in others; rural weavers brought their cloth to town for finishing, while urban merchants sometimes provided capital-intensive items such as a loom or wool which the weavers could not afford. It is now agreed that the demise of the older urban cloth industry should not be exaggerated. Although the market for quality cloths suffered competition from Flanders and Brabant during the later thirteenth century, evidence suggests a compensatory growth in the manufacture of cheaper worsted cloths, for which the large and increasingly impoverished population provided a ready market. Moreover, despite the challenge, English quality cloth continued to find overseas customers into the fourteenth century. Arguably, it was at this time that the foundations were laid for later English domination of the European market with high quality woollens. A gradual change was taking place in the balance of production between older regional centres and the emerging cloth towns in East Anglia and the Cotswolds, which by the fifteenth century had acquired massive perpendicular churches, substantial cloth halls and weavers' cottages destined to become today's bijoux residences. Although these towns took time to grow, already by 1327 more weavers could be found in Lavenham and Long Melford in Suffolk than in neighbouring villages.[20]

If cloth was the most important manufacture in many towns, it was by no means the only one. Literally hundreds of different craftsmen laboured in cramped workshops to produce goods for the market. Many have passed on occupational names to their descendants, although the nature of the craft can now be obscure. It is not immediately obvious today, for example, that fletchers made arrows or horners made horn spoons or combs. Soon carters and smiths may follow them beyond living memory. The creation of a single article frequently involved several crafts. A saddle, for example, required a fuster (joiner) to prepare the basic wooden frame, a lorimer to fashion the

---

[20] Miller and Hatcher, *Medieval England: Towns*, 107–28; Bridbury, *Medieval English Clothmaking*, 5–9; Childs, 'The English export trade', 137–8, 146–7.

accompanying metal bridle and bit, and a painter to provide the decoration. Similarly, a finished cloth would have passed through the hands of those who carded and spun the wool, a weaver and, depending on the type of cloth, a fuller, a shearer and a dyer. All these were skilled operations but, in smaller towns especially, crafts were often combined with other activities. Nor were these other activities always of a commercial nature. Burgesses, by definition the most solidly established members of the community, held land in the town fields and were part time agriculturalists.

Manufacture, even in the cloth industry, was essentially carried out in small workshops requiring a modest input of capital. The number of separate crafts involved in the production of a finished item was as much a practical response to an inability to finance and operate an integrated enterprise as a reflection of the variety of skills required. It reinforces the suggestion that the English economy had not yet developed to a high level of sophistication despite the financing and co-ordination of merchants who marketed the finished product. England in the later thirteenth and early fourteenth centuries thus appears to have been a relatively underdeveloped economy, a primary producer, lacking the expertise and infrastructure to process its rich natural resources effectively. This is borne out by its principal exports as revealed by records of customs duties newly imposed in 1275. Export of raw wool far exceeded in value that of cloth.[21] The other raw material for which England was prized was tin. Until supplies in central Europe were tapped during the course of the thirteenth century, Devon and Cornwall enjoyed the only exploited deposits available. An essential ingredient of a number of alloys, chiefly bronze and pewter, a ready export market was assured from Roman times onwards. By the first decade of the fourteenth century, manufactured pewter was being exported, but it was far less important than the export of tin itself. Significantly, remaining exports were largely animal products, such as hides and cheese, together with grain and fish, all redolent of an agricultural economy.

Although the exercise is fraught with statistical hazard, attempts have been made recently to assess how far the economy as a whole was commercialized. The conclusions are interesting but highly speculative. Moreover, although the situation c.1300 has been taken as a point of comparison, the thrust of the investigation has been into the state of the economy at the time of the Norman Conquest. Nevertheless, a number of prerequisites for a developed economy have been identified and it is possible to decide how far they were present in England in the time of Edward I and Edward II.

[21] Childs, 'The English export trade', 132–3.

The first of these prerequisites is monetization. Here there can be no doubt. Money transactions were widespread, despite a good deal of subsistence farming and unrecorded barter. The poorest peasant needed to market enough produce to meet rent obligations. Even villeins performing labour services commonly owed a proportion of their rent in cash. Specialization of labour was also well established, even though few were engaged exclusively in a single occupation. Individual trades were habitually segregated into particular quarters within towns, especially where, as in the case of butchery and tanning, they caused pollution. Markets in both labour and land were increasingly evident. In 1267, Henry III was able to write to the king of France that land was commonly sold at ten times its annual value.[22] Meanwhile, many landlords preferred to employ wage labour rather than exact labour services. A market in capital had evolved to the extent that money could be borrowed on manageable terms where risk was low, but merchants engaged in less certain enterprises could only raise finance on a partnership basis and frequently faced ruin. This was particularly true of overseas ventures, where shipwreck was a very real hazard. Opinion is divided as to how far, if at all, the economy became more commercialized between 1066 and 1300, but it has been suggested that the balance between subsistence and the market in gross domestic product might be roughly comparable to the fifty per cent split of mid-twentieth-century Africa or possibly the slightly more market-orientated India at the same date. This perhaps offers the best imaginative feel for conditions which, in England, are now remote from our experience.

The English economy in the thirteenth and early fourteenth centuries has been judged perforce on its export performance, since internal trade is impossible to quantify. It is likely, however, that exports accounted for only about four per cent of the £5 million gross domestic product estimated by Nicholas Mayhew.[23] Although exports only tell a small part of the story, they do perhaps indicate how change was taking place. The seeds of a strong, new trade in native cloth were being nourished by unwittingly protectionist customs policies adopted by the crown. Customs records show a strong underlying rise throughout the fourteenth century, despite marked short-term fluctuations. On a very different plane, Edward II's tomb set the precedent for a small but highly successful industry in carved and painted alabaster. Anyone who has seen the magnificent collection of panels depicting the deposition of Christ in the Musée de Cluny in Paris cannot doubt that they were produced on a commercial scale to a standard design. By the later fourteenth century,

[22] Cal Pat, 1266–72, 141.
[23] Britnell and Campbell, A Commercialising Economy, chs 1–4, esp. 57–9.

successors to the prosperous English merchants of earlier decades were men rich enough to service the crown's borrowing needs. Whereas formerly the crown had relied heavily on Italian banking houses, particularly the Riccardi and the Frescobaldi in the late thirteenth century and the Bardi and Peruzzi early in the following century, it was an English merchant, William de la Pole, who emerged as the king's principal source of loans when the Bardi and Peruzzi went bankrupt in the 1340s.

Who finally were the merchants who powered commercial life under Edward I and II? Many of them were small scale, often part-time traders. At the opposite end of the spectrum, there were the wealthy aliens, great merchant bankers of Italy, members of the German Hanse, merchants from Cahors, Gascony, Spain and, when politics permitted, the Low Countries. London and the greater ports in the late thirteenth and early fourteenth centuries were cosmopolitan places. Hull and Boston were thronged with merchants from Norway, Germany and the Low Countries, while the ports of the south-west were patronized by men from France and Iberia.[24] These overseas traders were not absorbed into the host community on an equal basis. Although blessed by wealth, aliens were significantly disadvantaged by their status as outsiders. Medieval society controlled the behaviour of its members through social sanctions imposed by neighbour and kin, reinforced by a system of mutual responsibility. Anyone outside this system *ipso facto* represented a threat. The insecurity this engendered can be seen from the advice offered to those crossing to England by Giovanni Frescobaldi in the early fourteenth century: 'Wear modest clothes, be humble, be dull in appearance'. Since outsiders were by definition deprived of the network of support commonly enjoyed by those at home, he further recommended that they stick with their fellow countrymen and ensure that their doors were bolted early and securely.[25] To the danger of theft or attack by the mob in times of unrest was added the hostility of native merchants with whom they competed. Small wonder therefore that the favour and protection of the crown was vital to them. This Edward I provided in large measure, to the disgust of his English subjects, particularly to the merchants of Gascony, which held a special place in his affections. The price for royal patronage was high, however. The Riccardi were ruined by the withdrawal of royal favour in 1294. Poncius de Mora, a Cahorsin wool merchant favoured by appointment as the king's wine buyer, was nevertheless living in poverty by 1300. In the following century, it was royal debt that caused the failure of the Bardi

---

[24] Childs, 'The English export trade', 135–6.
[25] Lopez and Raymond, *Medieval Trade*, 423–4.

and Peruzzi.[26] Fortune was fickle; if aliens could rise high, they could also fall far. The picture was not altogether gloomy, however. Even before the reforms instituted by the crown in 1285, there is evidence of alien merchants acquiring property and being admitted to citizenship in London. Some aliens went into partnership with Englishmen. Others, such as the Italian Hugh Gerrard trading through Newcastle upon Tyne, married into the local merchant community. Overseas merchants in Southampton were commonly taken into the houses of denizens (natives), while in London there was a sizeable community of Italians who had chosen to settle in the city on a permanent basis.[27]

By 1300 there were numerous English merchants who, while not yet in the same class as the merchant princes of the Continent, were nevertheless men of wealth and power within the local community. This is reflected in what we know of their lifestyle. Less luxurious than that of aristocratic Elizabeth de Burgh, it was nevertheless very comfortable by the standards of the day. A building account for a London furrier's house of 1308 reveals a hall with a large bay window with living quarters for the family upstairs and a stable with rooms and garrets for other members of the household. Archaeological finds at the house of Richard of Southwick (d. c.1290) in Southampton show that he owned pewter vessels, imported glass and painted claret jugs from the Saintonge in south-west France from which he could pour the town's principal import, as well as high-quality local ceramics for the rest of his household. A man who was far from being the richest merchant of his generation, he even kept a small African monkey, presumably as a pet.[28]

As in the countryside, the story has been predominantly that of men. However, the domestic nature of so much trade and industry inevitably drew female members of the family into active participation. Evidence for London at the end of the thirteenth century shows not only wives working in partnership with their husbands and widows carrying on the family business, but also single women trading on their own behalf. Those married to a citizen could, if they wished, operate as individuals, answerable for their own debts. These opportunities should not be exaggerated however; women were more prominent in selling, particularly textiles and more expensive goods, than in manufacture. Should a husband die, there was often pressure to wed a fellow tradesman lest

[26] Miller and Hatcher, *Medieval England: Towns*, 200–6.

[27] Nightingale, *Medieval Mercantile Community*, 93; Lloyd, *Alien Merchants*, 40 and *passim*; Platt, *Medieval Southampton*, 69; S. Dempsey, 'The Italian community in London during the reign of Edward II', *London Journal*, xviii (1993), 14–22. For England's trading activities overseas see chapter 8.

[28] F. Barker and P. Jackson, *London: Two Thousand Years of a City and its People*, London, 1974, 36; Platt, *Medieval Southampton*, 103–4.

marriage to an outsider damage the interests of the heirs or other members of the craft. A widow might be entitled to be a freewoman of the city with full trading rights providing that she did not remarry, but she also carried a concomitant obligation to carry on if there were apprentices who had not yet served out their terms.[29] Although there are few early gild records for other towns, it is unlikely that arrangements governing the participation of women were significantly different.

Below the level of organized crafts, women had carved a useful though not exclusive niche for themselves in brewing and selling ale. They were also heavily involved in all sorts of food preparation and retailing. Those found infringing the 1301 York ordinances included bakers and cooks. In late thirteenth-century Norwich, they were found breaking the law by buying grain and shellfish outside the town and bringing it in to sell at a profit. The quantities involved in these illicit transactions were almost certainly small. Female trading, both in the choice of commodity and in volume, appears to have been an extension of their domestic role. Their appearance as hostel-keepers also conforms to this pattern. Worsening conditions among the poor towards the end of the thirteenth century and the crises of the fourteenth may have forced more women into augmenting the family income by such means. It may also have driven more women into prostitution, particularly those who had migrated to towns in search of employment and who were without the protective supervision of their kin. That it was a recognized aspect of town life may be inferred from provision made in the York ordinances for the removal of the roof and doors of known brothels and the order in Bristol that prostitutes wear a striped hood to distinguish them from other women.[30] Then, as now, it was a dangerous occupation; towns were not guaranteed to be a route to female independence and fortune. Many, however, found safer work as domestic servants and achieved greater independence than they would have enjoyed in the countryside. For women, like unfree peasants, town air offered a breath of freedom to exploit as they might.

Despite continuing restriction on free trade through tolls, and uncertainties in overseas trading relations, the growth of towns in size and number by the end of the thirteenth century meant that England had developed a larger trading base than its lower population would actually need in the later Middle Ages. As in modern developing economies, urban streets were crammed with those making a precarious living doing and selling whatever they could find. Even those who were

[29] D. Keene, 'Tanners' widows, 1300–1350', in Barron and Sutton, *Medieval London Widows*, 1–27 and also xxvii-viii.
[30] *Women in England*, 27–34, 185–91, 210.

relatively well established lived in squalid, overcrowded conditions. Pigs were the least of the hazards to be encountered in the gutter. Medieval towns were not healthy places for rich or poor. When we know about urban death rates in the later Middle Ages, they are horrifying. Monks entering Westminster Abbey or Canterbury Cathedral Priory had a life expectancy of less than thirty years for much of the fifteenth century.[31] Mortality at that period was exceptionally high. The subjects of Edward I and Edward II were spared epidemics on the scale that haunted society from the mid-fourteenth century. However, open sewers and the close proximity in which people lived no doubt ensured that many died prematurely. This did not deter people from flocking into towns. Indeed, it is unlikely that they could have sustained their population without such constant inward migration. Even the most important members of society found it necessary to have a London base. For all the debate about the prosperity of towns at this date and the relatively small proportion of the population living in them, it is clear that they played a vital role in English society.

---

[31] Harvey, *Living and Dying*, 127–9; Hatcher, 'Mortality', 32.

4

The Church

The overwhelming presence of the church, together with the distinctive nature of feudal bonds, formed the essence and distinguishing features of medieval society. That worship of a higher power and preparation for the afterlife should play so large a part in people's concerns is not surprising. Even for the wealthiest, life was unpredictable and often brutish, while almost all natural phenomena were inexplicable. No wonder that events were attributed to supernatural intervention and that so many felt vulnerable in the face of it. In such circumstances, the promise of protection and salvation offered by Christian teaching proved infinitely comforting.

By the thirteenth century, the church had extended its activities and infrastructure far beyond its distant initial mission. Viewed as a whole, it was not only immensely rich, but everywhere a familiar and monumental physical presence. In the countryside, stone or flint churches were by far the largest and most solid edifices to be found in most communities, asserting the primacy of the spiritual over the material. Cathedrals and monasteries dominated their environs to an even greater degree. High walled monastic precincts were not unlike Victorian prisons in their symbolic and practical claim to privacy in the public interest. Only castles could rival the great religious institutions in size, but secular buildings could never compete with the richness of decoration and the aura of mystery associated with holy places, heightened by appeals to the senses through incense, bells and guttering candles.

Although customarily referred to as though it was an entity, the church was in reality a complex mesh of widely differing persons and bodies. At its widest, it comprised the whole of society, lay and clerical. More narrowly, it consisted of those in holy orders or men and women who, while not ordained, had nevertheless taken vows to live a celibate life usually under some form of rule. It is this narrower group which is generally meant when referring to the church, but, even then, the variety of individuals and institutions encompassed within the single term remained huge.

The church which survives today as the Anglican Church with its parochial system and hierarchy of archdeacons and bishops, culminating in the archbishops of Canterbury and York, constituted only one part of the medieval church – the so-called secular church. The other part consisted of the regulars who belonged to one or other of the religious orders and whose name derived from *regula*, meaning rule.[1] In many ways the secular hierarchy mirrored that of lay society. Those at the top were generally drawn from well-born families, of knightly or aristocratic background, even where their advancement was a reward for administrative service to the crown. Such was Chancellor Robert Burnell, bishop of Bath and Wells between 1275 and 1292. By contrast, the parish priests who served at the base of the pyramid were often peasants, distinguishable from those whom they served only by a little learning. This was even more true of the countless numbers of unbeneficed clergy who earned a frugal living as chaplains or minor officials. Life at the bottom of the ecclesiastical heap must have been the lot of many of those recorded as being in holy orders in the Spalding censuses.[2] For men such as these, a patron, most probably their lord with livings in his gift, was the only hope of advancement.

It was the secular church present in each community which most directly served the spiritual needs of the laity. Although by this time well organized and equipped in terms of buildings, it nevertheless confronted intractable problems of funding and providing sufficiently well-educated incumbents to fulfil its function properly. The parochial clergy were supported by their glebe (land attached to the church) and tithes, supplemented by dues paid at certain times of the year and for certain services such as officiating at burials. Unfortunately by the later thirteenth century, both the right to present priests to parish churches and much of the tithe income had fallen into the hands of religious houses. Eleventh-and twelfth-century attempts by church reformers to wrest control of parish churches and their tithes from the lords who had built them had led to compromise gifts of advowsons (the right to present) to the religious rather than their surrender to episcopal control. Lords were thus enabled to comply with church reform while at the same time providing benefactions for the good of their souls. In itself the transfer of advowsons to the religious did not significantly worsen the situation, since lay and ecclesiastical patrons were equally likely to

---

[1] Confusingly, secular is today used as a synonym for lay, as in the second paragraph of the chapter. The meaning is usually clear from the context.

[2] See chapter 1.

use the benefice to support their officials, with the consequent effect of non-residence. However, for an ecclesiastical patron it was often a short step from presenting a clerk to the benefice to placing the institution itself in the position of rector, thereby appropriating the major tithe revenue from grain and leaving the parish to be served by a vicar (literally a deputy) on a much reduced income. A surviving handful of magnificent medieval tithe barns bears witness to the scale of wealth siphoned away from parishes in this way. A combination of absentee rectors and impoverished vicars meant that few parishes were served by well-educated incumbents or able to fund an education for those they had. This inevitably imposed a ceiling on the quality of teaching available to the rural laity and presented the church with a structural problem which worsened in the later Middle Ages as religious houses sought to shore up their finances through further appropriation. Nor was this problem solved by the Reformation, because the income from appropriated rectories merely passed into the hands of the lay successors to the religious. However, to recognize these difficulties is not to devalue the quality of spiritual life which flourished in many parishes and which has been defended so vigorously for the later Middle Ages by Eamon Duffy, but it was a spirituality which drew heavily on visual culture, on ritual incorporating many of the traditions of the ancient countryside and on rote learning.[3]

Just as one has to turn to the paintings of Longthorpe Tower to gain an imaginative insight into the world of the knightly family, so one can turn to the fabric and decoration of parish churches for that of the medieval villager. Today's churches are a poor guide to their medieval past. The plain interiors dictated by modern taste would once have been a cluttered riot of colour. Carved roods (crucifixes) and lively depictions of the Last Judgement, which often covered the chancel arch, can have left the populace in little doubt as to the central messages of Christianity. Further paintings round the nave might recount Bible stories, the lives of saints or moral themes such as the dangers of idle gossip, the seven deadly sins or the seven works of mercy.[4] The role of the laity was largely to observe and absorb, particularly the elevation of the host at the Mass. By the later thirteenth century, the host had become the most important Christian image, eclipsing even the cross. The introduction of the feast of Corpus Christi into England c.1320 enhanced its importance still further, a process which gathered pace as the century progressed, with the appearance of Corpus Christi gilds and Corpus Christi sermons and processions.[5] Popular piety expressed itself not in the

[3] Duffy, *Stripping of the Altars, passim.* See also chapter 5.
[4] Rouse, *Medieval Wall Paintings,* 38–70.
[5] Rubin, *Corpus Christi,* 199–200.

scriptures or theological argument so beloved of the Lollards and post-Reformation divines, but in simple devotions before statues of the Virgin and saints, where offerings of candles marked humble requests for intercession. Nor was this something deplored by the ecclesiastical authorities. The bishop of Exeter's synod in 1287 required that every church in the diocese be provided with two crosses, one statue of the Blessed Virgin Mary and further images of local saints.[6] The few statues to survive Reformation iconoclasm give scant impression of their full medieval splendour. Garish to our mind, many were brightly painted and lovingly dressed, decked in whatever jewellery the community and grateful suppliants could afford. They, along with parishioners, played an active part in public life as they were carried in procession at celebrations of the major festivals.

By the later thirteenth century, these visual aids to learning were reinforced by systematic instruction. The Lambeth council of 1281 introduced a preaching programme including the Creed, the Ten Commandments, the seven virtues, the seven vices, the seven works of mercy and the seven sacraments, to be delivered to parishioners in the vernacular four times a year. William of Pagula's *Oculis Sacerdotis*, written in the 1320s, assisted further with guidance to the clergy on confession and the seven sacraments, together with teaching for the laity. The emphasis was severely practical and in places more akin to social rather than spiritual education. In the section on the sacraments, eight reasons were given why husbands should love their wives and eight reasons why marriage should be commended. On confession, the priest was enjoined to ask a penitent, 'if he was drunk, how he got drunk, whether perchance because he did not know the power of the wine, or because of guests, or because of an exceeding thirst coming upon him'. Expectant mothers were advised to avoid heavy work and, when delivered, to breast-feed.[7] If this was a long way from the theological learning to be found in the universities, it nevertheless represented a real achievement in ensuring that parishioners were equipped with the key knowledge and guidance to live a Christian life.

The Thorpe family of Longthorpe was very much part of this spiritual tradition, as the wall paintings in their chamber show. Knights and barons had more opportunities for learning, but this remained for the most part devotional rather than intellectual. The wealthier among them obtained their bishop's permission for private chapels and were served by private chaplains. Illuminated manuscripts, which in the twelfth century had been the preserve of the religious, were increasingly

---

[6] Camille, *Gothic Idol*, 224–5.
[7] Duffy, *Stripping of the Altars*, 53–5; Pantin, *The English Church*, 197–202.

commissioned by wealthy lay patrons. Richly painted psalters, books of hours and lives of saints became devotional works for study in the home or for liturgical use in their chapels or parish churches. Such was the Luttrell Psalter. Texts were produced for a specifically lay clientele, such as the manual of practical instruction for the Mass written c.1310–25 in French and illustrated by the same fine artist as the Queen Mary Psalter. Entitled 'What you should do and think at each stage in the Mass', the text was augmented by thirteen pictures showing variously the priest, the server and the congregation. Rather than remain passive recipients of what the clergy offered, the interaction of words and image in this and other manuscripts enabled those with sketchy Latin but with the privilege of wealth to play a more active part in their spiritual development. Robert Mannyng, a Gilbertine canon, addressed an even broader audience in his lengthy vernacular poem *Handlyng Synne*, written between 1303 and 1317. Translated from an earlier Anglo-Norman work, its lively tone and vivid illustrative anecdotes based on local East Anglian and Lincolnshire incidents and folk culture made it instantly accessible to laity and parish priests alike.[8]

Until the recent upsurge of Catholic writing, it was common to view the medieval church through the distorting glass of post-Reformation Protestant values. The verdict was inevitably disparaging. The worst aspects of relics and pilgrimages were emphasized, while pluralism and non-residence were condemned, with scant appreciation of the social norms of a patronage-based society or the genuine attempts of senior churchmen to tackle abuses. Historians are now much readier to assess the medieval church on its own terms. Despite the underfunding and episcopal worries about the educational attainment of ordinands, by 1300 parish life was well adapted to the needs of a largely peasant society. Those in search of intellectual engagement with Christian doctrine and a more sophisticated approach to spirituality looked to the other, equally important, half of the church.

The regular orders, excised by Henry VIII at the Dissolution, were diverse in origin and nature and even, if somewhat grudgingly, provided a vocation for women. The oldest and richest religious houses were founded in the pre-Conquest period for monks or nuns following the rule of St Benedict. To these were added in the eleventh and particularly the twelfth centuries foundations where Cluniacs and, later, Cistercians might follow reformed versions of this rule, and canons (priests who lived a common life) might follow the rules of St Augustine, St Norbert or St Gilbert of Sempringham. The last was the only native religious

---

[8] Alexander and Binski, *Age of Chivalry*, 37, 148–51, 236, no. 110; Platts, 'Robert Mannyng', 24–5.

order and unusually included ten joint houses for men and women, although they lived separately within a common precinct. This fertile period for religious endowment had also seen the advent of Templars and Hospitallers, men who combined the vocation of monk and soldier and whose origin and focus lay with the Holy Land. It is significant, however, that no more orders of this sort were established in thirteenth-century England.[9] Society was changing. Western monasticism had risen from the ashes of the Roman Empire as a refuge in a disintegrating world and remained relevant into the twelfth century. Contemporaries saw a connection between the surge in religious foundations and the unrest of King Stephen's reign (1135–54). Aelred of Rievaulx is said to have realized that 'in those days, it was hard for any to live the good life unless they were monks or members of some religious order so disturbed and chaotic was the land reduced almost to a desert by the malice, slaughters and harryings of evil men'.[10] By the thirteenth century, however, a larger population, more buoyant economy and, above all, more settled government meant that the need to retreat from a chaotic world in order to save one's soul had greatly diminished.

The loss of their *raison d'être* did not mean the disappearance of older houses. It is one of the ironies of history that just as popular enthusiasm for the enclosed orders was beginning to wane, the crown for the first time established effective legal title allowing them to protect their landholdings from seizure. Houses which had been plagued by invasions of their property and attempts by heirs to claw back benefactions were now able to defend their estates from depredation effectively. The thirteenth century thus inherited a large number of religious institutions, some such as Westminster Abbey or Glastonbury rich enough to rival the greatest magnates in their annual income, but which were no longer at the cutting edge of Christian observance.

Exactly how much of the country's wealth was tied up in the enclosed orders is not an easy question to answer. Although historians owe almost all their knowledge about the medieval economy to records from the great monastic estates, a comprehensive picture of their holdings is elusive. There were some 800 religious houses by the thirteenth century, but wealth was unevenly spread between them and also in its geographical distribution. Where concentrated, monastic wealth had a profound effect on the regional economy. The oldest and richest houses were concentrated in central and southern England, largely because this

[9] The Carthusian order, combining life as a hermit with life in a community, founded on the Continent in 1084, was exceptional in not becoming well established in England until the later fourteenth century. For the chronology of foundation and wealth of religious houses at the Dissolution, see Knowles and Hadcock, *Medieval Religious Houses*.
[10] *Life of Aelred*, 28.

anciently settled fertile region was the home of their earliest benefactors.[11] The group of tenth-century foundations in the Fens reflected both Christian recolonization after the destructive Danish invasions of the ninth century and a subtle means of asserting royal control in a border region. The extent to which this early religious settlement continued to dominate the east Midlands can be seen from the 1279 hundred rolls. There were few estates, particularly in north Huntingdonshire and the Fens, which did not belong to one or other of the great abbeys of Peterborough, Ramsey, Ely, Crowland and Thorney or one of the smaller houses like Sawtry Abbey, also to be found in that area. Although the same source makes it clear that nearby counties of Bedfordshire and Oxfordshire lacked religious institutions on the same scale, the overall impact on the region was considerable. Monastic precincts formed the nucleii of towns which grew up to service their needs. Bury St Edmunds is an unusually well-documented case, thanks to a unique entry in Domesday Book.[12] More significantly, monastic estates tended to differ in structure from those of the laity. Kosminsky's analysis of the 1279 hundred rolls showed that ecclesiastical manors were generally larger and more traditionally organized.[13] Insofar as the classical manor existed, with its demesne (lord's land) and villein tenantry, it was chiefly to be found on monastic estates in central lowland England.

Monastic settlement affected the north of England just as much, but in a different way. With a few exceptions, houses belonging to the austere Cistercian order were located north of the River Trent on unpromising moorland. At the time of their foundation, this barren terrain appealed both to the monks' wish for poverty and seclusion and their patrons' inability to spare better land for their grants. It is yet another historical irony that these meagre endowments proved ideal for the sheep flocks which brought extraordinary wealth and subverted the Cistercian commitment to simplicity. As Pegolotti's list shows, in the early fourteenth century Cistercian houses were prominent suppliers of wool to overseas merchants.[14] The monks were recognized for their capability as breeders and producers of high-quality, well-graded fleeces. Unfortunately, this was not always matched by their business acumen. By the later thirteenth century, it had become customary to sell wool for several years ahead of production in order to finance ambitious building projects or to service debt. Risky at the best of times, this led to disaster when scab became prevalent after 1275 and the weight of fleeces declined dramatically. By 1291, Fountains was in debt to the tune of more than £6,000,

[11] See map 3.
[12] VCH Suffolk, i, 508–9.
[13] Kosminsky, Studies in Agrarian History, 108–12.
[14] See pp. 49–50.

MAP 3   Distribution of black monk houses in 1100

a heavy burden even for the richest of the Cistercian abbeys.[15] At smaller houses, the debt might be smaller too but the situation no less desperate. Relations between the monks of Pipewell Abbey in Northamptonshire and merchants from Cahors in France reached such a pass by 1290 that they had to call on arbitrators. The resulting agreement, enrolled in the royal Chancery, is informative about the preparation of wool for export, but regrettably less explicit about the 'divers trespasses and damages' inflicted by the abbey. Its own records reveal a sorry tale of debt which continued well into the next century, and the mysterious disposal of a London house. Opinion differed as to whether it had been sold on the abbot's authority or by a monk using a forged abbey seal.

<hr/>

[15] Stephenson, 'Wool yields', 376–81; Denholm-Young, *Seignorial Administration*, 53–7.

Whatever the truth of the matter, the abbot resigned his office in 1294.[16] The plight of other abbeys may have stopped short of disrepute, but their indebtedness was often comparable.

With the exception of the Gilbertines, the distribution of houses of canons was less geographically specific. In their case, however, it was striking. Of the twenty-three houses, all but a handful were in Lincoln-shire and Yorkshire.[17] In the words of the order's most recent historian, 'Gilbertine priories were, like their Augustinian cousins, local houses for local men and women.'[18] In this respect, they were typical of the majority of twelfth-century foundations. The days when magnates surrendered great swathes of countryside to their chosen institution were long gone. Needs of family and followers over the centuries had left little land to spare even among the aristocracy, and adequate provision for their souls had already been made. The most generous benefactors of the twelfth century were those grown newly rich in the service of the crown, for whom the Augustinian canons exercised a strong appeal. Among the twelfth-century foundations, only Cirencester (Augustinian), Fountains (Cistercian), Reading (Benedictine) and St John's Clerkenwell (Hospital-ler) ranked alongside the greatest of the houses established in the tenth and eleventh centuries and recorded as having net incomes at the Dissolution of more than £1,000 per annum.[19] Founders and patrons were drawn increasingly from lesser ranks, knightly families wishing to emulate those higher in the social scale, with correspondingly more limited resources. Their grants often consisted of estates within villages where lordship was shared, advowson rights or even isolated plots of land. The influence of such foundations on the local economy was accordingly more limited.

The spiritual legacy of these orders to the thirteenth century was more modest than their wealth might suggest, but should not be underestimated. Even the largest and oldest houses continued to attract small offerings, as the habit of giving filtered down the social scale to the peasantry. For some rural tenants, prayers or a candle burning at an altar in their lord's abbey or priory church must have seemed an even more potent guarantee of blessing than anything the parish church could offer. For those men and women who felt a vocation to the enclosed life, their local house was an obvious choice. More often still one suspects it was the obvious choice for parents deciding on the future of younger sons or daughters. The large number of nunneries in Yorkshire and

[16] *Cal Close, 1288–96*, 192–5; BL, Cott. Otho B xiv, fos. 155v–94v.
[17] See map 4.
[18] Golding, *Gilbert of Sempringham*, 308.
[19] Knowles and Hadcock, *Medieval Religious Houses, passim*.

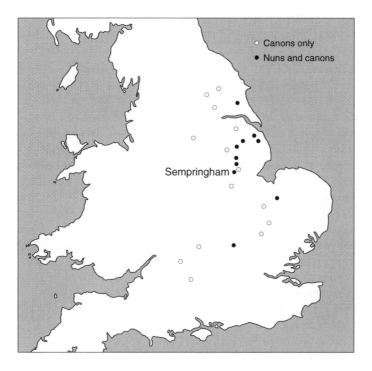

MAP 4   Distribution of Gilbertine houses in 1300

Lincolnshire, including those of the Gilbertine order, probably owed their existence to the needs of the unusually large number of small knightly families in that region. The sisters of Geoffrey Luttrell were nuns at nearby Gilbertine houses, so too was his daughter Isabella.[20] Placement in a nunnery was a respectable solution to the financial embarrassment presented by too many daughters in need of dowries. It was customary to make an offering to the house on entry, but the cost was more manageable. For some of these girls it would have been a happy enough solution, but the frequency of apostasy (abandonment of vows) during the thirteenth century suggests that vocation often came second to convenience. As with parish life, however, it is easy to focus on inadequacies and abuses, while failing to appreciate less well-documented pious observance.

The quality of spiritual life within the old orders is not easy to gauge. The Gilbertine order envisaged punishment for theft, conspiracy, arson

[20] Camille, *Mirror*, 57, 118.

and illicit homosexual or heterosexual relations, albeit for the lay brothers rather than the canons or nuns.[21] Equally, it was a Gilbertine canon
who was moved to write *Handlyng Synne*. That discipline might prove a
problem is not surprising, given the way in which many of the religious
were recruited. In 1276, the archbishop of York's register records that
one canon from the Augustinian priory of Felley kept a mistress 'newly
impregnated' in Nottingham, while another kept his in Annesley.[22] Such
scandals erupted from time to time, but a more insidious challenge to
tranquillity and worship arose from the tensions present in any small
community. The same register in 1275 ordered the subprior of New-
burgh Priory in Yorkshire not to lose his temper in chapter meetings, the
cellarer to be less surly with his colleagues and visitors, and the canons
not to gossip with outsiders in the old prior's chamber.[23] The bishop of
Lincoln was called upon to impose penances for similarly trivial misdemeanours following his visitation of St Michael's nunnery at Stamford
in 1298, while in the previous year the nuns had actually come to
blows.[24] Life in many houses was disturbed by their benefactors using
them as convenient places for retirement, the education of their children
or the medieval equivalent of hotels. The canons of Watton Priory
(Yorkshire) were not the only ones to have to call on royal aid, when
in 1272 they needed to rid themselves of a patron who had descended
with 'a great crowd of women with dogs and other animals'.[25]

The reliance of poorer houses on the income brought by boarders
undermined good discipline, as did the debt and maladministration
found in many places by the late thirteenth and early fourteenth centuries. Nunneries in particular ran the risk of recruiting more than their
slender resources could support. Nor were the Cistercians the only order
to miscalculate their capacity to fund new buildings or to make impru-
dent contracts with overseas merchants. For some houses, the wars and
agricultural crises of the early fourteenth century were the final straw.
Laying off their servants was not sufficient to rescue the canons of
Bolton Priory in the Yorkshire Dales. In 1320, they were forced to
disperse themselves among eight other houses in the north of England
to allow their finances to recover from the disasters which culminated
with the Scots who 'plundered their animals and beasts at various times
and have destroyed their villages, manors and places with fire and
flame'.[26]

[21] Golding, *Gilbert of Sempringham*, 159.
[22] *Register of Walter Giffard*, 319–20.
[23] Ibid., 329.
[24] BL, Cott. Vesp. E xxii, fos. 33, 35v–6.
[25] Golding, *Gilbert of Sempringham*, 320–1.
[26] Kershaw, *Bolton Priory*, 17. See chapter 2.

For an insight into life in one of the less vulnerable, old black monk houses one can turn to the *De Gestis Abbatum* (Deeds of the Abbots) of Thorney Abbey. Writing in the early fourteenth century, the author warmly praised the three abbots whose rule spanned the years 1261–1313, a time when the abbey was thriving. His enthusiasm, however, was reserved primarily for their material rather than their spiritual achievements. Major building works at the abbey and on many of the estates were admiringly described, as were purchases of property and doughty legal battles with neighbouring abbeys. Insofar as worship was mentioned, it was in the context of the acquisition of jewelled chalices and vestments richly embroidered with gold stars, leopards and griffons. The simplicity and compassion of Abbot Odo were a matter for approval, but one judges that these qualities alone would not have commended him as leader. The emphasis was on beauty and grandeur, but it is important to remember that these were characteristic of the black monks' commitment to worship to the glory of God. They may have appeared inappropriate to later reformed orders, but they did not mark a radical departure from their own ideals. Yet, for all its splendour, it is noticeable that this house too was in trouble by the 1320s, when Abbot Reginald succeeded to a debt of 1,300 marks.[27]

If the ardour of the oldest houses had often become subsumed in liturgy and display, they still maintained a tradition of learning and artistic creativity, although it was no longer exclusive to them alone. The *scriptorium* of Peterborough Abbey continued to produce texts and illuminations of a high quality for their own use and for others. The writing of chronicles also extended into the fourteenth century at many houses. Some, such as the chronicle of Bartholomew Cotton, a monk of Norwich who died in 1298, were begun from scratch. Others, such as that of Bury St Edmunds, found their way into other houses, where they were adapted and continued by new scribes. It is known, for example, that a customized copy was made for Peterborough Abbey *c*.1295, with 'Peterborough' substituted for 'Bury' in the text where appropriate.[28] In the fourteenth century St Werburgh's, Chester, could still produce a historian of the calibre of Ranulf Higden, whose *Polychronicon* (Universal Chronicle) drew on a wealth of classical and medieval learning. Devotional reading remained an important part of the daily monastic timetable and many houses amassed large libraries for this purpose. Durham was perhaps unrivalled, with more than 500 volumes, but collections of several hundred were quite common. Higden, who is not known to have studied outside Chester, found Pliny and Bede as well as

---

[27] CUL, Add. MS 3021, fos. 448v–65.
[28] Gransden, *Historical Writing*, i, 402–3, 440.

scientific and homiletic literature in his monastic library. The only major gap in his reading, and perhaps a significant one, was the scholastic work produced at Oxford in the previous century.[29] Texts of all sorts in Latin, English and French were gathered into anthologies, often reflecting a surprisingly wide range of subject-matter. A Reading Abbey collection included French fables and the only surviving complete text of Marie de France's Breton lays, as well as music, English songs and Latin poems. This anthology was unusually secular in tone, but even in the more common religious compilations monastic copyists showed that they were influenced by the contemporary world. An increasing inclusion of vernacular material indicates a living tradition of study, not just a sterile reproduction of ancient works.[30]

Our dependence on visitation records for an assessment of the daily life of monks and nuns inevitably highlights their failings. Racy incidents of gross misconduct can easily be found, but should be balanced against leaders such as Prior Philip of St Mary's, York, (d. 1296) or Abbot John de Gamages of Gloucester (d. 1307?), who were renowned for their holiness. Nevertheless, David Knowles, the greatest historian of religious orders this century and himself a monk, surveying the visitation evidence with an informed eye, concluded that the prevailing standard of observance could best be described as one of 'decent mediocrity'.[31] The true heirs to those whose life of privation and sanctity had inspired the old orders were the anchorites, who were scattered in surprisingly large numbers throughout the country. These were men and women who took lifelong vows to live in seclusion, of whom 198 are known in the thirteenth century and 214 in the fourteenth. Significantly, some were members of religious orders seeking a more austere life. Such was Walter, an Augustinian canon for thirty years, who became a recluse c. 1270 and ten years later produced a rule. Another rule compiled by a fourteenth-century abbot of Bury St Edmunds, reveals that one of his monks wished to become a hermit, while an early fourteenth-century abbey register shows forty-two hermitages in the neighbourhood of the abbey.[32] That the religious sometimes wished to leave their communities for a more rigorous way of life attests at the same time to both the seriousness of spiritual purpose still to be found in the old orders and their inability to satisfy it.

A high proportion of anchorites were women, probably the majority. This is telling. The medieval church had a distinctly ambivalent attitude

[29] Burton, *Monastic Orders*, 193–4; Taylor, *The Universal Chronicle*, 1, 46, 87.
[30] Frankis, 'The social context of vernacular writing', 176–7.
[31] Knowles, *Religious Orders*, i, 112.
[32] Warren, *Anchorites*, 18, 291–7.

to women, which coloured its response to their strongly felt sense of religious vocation. It has also not passed without comment that David Knowles devoted only three pages to nuns in his magisterial study *The Monastic Order in England*.[33] Women were of course debarred from holy orders and thereby excluded from a leading role in the secular church. Nor were the reformed orders always sympathetic to their wish to join; the Cistercians denied them affiliation until the early thirteenth century.[34] Some churchmen proved readier in their support, but this in itself sometimes posed problems. The ecclesiastical authorities became increasingly, and perhaps understandably, nervous about the relationships between a number of hermits and their female followers or the informal attachments that grew up between groups of women and monasteries.[35] The success of the Gilbertines has been attributed in part to the strictly defined position of nuns within the community, thereby protecting them from scandal. It is noticeable, however, that while the order arose principally as a result of Gilbert's wish to provide for his female followers, by the later thirteenth century the nuns were engaged in a long rearguard action to defend their resources from the hands of the canons.[36] With the exception of a handful of rich pre-Conquest nunneries, houses for women were generally poorer, second-class in the education they offered to their inmates and uncertain in their discipline. It is not surprising that the most distinguished female contribution to fourteenth-century mysticism should come from the anchorite's cell of Dame Julian of Norwich, rather than from within the old orders.

By the later thirteenth century, the old orders continued to be hugely important economically and still fulfilled a social need, with standards of observance respectable if no longer fervent. Nevertheless, each generation tended to find a means of expression appropriate to its needs, and bustling towns with their skilled inhabitants were making new demands on the church. This constituency was served by the friars, whose distinctive contribution was to abandon the cloister and live a life of poverty within the community. Known as mendicants because they lived by begging, they presented a sharp contrast to the wealth of many of their forerunners. Their impact was the more powerful because their dedication to preaching also set a new standard of teaching for the laity. In order to hold the attention of their audiences, they leavened their theology with vivid illustrative stories. A legacy to the present day is the invention of the Christmas carol, in which they set sacred words to

---

[33] Golding, *Gilbert of Sempringham*, 2, n. 4; Burton, *Monastic Orders*, 85.
[34] Burton, *Monastic Orders*, 101.
[35] Thompson, *Women Religious*, 22–6; Elkins, *Holy Women*, 33–42.
[36] Golding, *Gilbert of Sempringham*, 133–7, 162–3.

popular contemporary tunes, just as the Salvation Army with a similar mission adopted those of the Victorian music-hall. Whereas massive abbey and priory walls signalled the exclusion of the laity from all that took place within, so the vast naves of the friars' churches and the preaching yards outside them bear witness to the change of emphasis towards a more inclusive approach and the popularity of the newly available message. By the late thirteenth century, all four mendicant orders – the Franciscans, Dominicans, Carmelites and Augustinians – were well established in the major towns of the realm. Their modest lifestyle called for the sort of gifts that ordinary people could afford, typically a mark or so. This, combined with their seizure of the moral high ground due to their emphasis on poverty, ensured their success. Although the Gilbertines had no difficulty in recruiting until the early fourteenth century, it is significant that William of Kyme, dying at the end of the thirteenth century, chose to be buried in Bullington Priory, while his wife Lucy elected to lie with the Franciscans at York.[37]

The importance of the friars was not solely as popular teachers, however. The Dominicans from their inception had laid great emphasis on scholarship and had indeed chosen Oxford as their first base in England. By the late thirteenth century, the Franciscans too had modified their original ideals to encompass learning. That Oxford and Cambridge ranked as European centres of learning alongside Paris, Montpellier or Bologna by the later thirteenth century was almost entirely due to the friars' presence there, even though relations with the University authorities were sometimes strained. It was the friars who introduced scholastic theology to Oxford, making it an international centre for debate about the writings of St Thomas Aquinas. Scholars such as Duns Scotus (d. 1308) or William of Ockham (d. 1347) ranked among the finest of the Middle Ages. The friars, notably Roger Bacon (d. 1294), were also responsible for the introduction of the study of languages, mathematics and science, a mundane footnote to which was a realization of the value of convex lenses to long-sighted readers.[38] These developments were to have profound consequences. It has even been argued that western Europe's ultimate emergence as the scientifically dominant continent was due to the way in which distinctively quantitative habits of thought were adopted in the fifty years after 1275.[39] The old orders perforce were drawn towards the new learning. By 1291 Durham and Gloucester Colleges had been founded at Oxford

[37] Ibid., 342, 447.
[38] Burton, *Monastic Orders*, 203–6; Manguel, *History of Reading*, 293–4.
[39] Crosby, *Measure of Reality*, 17–19.

for monks from the north and south of England respectively, while the Gilbertines had established St Edmund's College in Cambridge.[40] Already on the defensive because of the visible contrast between mendicant poverty and their own wealth, they could not afford to lose the theological arguments as well.

Although structurally distinct, the secular and regular clergy did not function in isolation from each other. Cathedrals might be served either by monks, as at Canterbury, Norwich or Durham or by secular clergy, as at St Paul's, London, Lincoln or York. Canons, as priests, sometimes combined a ministry to the laity with a life of communal worship. The friars, by their nature, shared with the parochial clergy in preaching and teaching. Leading churchmen within the secular church might be drawn from among the religious. John Pecham, archbishop of Canterbury 1279–92, was a Franciscan, his predecessor Robert Kilwardby a Dominican. The interaction between secular and regular or even between different religious orders was not without its tensions, however. More often than not, hostility focused on the friars. It did not help that they were a fashionable choice as confessors among the elite, or that many of the laity echoed the example of Edward I, who interred his second wife and the heart of his mother in the Franciscan church in London.[41] The quarrel that broke out between the Franciscans and the monks of Worcester over the burial of Henry Poche in 1289 was unusual only in its bizarre detail. Henry, despite having chosen burial in the Franciscan cemetery, was laid to rest in the cemetery belonging to the monks. When this was challenged by the friars, they not only had him exhumed, but carried his corpse in triumph 'with noisy chanting through the main market place, inviting everyone they could to the spectacle'.[42] For the monks it was an affront to their dignity, but for parish priests the loss of burial dues and bequests could cause severe hardship. The threat to parochial income was addressed if not solved in 1300 by the papal bull *Super cathedram*. This permitted the friars to preach in their own churches, in public places subject to certain restrictions and in parish churches by invitation only. Parish priests were also to receive one quarter of any bequest to the mendicants.[43]

An institution so deeply embedded in the fabric of society inevitably raised problems for its host community to add to those of its own. The fact that literacy often remained the preserve of the clergy and anyone in a literate occupation was by definition a clerk, placed the church at the

---

[40] Burton, *Monastic Orders*, 191; *Durham Priory*, 343–4; Golding, *Gilbert of Sempringham*, 173.
[41] Burton, *Monastic Orders*, 120.
[42] Gransden, *Historical Writing*, i, 449–50.
[43] Burton, *Monastic Orders*, 126–7.

heart of government.[44] Not until 1340 was the first lay Chancellor of the realm appointed, in what proved to be a short-lived experiment. Bishop Burnell was unusual in serving Edward I as Chancellor for as long as eighteen years, but the office was normally held by a bishop or other senior churchman. The roll-call of Treasurers was almost as illustrious. Clerics were present at every level, from the royal Council to the lowly scribes who staffed the departments of government. In principle there was a fruitful symbiotic relationship between church and state; the crown enjoyed the services of able administrators, who were rewarded with ecclesiastical preferment, while the papacy depended on the secular power to enforce its authority. Most provisions (appointments) were to offices without cure of souls, such as canonries in the secular cathedrals, but the vast expansion of royal administration, particularly in the 1320s, strained the church's capacity to supply a sufficient number of benefices without undermining its ability to perform its ecclesiastical duties.

Ecclesiastical wealth presented another source of tension, not least because in much of the country churchmen were also secular lords. Although the distinction between spiritual office and temporal property and the allegiance appropriate to each had been defined during the twelfth century, the very possession of substantial landholdings drew prominent churchmen into the political arena. Sensitivities in abeyance under archbishops as diplomatic as Walter Reynolds, could boil over into confrontation when a character as assertive as Archbishop Pecham held office. The status of bishops and many abbots as tenants-in-chief brought them into Parliament, where they often stood alongside the baronage in disputes with the crown. Seven bishops featured among the twenty-one Ordainers in 1310 and Bishops Orleton and Stratford were party to Edward II's deposition. However, it was in the nature of the complex relationship between church and state that the ecclesiastical hierarchy could not be straightforwardly and unanimously identified with the reformers' cause. Churchmen were among the most active mediators between Thomas of Lancaster and the king in 1317 and 1318, while in 1326 Bishop Stapledon of Exeter paid for his loyal service to the crown by decapitation with a breadknife at the hands of the London mob.[45]

A less acute, but no less intractable, problem arising from ecclesiastical wealth was the alarmingly voracious way in which the church appeared to be acquiring land. The nub of the problem was that ecclesiastical institutions, unlike individual lay landlords, never died and

---

[44] See chapter 5. For the following see Heath, *Church and Realm*, chs. 1 and 2, and Wright, *The Church*, *passim*.
[45] See chapter 7.

were forbidden to dispose of their property, so the church's landholdings grew ever larger. Worries about the consequences of this perpetual tenure, known as mortmain tenure, were voiced from the beginning of the thirteenth century. They had gained an added edge by the later thirteenth century as some knightly families found themselves in financial difficulties following the civil war.[46] Edward I grasped the nettle in the Statute of Mortmain of 1279, which forbade the acquisition of any further land by the church.[47] The practical consequences of this were not as severe as might first appear. The blanket ban was soon softened by the issue of licences permitting gains notwithstanding the statute, and churchmen exercised some ingenuity in evading it through the use of nominees. Thus, although the legislation made acquisition more complicated and expensive, it did not prevent it. Curbs on the expansion of ecclesiastical holdings were governed by independent considerations of fashions in benefaction and the ability of churchmen to fund purchases rather than legal embargo.

Houses belonging to the old orders appeared to the laity as much the most threatening predators. This was not because of what they were given, since they rarely attracted patronage on any scale by this date, but during the later thirteenth century many houses were active purchasers of knightly estates. This was particularly evident in Northamptonshire and Huntingdonshire in the area bounded by the River Nene, where several large monasteries had interests. Most dramatic was Ramsey Abbey's single purchase of land at Barnwell, Hemington and Crowethorpe at a cost of more than £1,600. More commonly, single manors were bought costing a few hundred pounds. While there can be no doubt as to the fact of these purchases, their significance is open to debate. Some historians have taken at face value contemporary fears that military tenure was being undermined so relentlessly that the safety of the realm was at risk. A cooler inspection of the evidence suggests that while individual families often faced ruin and extinction, their disappearance was balanced by a constant stream of others who were newly establishing themselves. In many ways the real threat to knightly tenure was posed by individual churchmen, often themselves of knightly stock, who had made their fortunes as administrators and wished to provide for their families. Robert Burnell was a prime example of this. At his death, he had acquired estates scattered over nineteen counties, a feat that even the richest monastery would have found it impossible to match.

On closer investigation, many monastic purchases also prove to have been defensive. Abbeys like Peterborough were recovering manors

---

[46] See chapter 2.
[47] For what follows see Raban, *Mortmain Legislation, passim.*

reluctantly granted in fee to knights following the Norman Conquest in order to meet the military requirements of the king. Houses were also buying land from their own tenants, whose sale to an outsider might have presented them with future problems. They may even have been influenced by considerations of 'good lordship', where their purchases helped tenants who had fallen into debt. The plight of Geoffrey of Southorpe would have been a good deal worse had Peterborough Abbey not recovered his last remaining manor in 1286 from Stephen of Cornhill, a London merchant to whom it had been mortgaged, and given him ten marks and two horses to enable him to ride away into genteel retirement with the Carmelites.[48]

Monastic purchase was high profile, especially where religious houses dominated an area, but it was not unique. The same pattern of behaviour can be found on the estates of lay tenants-in-chief, but churchmen were more reliant on purchase. Without recourse to marriage or military conquest and with the stream of benefaction run dry, purchase remained the only option. For some houses, faced with declining income and rising expenses, it seemed to be the only way to bring in extra revenue. Moreover, although the great religious houses were incomparably richer than the knights who were forced to sell, the ways in which they paid for their acquisitions reveal that few had large quantities of ready cash at their disposal. Vendors were sometimes offered life leases or payment by instalments. Despite its prevalence, the image of wealthy ecclesiastical predators was far from the truth.

It thus appears that the main points of tension between the church and lay society were generated within the realm; the one possible source of conflict which rarely manifested itself in an acute form was that between king and Pope. Boundaries between their respective authority had been painstakingly worked out in preceding centuries through a process of challenge and compromise on each side. Formal complaints put to the king by the English clergy in 1280, 1309 and 1316 showed no concern with matters touching papal rights and privileges. Royal taxation of the church's property remained as the most likely source of dispute. In 1296 Archbishop Winchelsey, opposing Edward I's excessive demands, received support from Boniface VIII whose bull *Clericis laicos*, forbade the taxing of the clergy without papal sanction. More often, however, the papacy undermined the position of the English hierarchy by allowing the crown to divert papal taxes into the royal coffers. Such complaisance owed something to the hope that one of the two Edwards might undertake a further crusade, but even more to the Popes' own political vulnerability. The Gascon origins of Clement V and John XXII, together

---

[48] King, *Peterborough Abbey*, 43–4. See chapter 2.

with the favours they received from the Plantagenets, also predisposed them towards cooperation wherever possible. This did not entirely preclude the assertion of moral leadership, particularly in the face of Edward II's more outrageous behaviour, but the papacy rarely impinged significantly on English affairs.[49]

The pan-European nature of Christendom meant that problems originating in other countries could sometimes spill over from the continent to England. The most spectacular and unpleasant example of this was the sudden and savage attack on the Templars by Philip IV of France in 1307.[50] Sustained torture led to a series of confessions ranging from blasphemy and sodomy to obscenity. That the accusations were largely baseless is indicated by their similarity to long-established folk traditions regarding magic and heresy in which worship of idols and cats featured prominently. The order had been a source of concern for a generation and the possibility of amalgamation with the Hospitallers had been mooted from time to time following the Council of Lyons in 1274. Criticisms had sharpened after the fall of Acre in 1291, but contemporaries suspected with some justice that the French crown was motivated more by the prospect of Templar wealth than a desire for reform. Clement V, weak and under threat, found it more politic to assume control of the prosecution than attempt to defend the beleaguered knights, thus extending the attack to the whole of Christendom. In England, Edward II at first refused to credit the accusations nor, when the demands of the French king were reiterated by the Pope, was he keen to sanction the use of torture. In contrast to France, the imprisoned knights were well treated, some even being allowed their own servants and possessions. The northern bishops staunchly asserted that 'Torture has never been used in the kingdom of England.' Indeed, it was so alien to the English judicial process that the two inquisitors who came to England to gather evidence complained to Archbishop Winchelsey in 1310 that no competent torturers were to be found.[51] The persecution of the Templars (and their confessions) never attained the same height in England as in France, but Edward II sacrificed them to his need for papal support in his efforts to defend his favourite, Piers Gaveston. Estates worth some £3,000 per annum also proved too much of a temptation to resist. The Order was suppressed at the Council of Vienne in 1312, but it was not until 1324 that a statute was enacted to wrest the Templar lands from royal control and transfer them to the Hospitallers as Clement V had intended.

[49] Wright, *The Church*, 188. See chapters 7 and 8.
[50] The following account of the Templars draws on Barber, *The New Knighthood*; *idem, Trial of the Templars*; Partner, *Murdered Magicians*.
[51] Menache, *Clement V*, 229–33; McHardy, '*De heretico comburendo*', 112.

The seizure of Templar property was just one of the straws in the wind. On the surface the church in all its aspects enjoyed an unassailable position in society. Nothing on the political scene approached the quarrels between Henry II and Thomas Becket or King John's troubled relationship with Innocent III. In the parishes, the quality of teaching on offer to the laity had reached heights inconceivable even a century earlier. Additions of great splendour in the Decorated Gothic style were being made to ecclesiastical buildings all over the country, ranging from major rebuilding following disasters at Norwich and Ely Cathedrals, to new windows, aisles or porches in countless parish churches. Churchmen were playing a respected role not only in matters spiritual and intellectual, but also in government. However, one can see already the seeds of the less happy situation prevalent at the end of the fourteenth century. The credibility of the papacy was increasingly called in question by residence in Avignon and its willingness to act as royal tax gatherer. The wealth of the old orders was a growing cause for concern. Mortmain legislation and the revolt of the tenants of Bury St Edmunds in 1327 were early symptoms of the hostility which culminated in the later fourteenth century in the nickname 'possessioners' and Lollard calls for disendowment. The popularity of the mendicants and attempts to raise the level of parochial instruction ironically led to a more assertive laity, to some of whom a vernacular Bible and the teachings of the Lollards would prove attractive. Even the institutional sophistication of church and state were to prove double-edged as they brought inflexibility just when the church needed to adapt and to shift its resources away from the old orders and the reward of royal officials into pastoral care. Yet all this is more evident to historians than it was to contemporaries. Their feelings about the church must have been as complicated as the institution which embraced them so thoroughly.

5

Culture

The time is long past when a chapter on culture can be confined to a survey of the arts and architecture of the aristocracy. The term is now understood much more broadly. At the same time fundamental to society and elusive, culture comprises the values by which people live and the ways in which these achieve practical expression. It touches every aspect of life and takes myriad forms. Like other societies, every social and occupational group in England in the late thirteenth and early fourteenth centuries had its own code and conventions, as did those defined by their gender, age or ethnicity. Arguably there was a sense of national identity, certainly there was a sense of regional and local identity. There were no impermeable barriers between these cultures; too much of life was lived in common. Some of them have left copious traces, others none at all. All this makes the task of separating and interpreting the various threads a demanding exercise, but without attempting it the England of Edward I and Edward II cannot be properly understood.

If inadequate and intractable evidence is the normal lot of medievalists, those concerned with culture face the greatest challenge of all. They are forced to be creative in their approach to texts and imaginative in recognizing the potential of other forms of evidence. There are, however, limits to what ingenuity can achieve, because historians can only comprehend this raw material in terms of their own experience, which is necessarily very different from the world they are studying. Archaeologists and social anthropologists, who face even more demanding problems of evidence, have much to teach us about these limitations.[1] One important lesson is that objects do not necessarily have the same resonance for an outside observer as for those for whom they were made. This

---

[1] I. Hodder, *The Present Past: An Introduction to Anthropology for Archaeologists*, London, 1982, provides a stimulating examination of the problems.

is readily comprehensible in the case of a painting or sculpture made for religious purposes and now often viewed solely as a work of art, but might not be so easy to recognize in the case of more mundane things or where the objects in question belong to some aspect of society which has seen a less obvious shift in values. The fact that context can often affect meaning introduces further uncertainty in forming reliable judgements. To take a modern example, a safety-pin holding together an item of clothing signifies something very different from the challenge to conventional society intended by a safety-pin through someone's nose, nipple or other part of the body. As contemporaries, we have no difficulty in decoding such social signals, but they would be completely baffling to anyone unfamiliar with England in the late twentieth century. Such a person might also fail to register that a safety-pin, essential until recently in securing a baby's nappy, has within a few years been made redundant by disposable nappies and advances in adhesive fabrics.

Even straightforward works of art present a whole host of interpretative problems where perceptions central to their visual impact have changed. The language and meaning of colour have varied over time. The modern world sees colour primarily as a matter of hue, while our medieval predecessors saw it in terms of brightness. There were, moreover, overtones of value which would now escape us. It is no accident that the colour language of heraldry incorporates the silver, gold and furs appropriate to the elite or that the Virgin Mary came to be dressed in blue, a costly pigment made from ground lapis lazuli.[2] A more literate society has also lost contact with the symbolic language familiar to those whose communication was largely oral or visual. In these circumstances it is easy to misunderstand or simply fail to recognize that a message is intended. It is not uncommon for illuminated manuscripts to have astonishingly irreverent, bawdy or scatological illustrations alongside sacred texts. Sometimes they are a play on words, as when the Latin *culpa* was split at the end of a line to read *cul* (bum), or mock the seriousness of the subject-matter with weird figures or allusions to popular culture, but, if truth were known, often we can only make an informed guess as to the artist's intention.[3] The juxtaposition of opposites was a favourite medieval device, so where we might scent blasphemy, in fact heightened seriousness would have been understood. Much the same applies to the purpose of comic figures on corbels found in west country churches *c*.1320. Their clowning emphasized the holiness of the building.[4] Meaning in medieval art was often

[2] Gage, 'Colour in history', 105; *idem, Colour and Culture*, 80–2.
[3] Camille, *Image*, 22–47.
[4] Alexander and Binski, *Age of Chivalry*, 418–19, nos 502–5.

PLATE 4   Marginalia, replete with sexual symbolism, from the Grey-Fitzpayn
Book of Hours, *c.*1300 (*MS 242, fo. 55v*)

conveyed by subtle use of allegory. Michael Camille's close examination of the imagery of the Luttrell Psalter lays bare sober religious messages encoded in scenes of feasting, and the fear of famine lurking in obsessive depictions of food.[5] There are dangers here too, of course. Art historians are currently locked in debate as to how far one should view seventeenth-century Dutch genre paintings literally or whether they were intended as moralities.[6] Such questions are only now being explored by medievalists and, despite the hazards, are yielding a rich harvest of insight.

It goes without saying that the wealthier and more literate sections of society have left more information behind them. In considering culture, like any other aspect of the period, the majority must necessarily be viewed through the distorting lens of evidence left by the more fortunate minority. This applies as much to material culture as to more conventional written sources. Occasionally popular culture finds its own voice, as in the carvings on roof bosses or on the underside of misericords (wooden seats) in cathedrals and churches, but even these cannot be taken at face value. Apparently lively and spontaneous, misericords were often carved from patterns or copied from neighbouring churches. Nor were they free of convention. The women who featured in the scenes from everyday life were usually portrayed in their stereotypical role of

[5] Camille, *Mirror*, 82–93, 252.
[6] The most recent contributions to the debate are in W. Franits (ed.), *Looking at Seventeenth-Century Dutch Art: Realism Reconsidered*, Cambridge, 1997.

PLATE 5   A misericord depicting two figures dancing, from the stalls in Chichester cathedral, *c*.1320

gossip or scold.[7] One cannot assume, either, that the craftsmen who created them were given unfettered freedom in their choice of subject; their patrons may well have imposed their own views. Misericords are not easy to date. The lively dancers from Chichester cathedral choir stalls appear to have been created *c*.1320, but the more elaborate carvings of ordinary activities appear to come from the later fourteenth and fifteenth centuries.[8] For the earlier period we are more often reliant on illuminated manuscripts for information of this sort. Yet, as we have already seen, the cheerful everyday images of the Luttrell Psalter, with its brightly clad peasants engaged in the fields and at play, can be deeply deceptive.[9]

Historians sometimes look to present-day communities of an apparently similar kind in an attempt to circumvent the limitations of evidence from the past, but this too has its dangers. Inheritance customs can be fruitfully illuminated by looking at modern peasant societies. Primogeniture or ultimogeniture (inheritance of the first-or last-born) might appear unfair to those whose upbringing has been informed by egalitarian values. They are less so when anthropological studies reveal

[7] C. Grossinger, 'Misericords', in Alexander and Binski, *Age of Chivalry*, 123–4.
[8] See plate 5.
[9] See pp. 32–3, above.

the thought lying behind such arrangements. Although the eldest son might acquire the family holding, he might also inherit an obligation to provide dowries for his sisters and to establish his brothers in life. One can also discover the alternative logic involved in leaving the family holding to the youngest son, who, as last to remain in the family nest, would shoulder the burden of caring for elderly parents.[10] The disadvantage of using another discipline in this way can be seen from a sharp series of exchanges in the 1970s and 1980s over the nature of merchet payments. Professor Searle, drawing on the anthropologist's notion of dowry as a daughter's share in the family wealth, argued that merchet represented a form of taxation or compensation to the lord for the disposal of his property when she married. Yet, as she pointed out at the end of the third passage of arms, because the other parties to the controversy started from utterly different premises, there could be no meeting point in their conclusions.[11]

To achieve an understanding of a past society, recognizable to those who lived in it, is one of the most satisfying tasks facing the historian, but it is as well to remember that judgements might not only prove controversial among colleagues but, even worse, would appear laughable to the society in question if there were any means of knowing. Anyone doubting the dangers inherent in writing about another culture on the basis of inadequate information, might reflect on the description of the seventeenth-century English church by an unknown Armenian cleric:

> You wish to know whether the English are Christians? They are Christians. They even have their eucharist – such as it is. Once a year the minister goes up into the pulpit with a large basket of loaves on his arm: he flings the loaves about among the people, who scramble for them in the church.
>
> The English Christians also have another religious ceremony called the National Debt. This consists in offering a large sum of money every year to the Emperor of the French: a ceremony much disliked and murmured at by the people![12]

Religion was perhaps the single most important force in determining the conduct and values of medieval society. The rich and complex tapestry of ecclesiastical endeavour has already been examined in its

---

[10] J. du Boulay, *Portrait of a Greek Mountain Village*, Oxford, 1974, 20–1, 272–3; E. Freidl, *Vasilika: A Village in Modern Greece*, New York, 1962, ch. 4.

[11] E. Searle, 'A rejoinder', *Past and Present*, xcix (1983), 148–9.

[12] P. Hammond, *The Waters of Marah: The Present State of the Greek Church*, London, 1956, 5.

institutional and economic context in chapter 4, but religion also saturated the general culture of society. It governed daily life through the festivals and fasts of the annual cycle of the Christian calendar. Rites of passage – baptism, marriage and obsequies – were conducted and regulated by the church. Moral conduct and testamentary bequests were governed by canon law.

For the first time, in the thirteenth century the Latinate learning of churchmen was disseminated effectively, if somewhat selectively and simply, among ordinary men and women, but this belated indoctrination was far from complete. In acknowledging the overwhelming importance of the church, it is easy to forget that Christianity was not the only expression of religious belief current in England at this time. There was most notably a strong underlying vein of paganism, especially in the countryside.

Paganism was, of course, the survival of an older belief system which lingers with remarkable tenacity to this day. Indeed, it is debatable how far society has ever been thoroughly Christianized. Field-work in the north-eastern English fishing village of Staithes in the late 1970s showed the harmonious coexistence of Anglicanism, Methodism and paganism. Inhabitants simply drew on whichever tradition met their needs at any one time.[13] Who, even amongst the most highly educated, can claim that they never refer to good or bad luck or that they are totally immune from superstitious practices such as touching wood? Christianity was grafted onto this pagan stock. Pope Gregory the Great famously advised St Augustine to build altars on the sites of pagan temples and substitute Christian equivalents for existing ceremonies and festivals in order that the English might be weaned more easily from their former beliefs. As a result, there remained an ambiguity between Christian and pre-Christian belief and practice which helped ordinary people to explain and deal with the world around them, but which proved an enduring embarrassment to the church authorities. No one glancing at the face of the 'green man' peering out from the foliage of a roof boss in the cloister of Norwich Cathedral, rebuilt after a catastrophic fire caused by riots in 1272, or the strange figures in the margins of the Luttrell Psalter and the Grey-Fitzpayn Book of Hours, can doubt that the old ways continued to exercise a powerful influence, for all that they have left fewer traces.[14] Pilgrimages and the veneration of relics were another area where practice drifted uneasily between Christianity and paganism. Always alert to accusations of fraud or idolatry, the authorities were

[13] D. Clark, *Between Pulpit and Pew: Folk Religion in a North Yorkshire Fishing Village*, Cambridge, 1982.
[14] See plate 6. Rose and Hedgecoe, *Stories in Stone*, 26–30.

PLATE 6   A roofboss depicting a 'green man' from the cloister of Norwich
cathedral, *c*.1297–1325

especially anxious about local cults and miracles which came close to
magic.

Even more problematic was the continuation of outright pagan rituals
in the countryside. The incident recounted by the Lanercost chronicler
whereby in 1268 Cistercian lay brothers were found to have erected an
image of Priapus in the fields in order to ward off cattle plague is
particularly revealing.[15] Provision for lay brothers and sisters in the
new orders of the twelfth century for the first time enabled the fulfilment
of peasant vocations, but the Christian teaching made available to these
recruits was deliberately limited. Forbidden literacy, their spiritual education was confined to rote learning of the Lord's Prayer, the Creed and
a few other essentials. It was scarcely surprising that such people fell

[15] Camille, *The Gothic Idol*, 12, 356, n. 13.

back on their traditional aids despite living at the heart of orthodox worship. Although their conduct occasioned a *frisson* of shock in its overt reference to older fertility rituals, it must have been replicated by the rural laity in countless minor ways echoing measures practised from time out of mind or given a Christian veneer in the sort of rituals played out at seasons such as Rogationtide.[16]

If Christian and pre-Christian religion coexisted fairly harmoniously, medieval English society found it harder to come to terms with the presence of Judaism. The small community from Rouen which settled in England in the wake of the Norman Conquest and which had originally enjoyed serious intellectual debate with churchmen, found itself increasingly isolated and beleaguered. By the mid-thirteenth century, sympathetic communication between the two religions was much reduced, though never completely eradicated, and royal protection had been transformed into oppression. The story of the gradual erosion and final expulsion of English Jewry is not an edifying one, although it was a good deal more complicated than an earlier generation of scholars allowed.[17]

Multilingual and superior in learning to most of the host community, Jewish leaders such as Elias Menahem of London were patrons of scholarship and scholars themselves. Nor were his studies confined to religious texts. In 1280, his skills as a physician were in demand by the count of Flanders. Like many Jews, however, he made the major part of his living by lending money at interest, something forbidden, in theory at least, to Christians by the Lateran Council of 1179. Money-lending accorded well with the Jews' high degree of literacy and capital resources and met a real need in a society where assets were rarely liquid, but it also soured relations with the native population, especially when it put their land at risk.

Crucial to the well-being of the Jewish community was the attitude of the monarch. As with any aliens, their residence in England was subject to royal approval. They quickly acquired special standing as 'the king's Jews' and as such were generally afforded protection, although this broke down catastrophically in 1264 when Simon de Montfort's followers massacred 500 London Jews, and again in the pogrom that followed the accusations of coin-clipping in 1278–9. Even when it held, however, this protection had never been disinterested; the crown benefited from a prosperous and totally dependent community. Loans of the twelfth century had become punitive tallages (taxes) during the

---

[16] Camille, *Mirror*, 274.

[17] The following account of the English Jewish community and laws is from Mundill, *England's Jewish Solution*; Hyams, 'The Jewish minority', 270–93.

thirteenth, although there was a considerable gulf between the £31,000 or so levied under Edward I and the £10,000 or less that was actually raised.[18] Many fled the country. Of the remainder, those who were unable to pay were imprisoned, their chattels confiscated and their dependents deported. When the blow finally fell with the expulsion in 1290, the Jewish community had been reduced to around 2,000, less than half its number at the beginning of the century.[19]

Even before he came to the throne Edward I embarked on what has been dubbed the 'Edwardian Experiment'. Beginning with the Provisions of Jewry of 1269 and culminating in the Statute of Jewry of 1275, attempts were made to wean the Jewish community from usury and restore mortgaged land to Christian debtors. The impact of the statute, once thought to have been the final blow to English Jewry by removing its only source of income, is now understood to have been more subtle. Some debts had always been settled in kind as well as cash and this trend accelerated. Loans were made in advance of payment from the grain or wool crops, so much so that on their expulsion in 1290, the Jews of Lincoln were owed more than 2,000 quarters of grain and had captured some six per cent of the market in wool. The harsh climate in which they operated from the mid-thirteenth century meant that smaller operators in many Jewries disappeared, but the community as a whole showed some resilience despite its reduced numbers. In places, it had even achieved reasonable prosperity again by the eve of the expulsion.[20]

This fragile prosperity was achieved against a background of extreme vulnerability. Most ominous of all to a modern observer, the 1275 statute required that Jews over the age of seven wear on their outer garments a distinguishing badge of yellow felt, 6 inches long and 3 inches wide, depicting two tablets representing the Ten Commandments. Such regulations were not new, but attitudes were hardening. There is some evidence for the demonization of Jews by the host population. A caricature of a Jew on the Essex forest roll of 1277, clearly showing the badge, is captioned 'Aaron son of the Devil', while the earliest known example, on the 1233 Norwich tallage roll, shows a Jew wearing the characteristic pointed hat, being mocked by a devil.[21] Other caricatures reveal the hooked noses and straggling beards redolent of later stereo-types.[22] Otherwise rare stone houses, which Jewish financiers built to protect themselves and their property, bear witness to their sense of insecurity. That Belaset daughter of Benedict son of Moses, who is

[18] Mundhill, *England's Jewish Solution*, 106.
[19] Ibid., 26–7.
[20] Ibid., 185–98, 204–8.
[21] See plate 7. PRO, E32/12, m.3; E401/1565; Camille, *The Gothic Idol*, 183–4.
[22] Roth, 'Portraits and caricatures', i–viii; Rokeah, 'Drawings of Jewish interest', 55–62.

PLATE 7   A caricature from the Essex forest roll of 1277, under the contemporary caption 'Aaron son of the devil' and showing the badge that Jews were required to wear on their clothing)

reputed to have owned the house still standing on Steep Hill in Lincoln, might have felt vulnerable is entirely credible. It was probably her wedding which brought to Lincoln the nineteen Jews who were hanged after the discovery of Little St Hugh drowned in a cesspit in 1255, and she in her turn was caught up in the violence of the attack on coin-clippers in 1278–9.

The relationship between the Jewish and Christian communities was more complex than this dismal catalogue of events might suggest. Although Archbishop Pecham, at the behest of the papacy, was active in promoting anti-Jewish measures, attitudes were not uniformly negative. The friars maintained a scholarly interest in Hebrew texts and on occasion spoke out in defence of Jewish victims. The Franciscan Adam Marsh incurred popular opprobrium when he urged moderation in the aftermath of the discovery of Little St Hugh's body. The Dominican Archbishop Kilwardby pleaded on behalf of Elias Menahem in 1275. The houses of both Franciscan and Dominican friars in Oxford were located near to the Jewry, and although few took fraternization to the lengths of Robert of Reading, a Dominican who in 1275 converted to Judaism and took a Jewish bride (and subsequently died in prison), it was not unprecedented. That the friars should be the staunchest friends of the Jews is not surprising. It was this same quality of open-mindedness which promoted the scientific discoveries of Roger Bacon, regarded with equal suspicion at the time. The laity too were not invariably hostile. In 1286, Christian friends accepted the wedding invitation of a wealthy Jewish financier in Hereford in defiance of episcopal excommunication. Both events are known to us because they incurred the wrath of the authorities. No doubt there were many other friendly contacts and small kindnesses which have escaped record, as well as some better-documented fraternization over drink and in crime. The disappearance of Jewish money-lenders from the countryside after 1290 may have caused real hardship to peasants who relied on their advances against the harvest, particularly in famine years.[23]

There appears to have been a sincere desire to win converts from Judaism. Roger Bacon in his *Opus Majus* urged preaching to this end, and in 1280 the Dominicans prevailed on the king to command Jews to attend special Lenten sermons designed for their instruction. Despite his mother's straightforward anti-Semitism, Edward himself seems to have been motivated by genuine piety, probably strengthened as a result of his recent crusade. Close contact with the knights who accompanied him may have given him a sympathetic understanding of their financial problems and explain his determination to stamp out usurious loans. The Statute of Jewry fits well with his other reforming measures at that date.[24] It acknowledged that the king 'and his ancestors have received much benefit from the Jewish people in all time past' and insisted that they 'be safely preserved and defended by his sheriffs and other bailiffs'.[25] This was not an empty platitude. It was the king who was instrumental in calling a halt to the excesses of 1278–9. Arguably the change of policy from reform and conversion to expulsion in 1290 owed more to

[23] Mundill, *England's Jewish Solution*, 227.
[24] See chapter 7.
[25] *Statutes of the Realm*, i, 220–1.

Edward's need to cajole his subjects into granting him taxes than any real animosity towards the Jews themselves.[26] The ambiguity of the Jews' position is summed up by the contrast between the measures taken to protect them and grim reality. In 1290 it was provided that no one should 'injure, harm, damage or grieve' any Jew in the interval between the order for expulsion in July and its coming into effect on 1 November. The master of a ship carrying some of the forced emigrants abroad invited them to stretch their legs on a sandbank at Queenborough at low tide and then abandoned them to drown.

The association of Jews with the devil touches on another strand in the religious culture of the period. From the beginning of the fourteenth century, England shared in the emergence of witchcraft trials, which first manifested themselves on the continent, most conspicuously in the case against Pope Boniface VIII. The boundary between pagan magic and sorcery had always been uncertain and to this was added the suspicion of heresy. These early symptoms of the hysteria which swept Europe and the New World in succeeding centuries were conspicuously political in their targets. Worship of idols was central to the case against the Templars. Accusations of paying homage to the devil also featured among those of simony, pluralism, fornication and murder levelled in 1302 against Walter Langton, Edward I's hated Treasurer. A pretender to the throne in 1318 was accused of keeping familiars and acting at the devil's behest.[27] The authorities, as they had in the past, prosecuted less sensitive cases on the assumption that offenders were ignorant or deluded, but the foundations had been laid for their conversion to a genuine belief in the power of the devil, as the world began to transform itself in unsettling ways from the mid-fourteenth century.

Language, oral and written, was as important as religion in defining cultural identity, and is equally complicated. Put simply, English was the mother tongue of the majority; the elite, according to Higden, were 'taught French from the cradle and rattle'; and Latin was the language of church and government.[28] To these tongues, the Jewish community added Hebrew. While there is little doubt about Latin and Hebrew, what is meant by English and French requires examination. The sociolinguistic boundaries between the two languages were not clearly demarcated. By the later thirteenth century, English was the language spoken by most people as, little by little, the Norman French of the conquerors was undermined, a process accelerated by the loss of Nor-

[26] Mundill, *England's Jewish Solution*, 283.
[27] See chapter 4. A. Beardwood, 'The trial of Walter Langton, Bishop of Lichfield, 1307–12', *Transactions of the American Philosophical Society*, new series, liv, pt 3 (1964), 7; Childs, 'Welcome, my brother', 153–6.
[28] Taylor, *The Universal Chronicle*, 61.

mandy in 1204. Walter of Bibbesworth's late thirteenth-century manual 'How to speak French', compiled to instruct the children of Lady Denise de Montchesny, shows how knightly families were no longer automatically reared as Norman French speakers. Bilingual word lists and dictionaries were produced from the mid-thirteenth century to enable the middle ranks in society to achieve competence in the language they needed for advancement. Higden even claimed that peasants attempted to 'Frenchify their speech' to enhance their standing.[29] The common surname Latimer, deriving from *latimier* meaning interpreter, indicates how often help was needed at the point where French and English intersected, and how many people were available to provide it. Although it may have required more effort than had been the case a few generations earlier, educated Englishmen at the turn of the thirteenth and fourteenth centuries, unlike their predominantly monoglot descendants, were at home in three languages, able to move from one to another as appropriate. The higher clergy, as befitted their knightly or aristocratic background, probably spoke French among themselves, reserved Latin for formal use, but addressed their flock in English. Familiarity with all three languages was less likely among the laity, especially those who could not afford schooling, or among women, for whom it was not deemed relevant.

Although few outside the highest ranks of society may have been fluently bilingual or trilingual, the proportion of men and women in England at this date with at least a smattering of more than one language must have been very great. Grammar books produced at the turn of the century even suggest an attempt to teach the French of the Parisian schools to those who already had a grounding in Norman French, although in keeping with prevailing educational practice, Latin was the medium of instruction.[30] Despite such moves in educated circles, however, Norman French survived as an independent dialect until the later fourteenth century, enabling Chaucer to mock the French of the school of Stratford-atte-Bowe spoken by his prioress. It survived even longer with a distinctively English pronunciation, alongside Latin, as the language of Common Law, its very archaism eventually excluding all but initiates to the profession, and providing an excellent example of the way in which an occupational culture might operate to the benefit of its practitioners.

Tantalizingly little is known about the sound of spoken English at this time. Information has to be gleaned from written evidence with its inevitable limitations. Standardized texts in Middle English were rare

---

[29] Camille, 'The language of images', 36; Taylor, *The Universal Chronicle*, 169; D. Burnley, 'Lexis and semantics', in Blake, *The Cambridge History*, 412, 425.
[30] Rothwell, 'The Teaching of French', 41–4.

before 1300, so that in theory spelling could reflect differences in pronunciation between the five broad dialects, but less can be inferred from
this than might be hoped. Surviving manuscripts have often reached us
via several copyists, with each successive scribe contributing further and
confusing regional variants. Rhyme can offer some clues and there have
also been interesting speculations, such as the possibility that it was a
sign of cultivated speech to drop one's aitches. Such propositions are
difficult to substantiate, however, and hard fact remains elusive.[31]

Like any language at any time, both English and French were in a
constant state of flux, each influenced by the other. In the later Anglo-
Saxon period, both spoken and written English were each evolving
towards a single standard form. This process was disrupted by the Norman Conquest, after which English was no longer the language of
government and the pressure towards uniformity consequently relaxed.
The rigorous tradition of scribal training of late Anglo-Saxon England
also broke down, leaving scribes to adopt French letter forms and
employ a far wider variety of spellings. English also absorbed French
vocabulary and syntax, one indication of which was the growing use of
'you' and 'your' from the later thirteenth century in place of 'thee' and
'thine'. French literary genres and conventions regarding metre and
rhyme also became widespread. There were other reasons for change
too. It has been suggested that migration from the countryside further
north was the reason why Londoners abandoned their southern English
dialect in favour of one from the Midlands.[32]

One of the most important developments of this period was the
increasing use of writing.[33] The process had taken off in the late twelfth
century. By the time Edward I acceded to the throne, the volume of
writing emanating from crown, church and aristocracy had reached
massive proportions, even on the basis of what has survived. It is the
more remarkable that this increase happened despite the fact that most
of the texts were in a language that many did not understand and that
fewer still could read or write.

In dealing with practical matters such as the conveyance of land, the
problem of understanding was simply tackled by reading the document
aloud in translation. The same approach was adopted in court cases,
where evidence was often given in English or French, but formally
recorded in Latin. Ways were also found to enable the illiterate to
share in literate activities. Reading and writing did not necessarily go
hand in hand as they would today. The number who could read almost

---

[31] J. Milroy, 'Middle English dialectology', in Blake, *The Cambridge History*, 158–203.
[32] Blake, *The Cambridge History*, xiv–xv, 1–18, 537.
[33] Clanchy, *From Memory*, is the major work on this subject.

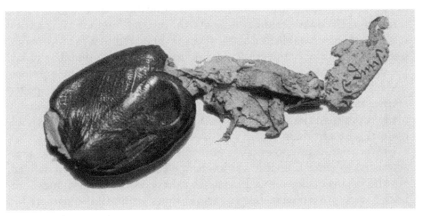

PLATE 8   The seal of an ordinary person showing a simple design on the face
and a thumb print on the obverse; no date

certainly exceeded those who could write, but even the ability to read
was not essential to sharing in written culture. Except perhaps in monasteries and academic circles, silent reading was not the norm, so listen-
ers could receive the written text at second hand. Indeed, it is likely that
public reading was the preferred form of leisure reading even for the
highly literate.[34] The interplay of text and illustration in books designed
for the laity further assisted the comprehension of unskilled readers,
with many illuminations providing visual or aural cues to the written

[34] Coleman, *Public Reading*, xi.

word.[35] The widespread use of seals proved a simple and effective answer for those who could not write but who needed to authenticate documents. Once reserved for the greatest in the land, countless misshapen lumps of wax bearing crude designs and often the thumb prints of their owners testify to the ubiquity of seals by the end of the thirteenth century.[36] The Statute of Exeter in 1285 even required that serfs had seals in order to authenticate their written evidence when they served on inquests.[37]

Just who could read and write remains uncertain. It seems likely that the upper echelons of society, lay and clerical, were able to do both, although how far most chose to exercise their skills must be open to question. Just as the rich and powerful today expect others to write for them, so it is probable that their medieval counterparts depended on scribes. Latin literacy was normally acquired through formal schooling.[38] The religious orders made their own provision, which often included a basic education in grammar and song for altar and choir boys. A few houses also contributed to education for a wider public through their own grammar schools or through support for nearby secular schools. Establishments of this sort operated in a far less organized way than the highly structured educational system familiar today. By the later thirteenth century, there appear to have been grammar schools funded by fee payers in most towns, teaching Latin as a spoken and written language, together with its literature. There were probably many more than the records suggest, lasting only as long as the schoolmasters who ran them.

Universities, also known as 'schools', shared many of the same characteristics as education at lower levels; the curriculum was well defined, but the means of delivering it somewhat haphazard. Oxford and Cambridge were pre-eminent, but at various times scholars also gathered in significant numbers at Stamford, Northampton and Salisbury. Students paid their chosen lecturers on an individual basis, but a measure of organization was gradually emerging. By the end of the thirteenth century, chancellors were appointed by the church for each university to ensure orthodoxy. The earliest of the colleges had also come into being alongside hostels for students. Nevertheless, provision for higher studies remained a long way from the salaried system and taught courses of today.

---

[35] Camille, *Mirror*, 193.
[36] See plate 8.
[37] Clanchy, *From Memory*, 51.
[38] The following account of schooling and the universities draws on Orme, *English Schools*.

As one might expect from its heavy emphasis on theology, canon law and the learning of the ancient world, education in the cathedral schools and universities was essentially the preserve of the clergy. Indeed the term *litteratus*, denoting those who were 'educated', was synonymous with *clericus*. For the most part, the laity acquired their literacy by other means. There was, however, an intermediate group, clerical by virtue of their Latin education, but secular in occupation, the ambiguity of whose position is still reflected in the dual meaning of 'clerk'. Their particular needs gave rise to alternative forms of professional training. Estate officials were served by teachers attracted to Oxford in the same way as scholars, but who offered specialist instruction separate from that of the university curriculum. Such was John of Oxford, who *c*.1280 wrote tracts on how to run a court or draw up accounts and conveyances. Some stewards and bailiffs no doubt learned their business on the job. This was certainly true of embryonic common lawyers. From the late 1280s there are references to 'apprentices of the Common Bench' who sat in a special enclosure in the court known as the 'crib'. Their 'text-books' were the Year Books which first survive from the early 1290s and which provided accounts of court cases together with commentaries, probably written by more senior apprentices. Only the disputations on points of law, known to have taken place in the early fourteenth century, approached the sort of teaching found in the universities.[39]

It is evident that literacy extended far beyond the clerical community. Whether in Latin or the vernacular, the wealthy could if they chose become sophisticated users of the written word through personal tuition. That they did not always choose to do so reflects a wider conception of education which encompassed the practical skills needed for aristocratic and martial pursuits. Convention dictated that these were often acquired in the household of a relative, family friend or patron. A significant proportion of the rest of the population mastered what might now be called pragmatic literacy, namely a sufficient grasp of the basics to enable them to function in a society where writing was increasingly important. As with the common lawyers, literacy for this group must often have been taught in the workplace in the course of training. Surviving indentures of apprenticeship are not common for this period, but when in 1291 John son of Gerard undertook to teach Hubert son of William de Tibenham 'his business in buying, selling and all other things' involved in the spice trade, it is likely that this would have included simple record keeping.[40]

[39] Brand, *The Origins*, 110–12.
[40] *Records of the City of Norwich*, i, 245–6.

Even less is known about female literacy, but almost certainly fewer women could read and write than men. Those who learned probably did so through the more informal channels of workshop and home. Yet, although their achievements may have been modest, the role of women in the transmission of literacy within the family should not be under-estimated. Denise de Montchesny is unlikely to have been the only mother ambitious for her children, but informal teaching of this sort was almost certainly confined to one of the vernaculars. Even within religious orders, women were normally excluded from a Latin educa-tion. Nuns were taught to follow the liturgy, but little more. Typically, when the bishop of Lincoln addressed the nuns of St Michael's Stamford in 1298, he used French, whereas he routinely wrote to the nearby monks of Peterborough in Latin.[41]

It was not so much the act of writing as its social consequences that made increased literacy so important. Without its widespread use, med-ieval English life would have been significantly different. An obvious example is the conduct of government. Centralized rule on the scale seen under the Plantagenets would have been inconceivable without writing. Less obviously, the availability of written records began subtly to influ-ence behaviour. In 1291 Edward I very consciously turned to written evidence to justify his claim to the Scottish throne, resorting first to monastic chronicles then to the royal archives.[42] By his son's reign, the Council in Gascony was finding itself seriously embarrassed by the loss of government records in the 1290s, because they had become essential to the settlement of land disputes and breaches of the peace.[43] Ordinary people too turned increasingly to written evidence, invoking Domesday Book to establish their rights as tenants of ancient demesne (tenants of the king in 1066) or the Feet of Fines (official copies) to enforce agree-ments made formally in court for extra security. The past had begun to assume an independent identity that could be used or interpreted, as well as being adapted over time to suit new needs in the same way as oral tradition. At a more mundane level, the co-ordinated agricultural enter-prises of some of the great landlords would not have been possible without written accounts and officials able to keep them. More signific-antly still, what had begun as a means of checking on the honesty of manorial officials had on some estates, by the end of the thirteenth century, turned into a tool of analysis. By the 1290s officials at the cathedral priory of Holy Trinity, Norwich, were able to calculate a

[41] BL, Cott. Vesp. E xxii, fos. 35v–6. See chapter 4.
[42] Clanchy, *From Memory*, 152–3.
[43] *Gascon Register*, i, xii–xiii.

figure for profit per acre on the prior's demesne, enabling them to assess whether or not he would have been better-off leasing.[44]

One should not overstate the impact of writing despite its obvious importance. England remained a largely illiterate society and even its most literate members often employed older oral habits. Even today we remain surprisingly reliant on oral tradition. Popular knowledge of law and custom is absorbed largely by word of mouth rather than any systematic study. Medieval lawyers carried this approach to extremes that we would now find unacceptable. Judges often drew on oral tradition as to the intention lying behind the enactment of statutes, treating the actual texts in a cavalier fashion, both misquoting and misapplying them. Before taking too superior a view of this, however, we should bear in mind a recent observation that despite the elaborate minutes we routinely draw up following meetings, most of us rarely consult them, relying instead on our memory.[45]

A lively debate currently centres on the suggestion that once again historians have been too keen to swallow the ideas of anthropologists, this time by making over-ambitious claims for literacy as the promoter of analytical thinking.[46] Exponents of such a view demote writing to a mere technology and call in question any absolute progression from oracy to literacy. Undeniably, oral and literate practices coexisted harmoniously in the Middle Ages and continue to do so today. The transition should therefore more properly be seen as a shift in emphasis between the two rather than one replacing the other. It would be misguided, however, to jettison all sense of literacy as an agent of change. Technologies are enabling, not least in the ordering and processing of data. Medieval accounts were no less significant than modern computers in opening the way to strategic information that was previously inaccessible. Nor should one underestimate the importance of the introduction of 'arabic' numerals, particularly zero, for mathematical operations.

Churchmen, united by their Latinity, their membership of a celibate, religious caste and subject to separate legal jurisdiction, stand out among the major cultural groups within late thirteenth-and early fourteenth-century society, but women comprised a larger and equally distinctive group. Despite participating in many other group cultures and varying greatly in social rank, they were united by experiences unique to their sex. These are largely beyond the historian's purview, however, owing to their restricted literacy. The most important way in which they differed from men was childbearing. Frequent pregnancies, even if not

---

[44] See chapter 2. Stone, 'Profit and loss accountancy', 33–57.
[45] Plucknett, *Statutes*, 103; Wickham, 'Gossip', 17.
[46] Coleman, *Public Reading*, 3–18.

always hazardous, dominated many women's lives.[47] It is not surprising, therefore, that there was a powerful female culture surrounding them. Something is known about customs regarding conception and childbirth, particularly where they engaged with religious observance. Some, such as the churching of women, a ritual of purification following childbirth, are still to be found in the Book of Common Prayer although no longer practised. Others more exotically pagan in flavour have disappeared. Such was the tradition at Bury St Edmunds, whereby the monks led a white bull garlanded in flowers in procession to the abbey church, so that women wishing to conceive could stroke its flanks before entering for orthodox prayers and offerings.[48] Phrases such as 'women's' talk' and 'old wives' tales' are eloquent testimony to the informal channels of communication among women over time and irrespective of background.

Knights were another group with a distinctive culture characteristic of the period. By the later thirteenth century the code surrounding knighthood had become well defined both in terms of heraldry and knightly conduct. Rolls recording coats of arms are common from the 1270s and show that there were more than a thousand armigerous families in England at that time. Arms were increasingly worn not just on the clothing of the knight himself but, as the portrait of Sir Geoffrey Luttrell so vividly shows, also on the trappings of his horse.[49] They were also to be found on tombs and monumental brasses, in stained-glass windows and as decorative stonework in churches and homes. Elaborate ceremonial governed admission to knighthood, even though it did not normally attain the heights of extravagance displayed in the Feast of Swans held in 1306 when Edward of Caernarfon was knighted; some 300 other young men were knighted at the same time and two gilded swans were borne in by minstrels at the ensuing banquet.[50] At the wealthier end of the knightly spectrum, tournaments were both training grounds and a ritual substitute for warfare. These often degenerated into real battles. Edward I himself was notoriously embroiled in what became known as the 'Little War of Chalons' in 1273, when he and his men travelling home from crusade challenged all comers. Roger de Leyburn, a Kentish nobleman and one of his closest associates, had disgraced himself even more in 1252 when he attacked an opponent with a sharpened sword in revenge for an injury at an earlier tournament.[51] A wide range of romance literature served to set a better example, but incidents such as

[47] See pp. 38–9.
[48] Leyser, *Medieval Women*, 122, 130.
[49] BL, Add. Ms 42130, fo. 202v.
[50] Coss, *The Knight*, 81–92, 121.
[51] Prestwich, *Edward I*, 84–5; Harding, *England in the Thirteenth Century*, 291.

these, involving men who were supposedly the embodiment of chivalry, illustrate how precariously the veneer of chivalric ideals cloaked underlying violence. Knights were essentially a warrior caste. It was an irony, therefore, that chivalric knighthood reached its apogee at a time when they were ceasing to be exclusively fighting men. Although military service still loomed large in a knight's life, wealth rather than valour was more often the qualifying criterion. During the course of the thirteenth century, the policy known as distraint of knighthood required those with lands worth £20 per annum to become knights. The distance knighthood had travelled from the adventurers who accompanied William the Conqueror is illustrated by the assumption by Edward I's reign that it was a status appropriate to judges.[52]

Notwithstanding the strong cultural identities of these individual groups, the upper echelons of society as a whole also enjoyed a homogeneous culture as inheritors of what is sometimes known as the Great Tradition – elite culture – as opposed to the Little Tradition of popular culture.[53] These two cultures could not live in isolation from each other. Even the most prominent members of the royal court spent time on their estates in close proximity with their tenants. Although lords were beginning to incorporate private accommodation into their castles and manor houses so that the family could withdraw from the great hall, a great deal of life was lived in common, particularly on important occasions or festivals and rites of passage such as marriage or death. Communal eating played an important part in cementing relationships within the community, and Langland, for one, disapproved of lords who neglected this obligation. The Rules of Robert Grosseteste set out the ideal – how people should be served, seated and fed. Above all, the bishop counselled that the lord 'be seated at all times in the middle of the high table, that your presence as lord or lady is made manifest to all'.[54]

Entertainment was tailored to suit all tastes, but the performances of minstrels on these public occasions are another casualty of a predominantly oral culture. Studies of the ballads of Robin Hood reveal how difficult reconstruction can be even when there is a large corpus of surviving material. A generation ago passions ran high over the question of the original audience for the ballads. Did they express the social protest of peasants or were they directed at the middling ranks of society? The tale of the knight's indebtedness to the abbot of St Mary's York in the early 'Gest of Robyn Hode' makes a knightly audience plausible. However, the very fact that we are dependent on a written

---

[52] Coss, *The Knight*, 60–1, 124.
[53] Burke, *Popular Culture*, 23–4.
[54] *Walter of Henley*, 402–5.

version decades later than the story's probable origin means that inevitably it reflects the interests and culture of a literate audience. A live performance in a lordly hall before all ranks would have differed considerably in content and emphasis and is utterly beyond our reach.[55] Music is even harder to retrieve. The lyrics of a large number of Middle English songs, which were often sung by dancers in *estampes* and *caroles*, have been preserved because senior churchmen inveighed against their polluting effect on the clergy, but the music itself has largely vanished. Even church music mostly survives as fragments cut up and used in the binding of books.[56]

Outside the great hall, seasonal rituals involving the whole community were a central feature of country life. Evidence for roisterings in animal disguise is plentiful in north-eastern England. Some of these traditions have lingered into modern times, along with Morris Men and bonfire celebrations, but once more it is impossible to recover their authentic flavour. As the survival of an ancient fire festival in the guise of Guy Fawkes Night demonstrates, traditions are subject to reinvention and modification to suit the needs of the day.[57] Urban festivities were no different. Descending to the present day in the form of mystery plays and pale protestant echoes of catholic carnival, they present equal problems of authenticity. Whether the gap between elite and popular culture has widened in the intervening centuries is debatable. The first stirring of the desire for privacy reflected in the construction of *solars* (private rooms) has evolved into the social isolation of dwellings for nuclear families or, increasingly, individuals living alone. Already by the late nineteenth century the gentry had limited their involvement in village mumming to benign spectatorship. On the other hand, it should be borne in mind that fanatical enthusiasm for football, television soaps and popular music is shared today by all social groups.

Finally, in a study of England at the turn of the thirteenth and fourteenth centuries, it is pertinent to enquire how far there was a notion of Englishness to which all levels of society subscribed. It has been argued that this had long existed in some sense, but that circumstances combined to give it added strength and definition from the reign of Edward I.[58] Language is an important determinant of national identity and English was fast gaining ground. As so often happens, warfare also sharpened perceptions, giving rise to stereotypes which consolidated

[55] Articles by R. H. Hilton, J. C. Holt, M. Keen and T. Aston in Hilton, *Peasants, Knights and Heretics*, 221–72; *Rymes of Robyn Hood*, 10–14, 71–112; Holt, *Robin Hood*, ch. 6.
[56] Wilkins, *Music*, 89–101.
[57] Camille, *Mirror*, 248–50.
[58] Clanchy, *England and its Rulers*, ch. 10; Turville-Petre, *England the Nation, passim*.

the identity of those creating them at the same time as depersonalizing the enemy. The English saw the Scots as savages, wild and hairy in dress and person, and the French as lecherous, cowardly and covetous. The French in their turn claimed that the English had tails. They were also widely regarded as drunken and perfidious.[59] The author of the *Vita Edwardi Secundi*, probably writing between 1310 and 1325, had a strong sense of the differing characteristics of the inhabitants of the British Isles, reserving for the English a dubious excellence 'in pride, in craft and in perjury'.[60] Anglo-Norman romances featured English heroes such as Guy of Warwick, Havelock the Dane and Richard Coeur de Lion. The Middle English versions, appearing from the beginning of Edward I's reign, were also becoming explicitly nationalistic in tone; when Guy de Warwick fights, it is 'for Inglond'.[61] Such tales were powerful in forming attitudes among knightly circles. For many centuries England had been ruled by a single monarch and, although royal authority at the periphery was a very different proposition from royal authority closer to London, this too promoted a sense of national identity, however nebulous. Notwithstanding these developments, it is likely that Englishness remained less important in defining self-identity than did membership of particular social groups. It is worth reflecting that even today, when national identity is so strongly established, a farmer in the Yorkshire Dales has little in common with a City stock-broker or a single parent in a run-down inner-city council estate, despite the existence of common educational qualifications, modern transport and national media. Now, as then, England is a country of many cultures.

---

[59] Camille, *Mirror*, 284–95; Coss, *The Knight*, 143; Clanchy, *England and its Rulers*, 248–9; Turville-Petre, *England the Nation*, 56.
[60] *Vita Edwardi Secundi*, 61–3; C. Givern-Wilson, '*Vita Edwardi Secundi*: memoir or journal', in M. Prestwich and R. H. Britnell (eds), *Thirteenth-Century England*, Wood-bridge, 1997, 172.
[61] Crane, *Insular Romance*, 21, 54, 59–66, 83.

6

Government and Administration

In thrall as we are to the modern state, with its National Insurance numbers and tax codes, motor vehicle licences, compulsory schooling and stringent rules about the production of food, the very different expectations of government in the late thirteenth and early fourteenth centuries can present something of a challenge to the imagination. For most of us, life is no longer a grim search for subsistence or the protection of someone more powerful than our oppressor. The role of medieval government in such circumstances was less to regulate the minutiae of daily life than to act as final arbiter. On a day-to-day basis, relationships with lords and neighbours were of greater importance than any relationship with the crown or its agents. Social relations were governed largely by networks of patronage linking members of the same affinity (lord's entourage), kin or community. The crown was drawn in only when these relationships broke down and aggrieved parties chose to resort to the king or to his courts. Not that this was a rare occurrence. By the later thirteenth century, popular demand had resulted in well-developed royal justice willing to recognize a wide range of actions and served by professional lawyers.

On this analysis, the exercise of royal power was essentially a response to pressure from below. Whilst this was undoubtedly true, it was far from the whole story. The king was himself a lord with direct authority over the most powerful tenants in the realm and with vast estates of his own to administer. The assumptions on which feudal society was based also conferred on the crown as liege (supreme) lord certain wider responsibilities. Chief among these was defence of the realm, a duty broadly conceived by the two Edwards to encompass campaigns in Scotland, Wales and Ireland as well as on the Continent. There was also an ecclesiastical as well as a secular dimension to government. Here the crown played a less direct role than modern practice might lead one to expect. Matrimonial, moral and testamentary matters were dealt with by church courts, as were criminal cases affecting the clergy. Thus, medieval government was at the same time less all-embracing than its modern counterpart, but more diverse in its nature and rationale.

Notwithstanding that it bore more lightly on the populace in day-to-day matters than our own, medieval government nevertheless generated vast quantities of writing. The crown would have been unable to dispense justice, manage the royal demesne or contemplate the level of military activity associated with the reigns of Edward I and Edward II without a highly sophisticated administration. Historians are doubly fortunate that much of its output has survived. However, although England never experienced the cataclysmic destruction of the French Revolution, this preservation should not be taken for granted. English medieval records encountered plenty of lesser hazards. When the king went to war, his officials and their working documents often followed in his wake. In 1319, twenty-one cartloads of Exchequer rolls were removed to York.[1] The Ragman rolls of the 1274–5 hundredal inquiry, so called because of the dangling seals of the jurors whose verdicts they recorded, suffered inevitable damage and loss as they were bundled around the country in the ensuing judicial proceedings.[2] There was no single designated repository for old records. Those responsible for them each made personal arrangements. In Edward I's reign, one chief justice of Common Pleas kept his past plea rolls in the New Temple while another kept them in the church of St Mary, Somerset. Other documents were kept in the Tower or at Westminster Abbey.[3] Nor was the custodianship of later generations always all that could be desired. In the seventeenth century, records stored in the Tower were described as 'peeping out of heaps of dust and rubbish a yard or two in depth'.[4] By the early nineteenth century, even Domesday Book was in peril. Stored in a cupboard on the stairs of the Chapter House at Westminster Abbey, its boards and parchment had fallen victim to book worm. It narrowly escaped an even more dramatic fate in 1834 when fire consumed the best part of the palace of Westminster in a blaze caused by the deliberate, if incautious, destruction of medieval tally sticks (receipts on notched pieces of wood).[5] In general however, one cannot fail to be impressed by the care taken by medieval officials and their much later successors at the Public Record Office to order, store and conserve this vast treasury of evidence. Nor should one forget the heroic, if

---

[1] Hallam, *Domesday Book*, 56.
[2] Cam, *The Hundred*, 44–5, 230.
[3] Clanchy, *From Memory*, 164–5.
[4] Fryde, *Tyranny*, 10.
[5] Hallam, *Domesday Book*, 150–1.

occasionally questionable, labours of nineteenth-and twentieth-century scholars who made these and other records more accessible in printed editions and calendars (summaries of contents).[6]

As a result of these endeavours, a remarkably detailed picture can be formed of the day-to-day workings of medieval government.[7] Thanks to Hubert Walter, Chief Justiciar and then Chancellor at the turn of the twelfth and thirteenth centuries, scholars are able to draw on office copies of documents leaving the royal Chancery, entered on the great series of patent and close rolls. These, together with incoming correspondence filed in bundles, are the solid core of the chancery archives. Further series were added as circumstances required, although some of these, such as the registers of correspondence under the Privy Seal kept from c.1290, have not survived. Each year detailed accounts for every county were rendered at the Exchequer by its sheriff. Known as the pipe rolls from the tubes in which they were stored, these survive in an unbroken run from the accounting year 1155–6. The Exchequer functioned as a court dealing with financial matters as well as an accounting office, and by the thirteenth century was greatly overburdened. Increasingly elaborate memoranda rolls were kept in an attempt to keep track of this business. Equally elaborate were the accounts kept by the Wardrobe, which encompassed not only the running of the royal household, but the much weightier task of organizing and arranging payment for the king's military expeditions. Another huge area of record keeping comprised the plea rolls of the royal courts. These survive for the central courts and for the general eyres (peripatetic legal proceedings) in an almost unbroken series from the beginning of Edward I's reign, although there are scarcely any records of county court proceedings. The results of the great series of inquiries commissioned by Edward I have also fared badly. Many still exist, but there are gaps which are at best frustrating and at worst a serious impediment to our understanding.[8] Tax records have been another common casualty although each assessment is known to have been enrolled.

In general, the best-kept records were those with long-established procedures and secure storage in London. Newer series were often less assured in what they should be documenting as well as more vulnerable to loss. This is illustrated by the early rolls of Parliament on which petitions and pleas were routinely entered, but until 1299 newly enacted statutes were not consistently recorded in one location. Record keeping

---

[6] The saga of the Rolls Series features some particularly hair-raising experiences. D. Knowles, *Great Historical Enterprises*, London, 1963, 101–34.

[7] Good recent overviews of government record keeping are Clanchy, *From Memory*, 68–73; Prestwich, 'English government records', 95–106.

[8] See pp. 120–1.

became more regular under Edward II, but the picture of parliamentary proceedings remains hazy, leaving historians to speculate how far the *Modus Tenendi Parliamentum*, a treatise of uncertain provenance written in the early 1320s, can be taken as a reliable guide. Yet, for all these slightly ragged later developments, record keeping in the period 1259 to 1327 was almost breathtaking in its range, as the merest glance at Giuseppi's *Guide to the Contents of the Public Record Office* reveals.[9] Ironically this indispensable tool of modern historians permits them to find their way round the huge volume of surviving material more easily than those who were originally responsible for creating it; thirteenth-century government was better at recording its actions than ordering its archives.

By the end of the thirteenth century this problem was acknowledged. If only because the information in the records was needed, steps were taken to remedy the situation. Between c.1282 and 1305, transcripts were made of all the important diplomatic documents from Henry III's reign onwards, including notes as to their location. Original documents relating to Aquitaine were placed in the keeping of a *custos*, who was not only responsible for their safety but also for briefing royal envoys as to their contents and offering advice on negotiating strategies. Plea rolls were systematically listed for the first time in the 1290s and similar attempts were made to organise the Wardrobe records in 1302.[10] The greatest step forward occurred in the 1320s when Bishop Stapledon, as Treasurer, undertook a general overhaul of the keeping, storing and listing of records. He recognized the danger of losses when documents passed from hand to hand and place to place, and he demanded the return of records still in the custody of officials. Influenced perhaps by work begun in 1318 to replace the lost Gascon archives with transcripts from English copies, he first commissioned a calendar of Gascon records. This was completed in 1322. In the meantime he had also commissioned a calendar of documents relating to Scotland, Wales and Ireland which was brought to a conclusion in the following year. This work was undertaken in parallel with a major sorting of Exchequer records and the creation of new categories.[11] Gradually, therefore, the crown was able not only to record its actions, but to bring its archives to some sort of accessible order. Only then could they be used effectively.

[9] i, *passim*.
[10] Clanchy, *From Memory*, 153; Cuttino, *English Diplomatic Administration*, 32–6, 112–16.
[11] Cuttino, *English Diplomatic Administration*, 119–26; Buck, *Politics*, 167–9. See also chapter 8.

Edward I and his son enjoyed one of the most advanced administrative machines in medieval Europe, unparalleled in its capacity to record. Despite this, and quite apart from the problems of storage and cataloguing it raised, its fitness for the purposes of later thirteenth- and fourteenth-century government was questionable. Its very precocity meant that it had been created for different conditions, with the result that it had to struggle to meet the heavier demands of Edwardian reform and warfare. In its favour was the fact that from an early date English government had proved able to evolve in response to fresh challenges. The question at the turn of the thirteenth and fourteenth centuries was whether the bureaucratic procedures, which were such an impressive achievement, had now become a barrier to such flexibility.

This was particularly the case with regard to financial administration. Exchequer proceedings had long proved too slow and cumbersome for the day-to-day needs of government. The problem was addressed vigorously in the early years of Edward I's reign. In 1275 changes were made in the way escheats (lands reverting to the crown) and wardships were administered and an interesting, if largely unsuccessful, attempt was made to exploit the royal estates directly rather than lease them out. Without the full co-operation of the sheriffs, whose interests were affected, the experiment was doomed to failure. Further reforms were instigated by John Kirkby when he was appointed Treasurer in 1284. Efforts were made to analyse the sources of royal revenue and to improve the collection of fines and debts. These met with some success, with income showing a significant increase in the years immediately following. There were limits to what could be achieved, however, not least because the crown exercised control over its magnates through their indebtedness and the process of accounting remained elaborate and slow. The Wardrobe, which had earlier evolved into a department better able to handle royal expenditure, was also experiencing difficulties in the face of the increasing demands made of it. Logistically it coped remarkably well, given a court constantly on the move and armies needing to be raised, equipped and provided for. Accounts were meticulously kept and, as the scale of operations became ever larger, Walter Langton established a system of final accounts drawn from the numerous lesser accounts of individual departments within the Wardrobe. These were then presented for audit at the Exchequer. Once more, however, the technical proficiency of government in keeping records exceeded its ability to translate them into further action. Such was the weight of business pressing on Wardrobe officials that it often took many years before the final accounts were completed. Those for 1300–1 were not ready until at least the middle of the following decade, while the last Wardrobe accounts to be audited in Edward I's reign were those for 1295–8.[12]

The need for reform became politicized under Edward II as magnates became increasingly concerned about the crown's inability to meet its financial commitments. An earlier generation of scholars interpreted the king's use of the household departments alongside the older departments of Exchequer and Chancery as an assertion of royal autonomy.[13] Certainly the manoeuvres to which the king was driven to gain possession of the Great Seal in order to validate the letter patent for Gaveston's earldom of Cornwall illustrate how easily Edward's wishes could be obstructed by administrative means. Nevertheless, increasing use of the Privy and Secret Seals kept in his own household was a practical necessity rather than anything more sinister. Similarly, the prominence of the Wardrobe and, to a lesser extent, the Chamber as financial as well as domestic departments, owed more to the need for speed and flexibility in day-to-day expenditure rather than any deep-laid royal plot. The Exchequer Ordinances of 1319 and 1323–6 were very much in the tradition of the reforms of his father's early years. Yet again, attempts were made to speed up the hearing of accounts and the collection of debts. Exchequer personnel were increased to cope with the ever-growing burden of business, and new categories of record were created. Twice a year a statement of issues and receipts was put before the Council and, most impressively, in 1324 there is the first extant estimate of Exchequer revenue based on calculations reached by averaging income from previous years.[14] Insofar as there was a driving force behind all these measures, it was the constant need to mobilize armies between 1294 and 1323 and the added burden of administering confiscated rebel estates thereafter.

Mutatis mutandis, the same pattern of difficulties confronting the administration can be seen with regard to judicial proceedings. Sweeping inquiries instituted by the crown from the time of Henry III and the introduction of new forms of action resulted in an upsurge of business for the royal courts. Whereas there were around fifty actions in use in the early thirteenth century, these had greatly increased a century later.[15] In addition, the widespread complaints about the conduct of royal

[12] Prestwich, *Edward I*, 102–3, 134–44, 241–4.
[13] J. C. Davies, *The Baronial Opposition to Edward II*, Cambridge, 1918; T. F. Tout, *Chapters in Administrative History*, 6 vols, Manchester, 1920–33, ii; idem, *The Place of Edward II in Administrative History*, 2nd edn, Manchester, 1936; Harris, *King, Parliament*, 186–7, 208–10.
[14] See chapter 7. Chaplais, *Piers Gaveston*, 27–8; Harriss, *King, Parliament*, 216–17; Buck, *Politics*, ch. 8.
[15] Musson and Ormrod, *The Evolution*, 118.

officials revealed by the hundredal inquiry of 1274–5 called for judicial hearings. Such an expansion of activity could not be absorbed without affecting the speed and effectiveness of justice, unless the system could adapt.

The structure of the medieval legal system echoes the complexity of the structure of the church and for much the same reasons; as circumstances required, new institutions had been added to the old rather than replacing them. Thus the Anglo-Saxon courts of the shire and hundred, for whose conduct the sheriff was normally responsible, continued to operate alongside newer seignorial and royal courts. Although all justice theoretically derived from the crown, it was necessarily heavily devolved. There were, moreover, strong communal traditions. In the freer areas of eastern England, village communities continued to regulate local affairs, but the circumstances of the Norman Conquest meant that manorial lords also had an important role to play in local justice. Their courts were generally permitted to deal with minor issues of law and order alongside specifically seignorial matters such as the transfer of villein tenements. The courts of the Wiltshire manor of Sevenhampton in the 1280s were typical. Villagers were fined for assorted livestock found roaming in the fields and brewers and bakers for breaking the regulations governing their trades. Complaints about assault and debt were settled and in 1283 someone was fined for building a wall on the highway. Alongside these everyday problems of a rural community, villeins rendered merchet, entry fines and the other obligations contingent on their status.[16] In addition to manorial courts, lords had gained control of many hundred courts and a handful of great liberties which would otherwise have been administered by the sheriffs. The greatest of these was the palatinate of Durham where, subject to the proper exercise of his authority, the bishop of Durham ruled as a *quasi* prince.

Royal justice had evolved more or less independently of these courts in order to provide remedies which could not be obtained elsewhere.[17] What had once been hearings before the king himself had long ago evolved into self-standing courts. The court of King's Bench (*coram rege*), which generally followed the king, dealt with matters touching the king's interest – largely criminal proceedings – and also functioned as a superior jurisdiction for appeals or difficult cases. The court of Common Pleas (*de banco*), usually located at Westminster to comply with Magna Carta's demand that it should be held in a fixed place, dealt

---

[16] R. B. Pugh (ed.), *Court Rolls of the Wiltshire Manors of Adam de Stratton*, Wiltshire Record Society, xxiv (1968), 56ff.
[17] The following account of royal justice draws on Musson and Ormrod, *The Evolution, passim*.

chiefly with questions of property, but like King's Bench could also handle criminal cases. Neither court fully solved the principal difficulty facing Edward I and Edward II of how to ensure ready access to royal justice in the shires. The chosen method, until its withdrawal in 1294, was by means of the general eyre. This brought itinerant justices to each county, where they delivered the gaols (dealt with those imprisoned pending judgement), heard civil litigation and pleas of the crown and also carried out any investigations with which they had been charged by the king. Although the general eyre was popular enough to attract large numbers of litigants, it was too diverse in its activities and too irregular in its appearance to prove wholly satisfactory. By the end of the thirteenth century there were experiments with alternative assize circuits, staffed by assize justices recruited principally from among the serjeants-at-law (barristers) of the central courts. At about the same date the first commissions of oyer and terminer were issued, in which designated individuals were ordered to hear complaints. These proved popular, not least because, unusually, they were speedy and enabled those seeking redress to suggest who should be appointed to deal with their case. In the early decades of the fourteenth century as many as 250 special commissions a year were being issued. *Ad hoc* arrangements were also instituted following the Ordinance of Trailbaston of 1305 (so called after the clubs – bastons – carried by criminal gangs) to deal with the backlog of criminal cases caused by the suspension of the general eyre, an experiment repeated in 1314 and again in 1321.

It is thus evident that medieval England was plentifully supplied with law courts and that, as in financial administration, new arrangements were forthcoming in the face of new needs. The question of their efficacy is another matter and a rather more complicated one. The whole question of what is meant by law and its enforcement is now approached with much more subtlety than would have been the case a generation or so ago. Medieval society saw frequent violence. It has been calculated that the murder rate in medieval Oxford was up to six times higher than in even the most violent of modern North American cities.[18] This is not surprising, considering the youthful age profile of the population, especially in Oxford, the habitual carrying of knives for daily needs and the fact that fermented grain was the staple drink. Throughout the realm, insanitary conditions and brutalizing poverty fostered crime and aggression. From another point of view, life was safer and more law-abiding than it is today. Most communities were small and their inhabitants reliant on each other, sometimes for their very survival. Deviant behaviour was unlikely to remain undetected or tolerated for long. Official

---

[18] Hammer, 'Patterns of homicide', 11–12.

arrangements for prosecution of malefactors reflected this situation. Males over the age of twelve were sworn into tithings (groups of ten men) within each village and bound to present before the courts any of their number who had transgressed. This rudimentary but effective means of policing was supervised by the sheriff, whose duty it was to hold twice yearly views of frankpledge in the hundred court to ensure that everyone belonged to a tithing. But while it is easy enough to see the framework within which day-to-day law enforcement operated, it is more difficult to assess the level of crime with which it had to contend and its success in dealing with it. The caution that we have learnt to exercise in interpreting modern crime statistics is equally applicable to those of the past. It is axiomatic that recorded crime is not the same thing as crime itself, particularly where rape is concerned. The importance attached to virginity and female fidelity in the medieval community must have resulted in even more women feeling reluctant to complain than is now the case. Allowing also for crime that was dealt with informally, one can be confident that the known crime rate is unlikely to have been the total crime rate.

There are also problems of interpretation specific to the medieval context. Apart from the inevitable gaps in the evidence, there were significant technical differences in the way in which medieval society approached the law. Courts were often regarded either as a final resort after less adversarial methods had failed, or as a means of bringing pressure to bear on opponents to come to terms in another forum. Arbitration was a well-recognized process.[19] The incidence of 'love days', occasions when those in dispute with each other might settle their differences, were seen as another useful resource.[20] The magnates suggested that Edward II and Thomas of Lancaster might come to an agreement by such means in 1317.[21] Those who chose to invoke royal justice manipulated the system with impressive assurance, sometimes making it hard to understand what was going on. Choice of King's Bench or Common Pleas might depend on the outcome the litigant wanted. Those seeking compensation brought civil pleas, while those in search of revenge or punishment activated criminal proceedings.[22] The formulaic language in which complaints had to be couched in order to be successful is also misleading. Complaints of trespass *vi et armis* (by force and arms) make the late thirteenth- and early fourteenth-century

---

[19] Powell, 'Arbitration', 52–5.
[20] Clanchy, 'Law and love', 60–6. For examples, see B. Farr (ed.), *The Rolls of Highworth Hundred, 1275–1287*, Wiltshire Archaeological and Natural History Society, xxi (1965), 145ff.
[21] *Vita Edwardi Secundi*, 81. See p. 148.
[22] Post, 'Crime', 217–18.

countryside appear a veritable battleground, but incidents did not necessarily involve serious violence. The large number of acquittals brought
in by local jurors should also not be taken at face value. Here the
informal ground rules governing court proceedings were very different
from our own. Where penalties were draconian and extensive use was
made of approvers (those turned king's evidence seeking to save their
own skin), jurors would not return a guilty verdict unless they were
satisfied that the punishment was really merited.

Contemporaries seem to have believed that the elusive real world
behind the stereotyped language and arcane procedures of the courts
was becoming more lawless and corrupt. Among the political poems
that survive from the period, 'The Outlaw's Song of Trailbaston' and the
'Song on the Venality of Judges' rail against unjust indictment and the
rapacity of the judiciary. The 'Poem on the Evil Times of Edward II',
also known as 'Simonie', lambasts officials of church and state alike.
The temptation to take these complaints too literally has to be resisted
however. The poems draw on a long tradition of satire directed originally at the church. This can be seen clearly in 'The Song of the Times',
which denounced the king's ministers in Latin and in a style which owed
much to sermons. The unsavoury characters so vividly depicted in this
literature may be no closer to real life than the mothers-in-law of the
modern stand-up comedian. Moreover, some of the targets may owe
more to political sensitivities than to misconduct. It is probably no
accident that the good justices in 'The Outlaw's Song of Trailbaston'
came from the south-west, while their evil colleagues had been imposed
from Westminster. However, scholars have detected a new bitterness and
specificity in the complaints dating from around 1300, which may
betoken something more than convention and resentment of royal interference in the localities.[23]

It is possible that the rising tide of criticism may reflect higher expectations fuelled by higher standards of law and order than earlier generations had enjoyed, but it is extremely plausible that the apparent
increase in petty theft of grain and livestock in the countryside during
the Great Famine did genuinely occur and that cattle-rustling was endemic in the unsettled conditions of the Welsh and Scottish borders. Nor
would it be surprising if a rise in crime coincided with the political
tensions of the 1290s and worsened with the misgovernment and civil
war of Edward II's reign. Abuses associated with purveyance and the
disruption caused when ex-soldiers were loosed on defenceless local
communities inevitably increased the general level of violence.[24] The

[23] J. R. Maddicott, 'Poems of social protest in early fourteenth-century England', in
Ormrod, England, 130–44; Political Songs, xxxix–xlix.
[24] Musson and Ormrod, The Evolution, 78; Hanawalt, Crime and Conflict, 238–60.

Coterels and Folvilles, notorious gentry gangs of the early years of Edward III's reign, began their careers in the last lawless years of his father.[25] They were a phenomenon new only in the outrageous lengths to which they carried their challenge to the rule of law. In 1305 Sir Ranulf Friskney, keeper of the peace, was accused of conduct seriously unbecoming the king's representative. He was found guilty of maintaining thugs who assaulted those attending markets and fairs and intimidated jurors. When John de le Fendik' attempted to bring a complaint against him, Sir Ranulf's henchmen broke into his house and beat and kicked his wife. Similar violence was offered to the king's purveyor, when he attempted to buy grain in Boston. Other cases heard in the Lincolnshire trailbaston proceedings of the same year tell sorry tales of damage to person and property. Some, such as the incident where a householder suffered extensive damage to his property and was then dragged to a tavern and made to drink a cocktail of beer and his own blood, have a wantonly cruel edge to them. Others suggest something more serious than casual brawls. Hugh son of Adam, having had his arm broken earlier in the summer, was again attacked at Michaelmas in the marsh of West Butterwick, suffering multiple breaks to both arms and having the soles of his feet slashed, perhaps leaving him crippled for life. Although in theory it was easy enough for the injured to haul their tormentors into court by means of bills (complaints in written form), the same process could equally well be used as a weapon of intimidation or in pursuit of grudges.[26] However, it is important to remember that similarly unpleasant cases can be found in any period and, as with punishment beatings in Northern Ireland or Mafia vengeance in Sicily, may tell us more about a community's preference for its own forms of justice when it is dissatisfied with those of the state than about the performance of the judicial machine itself.

Too negative a view of official law enforcement would be wrong. Until the later years of Edward II's reign, the royal courts were probably more successful in protecting legal title than personal well-being. The assize (action) of novel disseisin (dispossession) ensured that anyone deprived of their land could obtain swift recovery, thereby making it less rewarding for rival claimants or aggressors to take the law into their own hands. It had never been easier for subjects to bring bills of complaint before the crown, either in its courts or in Parliament. More

---

[25] Fryde, *Tyranny*, 150–2.

[26] The offences of the Folvilles included murdering a baron of the Exchequer and kidnapping a royal justice, for whom they demanded a ransom of 1,300 marks. E. L. G. Stones, 'The Folvilles of Ashby-Folville, Leicestershire, and their associates in crime, 1326–1347', *TRHS*, 5th ser., vii (1957), 117–36; *Early Trailbaston Proceedings*, 148–9, 157, 163–4.

than eighty per cent of the business in King's Bench in Lincolnshire between 1291 and 1340 was initiated by free peasants or lesser townsmen and it has been calculated that in the early 1330s around one in 200 of the population as a whole was involved in litigation in the court of Common Pleas.[27] Even allowing for the ways in which judicial actions were abused, it is unlikely that the courts would have attracted business on this scale unless there was some prospect of satisfaction.

The issue of corruption is also not as straightforward as it might seem. Impartiality was not a notion that sat comfortably alongside obligations to kin or lord. Nor were justices well paid. In medieval England, no less than today, promotion to the Bench led to a reduction in earnings. The chief justices of Common Pleas and King's Bench earned no more than £40 in addition to the £40 annuity that they were granted when they received their knighthoods. Rewards for lesser justices were correspondingly smaller. By contrast, senior clerics employed elsewhere in government might enjoy bishoprics yielding several thousand pounds a year.[28] In such circumstances, it was not surprising that bribes were taken and that justices became paid retainers of powerful lords. At the end of the thirteenth century, Peterborough Abbey was paying pensions amounting to £13. 13s. 1d. to six royal justices. Although the monks might legitimately have paid for expert advice, the fact that cases in which they were involved could be heard by their pensioners cannot have been satisfactory for their adversaries.[29] Edward I's dramatic dismissal and punishment of most of the judiciary on his return from France in 1289 is well known and seemingly reinforces its reputation for venality, but recent investigation has shown that the scale of the corruption among the justices of the central courts has been much exaggerated. It is also possible that the king's motives were in part financial, since subsequent fines amounted to almost a year's ordinary revenue. Punitive royal action probably exercised a deterrent effect, but judicial conduct was also influenced by a growing sense of professional ethics fostered as much by standards laid down in legislation and the oaths taken on appointment, as by any fear of retribution. Arguably, late thirteenth-century judges were well able to distinguish between proper and improper behaviour and often opted for propriety. Thus, continuing accusations of corruption may reflect the ease with which accusations could be brought and the law turned to the accusers' own ends rather than the extent of its actual incidence.[30]

[27] Musson and Ormord, *The Evolution*, 128–9.
[28] Ibid., 36; Maddicott, 'Law and lordship', 18.
[29] BL, Cott Vesp. E xxii, fo. 6. This list is partially printed in *Select Cases in the Court of King's Bench*, i, 143.
[30] Brand, *The Making*, 103–10.

This is not to deny that corruption was prevalent in many areas of government, including the law. It is hard to see how either Thomas Weyland, chief justice of Common Pleas until his dismissal in 1289, or his brother William, also a justice, could have accumulated their considerable estates on the basis of legitimate earnings and a peasant background. Nor were they isolated examples of men from modest beginnings who accumulated considerable wealth during their careers in public service. Geoffrey de Langley, who died early in the 1270s, also comes to mind. Belonging to one of the minor knightly families of Gloucestershire, he managed to carve out holdings worth at least £200 per annum during a career in which he was *inter alia* chief justice of the forest and, between 1254 and 1257, steward to the Lord Edward. It was men such as these whose families throve into prominence in knightly society and replaced older families overcome by debt and failure of the male line.[31] Most notorious of all was Adam de Stratton. During the course of a career in which his offices included the chamberlainship of the Exchequer, Master of Works at Westminster and steward to Isabella de Forz, he managed to acquire such wealth that when his misdeeds finally caught up with him in the 1289 purge, he was found to have more than £12,000 in cash at home quite apart from substantial holdings in land and ecclesiastical rents.[32] Lesser men enjoyed fewer opportunities, but there can be little doubt that minor officials equally often exploited the power conferred upon them by their positions.

It was the need to address these abuses and also to deal with widespread encroachments on royal rights that led to the great inquiries and the first Statute of Westminster. Edward I returned to England to assume his crown in August 1274 and almost immediately replaced the escheators (officials responsible for wardships and estates falling to the crown) and most of the sheriffs. Commissioners had already been appointed to enquire into the erosion of royal rights in eleven counties and this was extended into the countrywide proceedings of the 1274–5 hundred roll (Ragman) inquiry. Information was sought in response to some fifty articles of inquiry on matters ranging from the royal demesne and tenants-in-chief, their holdings and trespasses against the crown, to abuse of power whether by lords or officials. An even more ambitious inquiry was mounted in November 1279 when commissioners were again ordered into each county, this time charged with around forty articles seeking tenurial information so extensive that, if the information were available to us, it would dwarf Domesday Book in importance.[33]

---

[31] Ibid., 115–26; Coss, 'Sir Geoffrey de Langley', 167–8.

[32] Denholm-Young, *Seignorial Administration*, 77–84.

[33] Prestwich, *Edward I*, 92ff; Cam, *The Hundred*, 248–57; Raban, 'The making', 142–5.

These two hundred roll inquiries illustrate the strengths and limitations of later thirteenth-century bureaucracy. They demonstrate once again that machinery existed to amass information on a formidable scale, but also show that government was far less adept at putting its garnerings to effective use. The findings of the 1274–5 inquiry were assembled with remarkable speed between November and the following March. Even now they appear impressive in their quantity, although many survive only in the form of extract rolls probably compiled between 1280 and 1294.[34] Some of the complaints were trivial, such as the seizure of eight cockerels by the sheriff of Essex on the implausible grounds that they might be used to set fire to London by flying into the city with incendiary material strapped to their feet. Others were far more serious. The sheriff of Yorkshire and the keeper of the prison at York were accused of colluding to extract payment from Wylkes de Gloseburne by tying him naked to a stake in the prison and starving him into submission. Wylkes was, however, luckier than Thomas de Algarkirke, who was said to have been imprisoned by the prior of Spalding until his feet rotted off.[35] The sheer volume of the returns testifies both to the eagerness with which contemporaries seized the opportunity to express their grievances and their expectation of royal remedy. They were to be disappointed. The Statute of Ragman of 1276 made provision for special judicial hearings to deal with the indictments, but, as the Dunstable annalist laconically remarked, 'nothing useful came of it'.[36] This may have been due in part to the distractions of the Welsh war, but it also reflected the enormous scale of the undertaking. Eventually responsibility for legal action was transferred to the general eyres, but by then many of those who had been accused were either dead or untraceable.

Attempts to deal with those who had usurped royal jurisdictions or were holding markets, fairs or other privileges without royal authority were equally halting. Initially, the crown resolved to deal with the matter in Parliament. Magnates were summoned time and again to defend their possession, only to be dismissed because there was insufficient time to deal with their cases. It was decided therefore in 1278 that these so-called *quo warranto* (by what authority) hearings should be dealt with by justices in eyre and, at the same time, broadened to include investigation of title to all royal franchises, not just those which had been called into question. The issue was a sensitive one, as the irascible reaction

---

[34] Scales, 'The Cambridgeshire Ragman Rolls', 555–6; *Yorkshire Hundred and Quo Warranto Rolls*, 1–3.

[35] Prestwich, *Edward I*, 95–6; *Yorkshire Hundred and Quo Warranto Rolls*, 51; *RH*, i, 275a.

[36] *Annales Monastici*, iii, 263.

attributed to Earl Warenne shows.[37] Sometimes legitimate possession
was not susceptible of written proof. There were also political under-
currents, as the boundaries were negotiated between what the crown
might wish to recover and magnates might reasonably expect to retain.
A compromise was reached in the Statute *de Quo Warranto* of 1290
whereby tenure since 1189 was confirmed and, in 1294, outstanding
cases were dropped by the king 'as a favour to his people and on account
of the Gascon war'.[38] In the meantime, the burden of processing the
queries and accusations arising from the Ragman hearings added to the
volume of business coming before the justices in eyre. This, together
with the inclusion of all the 1274 articles of inquiry as *nova capitula*
(new articles) alongside the usual questions asked by justices in eyre in
1278, contributed significantly to the swamping of the courts.[39]

Whatever the outcome, at least the 1274–5 inquiry had a discernible
purpose and signalled the crown's determination to enforce good government. It is less clear what lay behind its successor in 1279.[40] By
contrast with 1274, the articles of inquiry showed no interest in official
misconduct. According to the commission, the king sought information
of a descriptive nature about royal demesnes and tenants, together with
rights of every sort, whether in town or countryside 'so that in future we
may know what is, and ought to be, ours and others may know what is,
and ought to be, theirs'. There were distinct echoes of the Anglo-Saxon
Chronicle account of the making of Domesday Book, in that findings
were to be 'written in books to be delivered to the king by the commissioners, in such a way that no one is spared'. It is hardly surprising that
such a comprehensive brief proved difficult to execute. Indeed, it is
possible that the whole enterprise fell at the first hurdle. Returns survive
for a few midland counties only, and even then they are patchy in their
coverage.[41] It is unclear whether other returns were lost or whether they
were never made.

Although not immediately obvious from the nineteenth-century
printed edition, the returns from both hundred roll inquiries were a
composite of material provided by landlords together with the verdicts
of hundredal, village and borough juries. Such a mass of information
posed a major challenge to those charged with reducing it to a coherent
final version. None of the commissioners in the 1279–80 inquiry completed their task; only those appointed to deal with Huntingdonshire
and Oxfordshire came anywhere close, and only then for one of the two

[37] See Chapter 5.
[38] *Yorkshire Hundred and Quo Warranto Rolls*, 4–5; Prestwich, *Edward I*, 347.
[39] Sutherland, *Quo Warranto*, 25.
[40] For the 1279–80 hundred rolls see Raban, 'The making', 123–45.
[41] See map 5.

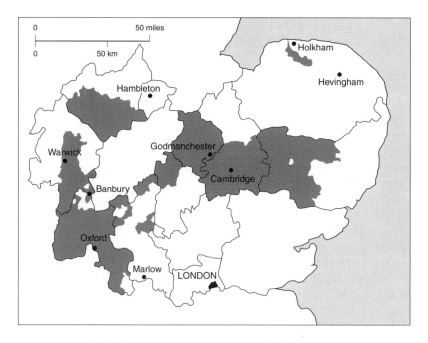

MAP 5   Hundreds for which returns survive from the 1279–80 hundred roll inquiry

counties for which they were responsible. Whereas it had proved possible for the findings of the 1274–5 inquiry to be summarized for more
convenient use in the extract rolls, those from 1279–80 defied any such
treatment. Unlike Domesday Book, there was no guiding hand to produce a summary text so consistent that it can be subjected to computer
analysis. In the eleventh century, this had been a remarkable achievement. Two centuries later it was unachievable; the tenurial situation was
far more complicated and the assembled information far more exhaustive. The material has proved a wonderful quarry for historians, but its
value to contemporaries was much more limited. Marginal flags high-
light information about royal franchises, indicating perhaps that action
was intended. Very occasionally a note actually calls for inquiry, but as
yet no one has shown that anything happened as a result of such
prodigious labours.

The hundred roll inquiries were the biggest but they were not the only
such undertakings, nor indeed the first. Large-scale investigations had
been an intermittent feature of English government since the Norman
Conquest. The immediate precedents, however, were the inquiries undertaken in the troubled years of the previous reign. In 1255 information

had been sought about the alienation of crown rights and official misconduct. Further inquiries took place in 1258 and 1259. It is likely that
Edward I consciously drew on these forerunners when seeking to establish his reforming credentials on assuming the throne. Not all were
associated with the need for reform, however. In 1279, in addition to
commissioning the second hundred roll inquiry, he instigated an investigation into how well the sheriffs had executed an order for distraint of
knighthood. The sizeable inquiry carried out in 1285, known as Kirkby's
Quest after John Kirkby, was part of his Exchequer reforms. Wide-
ranging information was sought about debts to the crown and other
sources of potential income. Although most of the returns have since
disappeared, like the returns for the 1274–5 inquiry they were in due
course condensed into extract form for more convenient use. However,
few even of these condensed versions survive.[42]

Although with hindsight it might seem as though the collection of
information in the 1270s and 1280s had become an end in itself, this
would be to underestimate the practical application of all but the 1279–
80 findings. Many of the problems they revealed provided the context
for legislation as well as resulting in the prosecution of individuals.
Edward I, hailed by Edward Coke, the great seventeenth-century jurist,
as 'England's Justinian', returned to England in 1274 full of reforming
zeal. The first half of his reign brought forth a stream of important
statutes. It would be anachronistic to see them as either a code in the
Roman fashion or a modern legislative programme. Rather they were a
reflection of his energetic pragmatism, his political needs and whatever
difficulties were confronting the courts or royal officials at the time.
Whether it was revising existing law or providing new remedies, the
common theme was practical solutions to immediate problems, but
whatever called them into being, the Edwardian statutes formed a
remarkable body of legislation enacted over a short space of time. As
such, and by accident, it came to constitute the foundation of English
statute law.

As well as being largely reactive, the process of lawmaking was still
very ill defined. Statutes had no set form. They were a heterogeneous
body of measures which became identified as statutes through usage and
subsequent collections made by lawyers and landlords for their own
purposes.[43] Some, such as the Statute of Mortmain were writs; others
were charters. Some were in Latin and some in French. Relatively little is
known about the process of drafting, other than that it was far less
refined than it would be today and that the king was unlikely to have

[42] Prestwich, *Edward I*, 236–7; *Feudal Aids*, i, viii–xvii.
[43] Plucknett, *Legislation*, 11–12; Prestwich, *Edward I*, 268–9.

been involved in the detailed work. Texts were not fixed, unambiguous or even, in the case of the Statute of Mortmain, internally consistent. As we have already seen, the written word had not yet come to enjoy absolute primacy over the oral.[44] This was well illustrated by Chief Justice Hengham in 1311 in a well-known riposte: 'do not gloss the statute [Westminster II, 1285], we know it better than you, for we made it...'.[45] In fact, many hands were involved in drafting major statutes, which were then brought to the king in Council or the wider body of Parliament for final approval and publication.

Statutes were as varied in content as form. The great Edwardian statutes dealt with many issues. The First Statute of Westminster (1275), enacted in the wake of the first hundred roll inquiry, had fifty-one chapters dealing with matters ranging from purveyance, wardship, tolls and rape to unwanted guests in religious houses. Much the same is true of the second Statute of Westminster enacted a decade later, where fishing for salmon out of season featured alongside far weightier concerns. These two statutes, together with the Statute of Winchester (1285), made important changes to the civil and criminal law. There was also a good number of other statutes, such as those of Ragman and *Quo Warranto*, which dealt with single issues as they arose.

Among the more important provisions of Westminster I was the overhaul of the working of the assize of novel disseisin. Introduced in Henry II's reign, revision was long overdue. The statute set a firm date (1242) before which actions were inadmissible, and permitted heirs to the original parties to continue litigation. Further refinements were made in the Statute of Gloucester (1278) and Westminster II. As well as land law, these 'portfolio' statutes contained an important body of commercial law. Merchants were in urgent need of an effective means of registering and collecting debts. This was addressed in Westminster I and II, as well as the more specialized statutes of Acton Burnell (1283) and Merchants (1285). In criminal law, the emphasis was on speed and efficiency. Among a host of measures, including the widening of the king's highway to protect travellers from attack, precise terms of imprisonment were introduced for the first time for specific offences.[46]

Legislation was not merely a response to legal and administrative needs. It was also enacted for political reasons. This is most apparent in the Statute of Wales (1284), setting out arrangements for the governing of Wales, following the second Welsh war.[47] On other occasions, the king was meeting the concerns of his magnates, especially when he was

[44] See chapter 5.
[45] Plucknett, *Legislation*, 72–3.
[46] See chapter 1. Prestwich, *Edward I*, 271–80.
[47] See chapter 7.

in particular need of their support. The Statute of Mortmain and the Statute of *Quia emptores* (1290) were each in their different ways a response by the crown to the anxiety of magnates about the way in which their interests were being damaged by the uncontrolled alienations of their tenants. While the Statute of Mortmain forbade further acquisition of land by the church, *Quia emptores* required those granting land to remove themselves from the feudal chain, so that the recipients held directly of the lord, who would then reap the benefits of any feudal incidents that might arise. Similarly, the legislation aimed at the Jewish community could also be seen as offering help to an indebted and resentful gentry.[48]

Parliament, like legislation, is an aspect of medieval government which it is easy to approach with hindsight. Its role in the conflict between the crown and baronage in the late 1250s and 1260s, once hailed as a constitutional turning-point, is now seen in the context of an ill-defined body whose later importance was only briefly prefigured while the magnates held the upper hand. Essentially Parliament was an extension of the king's Council, in itself an amorphous body comprising whichever officials and magnates happened to be in the royal entourage. The monarch normally worked closely with a handful of key ministers and favoured magnates, together with his household knights. At certain seasons such as Christmas or Easter, attendance at court would swell to include a wider circle of nobles and it then became convenient to involve them in discussion of current business. Over time, such wider groups came to be specially summoned and to be called parliaments, but this was only one of several contemporary terms indicating talk (*colloquium*, *tractatum*, *deliberacionem*, *consilium*) which before 1295 were often used interchangeably. It has been argued that the only distinguishing feature of a *parliamentum* was the presence of the king.[49]

The Provisions of Oxford (1258) envisaged Parliament meeting three times a year, whether or not the king chose to summon it, a measure not introduced effectively until the Glorious Revolution of 1689. Between Edward I's arrival in England in 1274 and his return to Gascony in 1286, parliaments were usually summoned twice a year, in spring and autumn, reflecting his exceptionally active rule. This did not harden into custom however. Meetings became less frequent in the 1290s and there were no parliaments at all in 1303 and 1304. The accession of Edward II saw a return to more regular meetings, but in his later years the king employed various devices to prevent them from causing him

---

[48] Prestwich, *Edward I*, 270, 274; *Statutes of the Realm*, i, 26ff; Raban, *Mortmain Legislation*, 12–18. See chapter 5.
[49] Prestwich, *Edward I*, 442.

embarrassment. Meetings were postponed or cancelled. He delayed his arrival or altered the venue.[50]

Business was varied, normally comprising whatever the crown found convenient to deal with in that gathering. The almost complete absence of records before the 1290s makes it exceptionally difficult to chart the way in which it evolved. Unfortunately the best-documented aspect of parliamentary business is that which holds the least interest for historians, the hearing of petitions. Indeed, it could be said that it held the least interest for monarchs too. Edward I complained that more important matters were held up while petitions were dealt with and Edward II made no time for them at all in the parliaments of 1309 and 1311. Important points of law were also held over to Parliament, when the king could have the benefit of a wider range of advice. This was a convenient way of sounding out legal and magnate opinion in conformity with contemporary notions of proper government. It was also useful strategy when matters touching the interests of tenants-in-chief were involved, as in the case brought by Llywelyn ap Gruffudd over Arwystli or early attempts to deal with the findings of the *Quo Warranto* inquiries.[51] Many of the proceedings must have been routine and technical, which perhaps explains why attendance at parliaments could be as low as thirty and the tendency of those present to depart before the proceedings had concluded.

If Edward I found Parliament a useful forum for implementing legislation as well as dealing with matters requiring wider consultation, the promulgation of the baronial programme for reform there set an equally important precedent. When the magnates sought to enforce proper conduct on the crown in 1300 and 1311, it was natural that they too should take that route. Another significant legacy of the mid-thirteenth-century civil war was the precedent set by the summons of knights and burgesses to the parliament of 1265, even though they were not invariably summoned thereafter nor even mentioned in the 1311 Ordinances.[52] While earls and bishops, together with a fluctuating group of abbots and lesser magnates, were always summoned in person, knights and townsmen were invited as representatives of the commons only when the business warranted. From 1295, representatives of the lower clergy were sometimes included too, although they had their own gathering in Convocation.

---

[50] *Documents of the Baronial Movement*, 110–11; Fryde, *Tyranny*, 66–7; *Handbook of British Chronology*, 526, 545–56.
[51] See chapter 7.
[52] *EHD, 1189–1327*, 527–39.

That the Commons ultimately became the dominant partner within Parliament was due to its last important function; the sanctioning of taxation. In summoning the clergy to the 1295 parliament, Edward I quoted the Roman law maxim 'what touches all should be approved by all'. In itself there was nothing remarkable in citing a well-known tag to those familiar with Roman law through canon law. What is significant was the way in which during the course of the thirteenth century it had become impossible for the king to levy taxation without the consent of representatives of all his (free) subjects. The implications of this for the unfettered exercise of royal power were demonstrated in the 1250s and 1290s. It is here that historians have to be most careful about anachronism. This ultimate control of the purse-strings permitted the development of a parliamentary democracy, but only over many centuries and after many confrontations. The initiative in calling Parliament lay with the monarch and, as Edward II showed towards the end of his reign, a ruler could amass sufficient revenue by other means to avoid its summons, unless faced with the demands of heavy war expenditure. For all the straws in the wind, Parliament in 1327 was still an ill-defined body with an untidy assortment of activities. It was not yet in any formal sense an institution central to 'the constitution'.

It is easy to lay emphasis on the shortcomings of government in the later thirteenth and early fourteenth centuries, thereby devaluing its achievements. The crown was often fortunate in finding outstanding servants, even if they were not always beyond reproach in their personal lives. Quite apart from enriching themselves, some such as Robert Burnell and Walter Langton were a cause of scandal for other reasons. Both kept mistresses even though they were bishops, the one siring numerous progeny and the other accused *inter alia* of murdering the wronged husband. The crown was equally well and somewhat less controversially served by its leading justices. Despite his dismissal in the 1289 purge and the long period of his subsequent disgrace, Chief Justice Hengham's worst offence was that he was too rich and independent-minded for Edward I's taste.[53] These men were exceptional in every way, but the general standard of senior officials, even under Edward II, was very high. However, the success of medieval government rested essentially on a host of clerks turning out immaculately written rolls year after year. The machinery of government which they operated grew increasingly sophisticated. It has been said that by the fourteenth century, the administration was 'literally honeycombed with specialists'.[54] If these bureaucratic developments sometimes meant that it was easier to

[53] Prestwich, *Edward I*, 140, 234.
[54] Cuttino, *English Diplomatic Administration*, 60.

initiate action than to carry it to an effective conclusion, this was not a problem unique to Edwardian England. Modern governments have proved no more successful in striking an effective balance between red tape and swift action. It was a tribute to the strengths of the system that it could operate and even refine itself under a monarch as deficient as Edward II. The ultimate test of medieval government did not come, however, until a generation after his death, under the onslaught of the Black Death in 1349. It triumphed. Notwithstanding the high death toll, officials stuck to their posts, enabling the administration to return to normal within a remarkably short space of time.[55]

[55] W. M. Ormrod, 'The English government and the Black Death of 1348–9', in Ormrod, *England*, 177–8.

7

Politics

Despite the existence of a sophisticated administrative machine able to handle prolonged, if infrequent, royal absences and major military campaigns, the king himself remained crucially important in late thirteenth- and early fourteenth-century England. Image mattered. Kingly demeanour, a certain piety and skill in the pursuits appropriate to fighting men were important attributes. It was Edward I's good fortune that he could in large measure match these requirements and the misfortune of his son that he could not. Neither could be faulted on kingly bearing. Walter of Guisborough described Edward I as 'handsome, tall and elegant, standing head and shoulders above ordinary people'. Edward II was equally well endowed. On his first campaign aged sixteen, he was described as 'a well-proportioned and handsome person, of a courteous disposition'.[1] Temperamentally, however, the two men had little in common. Edward I's remarkable energy focused on every aspect of rule. It is not too fanciful to liken him to Peter the Great or Prince Albert in his personal involvement in new town foundation and initiatives such as the search country-wide in 1295 for miners so that silver mining could be developed in Devon.[2] By contrast, his son was disinclined towards the business of government. Correspondence with his officials forms a litany of anxiety about procrastination and reluctance to deal with affairs of state. In 1320, the bishop of Worcester noted with relief the king's greater affability and willingness to participate in official matters, as well as the fact that he was getting up earlier in the morning. The younger Edward's preference for music and the pleasant day-to-day life of court contrasted with his father's more conventional enthusiasm for tournaments, hunting and hawking. It was not a simple difference between active and passive interests, however. Edward I enjoyed the quieter pleasures of

---

[1] *Guisborough*, 213; Johnstone, *Edward of Carnarvon*, 13.
[2] Miller and Hatcher, *Medieval England: Towns*, 71.

chess and his son enjoyed vigorous outdoor exercise. The problem was that Edward II's more active pastimes were not deemed suitable in a king. He relished rural pursuits such as ditching, thatching and black-smithing, together with rowing and swimming. Ranulf Higden was not alone in thinking that Edward's association with workmen, singers and actors showed a base nature. So widespread were these views that the pretender to the throne in 1318 could plausibly claim that Edward was the son of humble parents exchanged at birth for the royal infant.[3]

Had Edward II met the expectations of his subjects in other respects, these personal quirks would no doubt have been overlooked. Appearances were important, but reputation ultimately rested on solid achievement. This meant the ability to deliver good government and success in war. In attaining these, the two principal problems confronting medieval monarchs were magnates and money. It was axiomatic to the aristocracy that the king should rule with their counsel and within a framework of custom. The worst crises of the thirteenth and fourteenth centuries arose when they were driven to challenge the crown in order to ensure that this was the case. Disputes did not usually centre wholly on matters of principle, however. Quarrels and ambition also played their part. Medieval magnates were often fickle in their alliances and jealous of their status, or as the author of the *Vita Edwardi Secundi* more vividly expressed it, 'the love of magnates is as a game of dice'.[4] Relationships were always complicated by the web of marriage alliances between each other and the crown.[5] Strong leadership was needed to control men accustomed to power and military action, but it was in the crown's favour that their upbringing predisposed them to loyalty to the king as their feudal lord. That this loyalty became strained to breaking-point was more often than not due to the crown's need for funds. This was conspicuously so in the conflict between Henry III and his baronage, beginning in the late 1250s, and again in the later years of Edward I's reign. Although the ability to levy taxes permitted the crown to raise the huge sums required to wage war on an unparalleled scale, it also brought in its train the need to secure agreement from Parliament and the church. Assistance was rarely forthcoming without concessions, the redress of grievances and sometimes bitter wrangling, especially when campaigns were felt to be in the interest of the royal family rather than the realm as a whole.

---

[3] Johnstone, *Edward of Carnarvon*, 130–1; *Polychronicon*, viii, 298; Childs, 'Welcome, my brother', 152. See chapter 5.
[4] *Vita Edwardi Secundi*, 8.
[5] See Appendix 1.

Edward I came to the throne far better prepared than his son for the task of kingship. At thirty-three, he had already served a tough apprenticeship in the civil war of his father's reign.[6] By 1259, the Lord Edward as he was then known, was becoming a significant player on the political scene. Like many young men, he found himself irked by the controls imposed on him by his father. He had a particular grievance in that the treaty Henry III was about to conclude with Louis IX of France prejudiced Edward's interests in his duchy of Aquitaine.[7] Yet, although he flirted with the reformers between the autumn of 1259 and spring 1261, he came to appreciate that his ultimate interest lay in supporting his father. The political arrangements in the Provisions of Oxford drawn up by the king's baronial and clerical opponents in 1258 were fundamentally unacceptable to an aspirant monarch. They sought to control the king's choice of ministers, his exercise of patronage and his formulation of policy. They also imposed curbs on Edward's own freedom of action. The political aims of Henry III's opponents at this point were chiefly to avoid further debacles such as the ill-fated attempt to secure the throne of Sicily for his second son Edmund and to oust the king's hated Poitevin half-brothers and their followers. However, the peace terms put forward after the defeat of Henry and Edward at the battle of Lewes in 1264 made it clear that the controls initially designed as a short-term measure to deal with a wayward and incompetent monarch were not to die with him. They were to continue 'during the reign of the Lord Edward when he shall have become king, until a date which shall be settled hereafter'.[8] The defeat and death of Simon de Montfort, the baronial leader, at the battle of Evesham in 1265 freed Edward from this prospect, which, although alarming, was perhaps never very real. The crown could be assured of support from other rulers in resisting such far-reaching restrictions on its power, the implications of which were threatening to their own position. In the early 1260s, Henry had secured papal absolutions from his oath accepting the Provisions, while in January 1264 Louis IX, although personally sympathetic to Simon de Montfort, rallied behind his beleaguered fellow monarch and annulled the Provisions in the Mise (arbitration award) of Amiens. Without the co-operation of the crown, the reforms could only be implemented by means of coercion. Simon de Montfort was a more gifted general than Henry III and Edward's inexperience had been exposed at Lewes, but it could only be a matter of time before the unstable opposition fragmented and the crown was able successfully to reassert its control.

[6] The following section on the civil war period draws on Maddicott, *Simon de Montfort, passim,* and Prestwich, *Edward I,* ch. 2.
[7] See chapter 8.
[8] *Documents of the Baronial Movement,* 295.

The events of 1258 to 1260 have been described as the most formative of Edward's life.[9] He learned invaluable political and military lessons. The author of 'The Song of Lewes', supporter of the baronial cause, accused Edward of inconstancy, 'not holding steadily his word or his promise', while recognizing his 'unflinching bravery'.[10] Unlike his son, however, the Lord Edward had time to mature. The unwise and often wilful acts of youth which gave rise to such judgements had moderated before they could reflect on his reputation as king. Moreover, the climate of reform coloured his political education in a beneficial way. The Provisions were not solely concerned with control of the monarchy. They also attempted to respond to widespread popular concern about abuses in administration. The office of justiciar, in abeyance since 1234, was revived in order to 'put right the wrongs done by all other justices, and by officials, by earls, barons and all other persons'. Sheriffs were to be recruited from local knights and appointed for a year at a time. The Provisions of Westminster of the following year supplemented these broad measures with a host of more detailed arrangements aimed at specific grievances.[11] In launching his attack on corruption in the 1270s, Edward clearly drew on these earlier experiments with which he may well have had sympathy.

His apprenticeship was furthered in the years after the Battle of Evesham by the time he spent in Gascony and on crusade. Although conditions in the duchy differed from those in England, the need for a reforming hand was even greater. His presence there in 1254–5, 1261–2, and again in 1273–4 on his way back from crusade, enabled him to acquire valuable practical experience of ruling.[12] The crusade itself, on which he embarked in 1270, added immeasurably to his stature at home and abroad. Both ventures permitted him independence of action that he would have found hard to achieve in the shadow of his father. The other useful legacy of these early years was the development of a nucleus of well-tried companions and advisers on whom so much of his later success depended. Otto de Grandson accompanied him on crusade as did Roger de Leyburn, then his steward. Robert Burnell first appeared in his service in Gascony in the 1260s. His lifelong friendship with Earl Warenne also goes back to this period in his life. He was fortunate that an accident of chronology meant that most of his magnates were men of his own generation, making it easier for him to emerge as their leader through shared military adventure.

[9] Carpenter, *The Reign of Henry III*, 250.
[10] *Political Songs*, 93.
[11] *Documents of the Baronial Movement*, 106–9, 136–49.
[12] See chapter 8.

Henry III died in Edward's absence in November 1272. It is interesting that the new king did not make a swift return to England his priority
and perhaps a salutary reminder of the essentially continental character
of the English ruling house. The transfer of power is always the moment
at which an incoming king is most vulnerable and Gilbert de Clare, earl
of Gloucester, the most important of the magnates left behind, did not
have a record of unbroken loyalty. In the event, however, he honoured
his oath to support Edward and fulfilled it by suppressing the Londoners
who were rioting within earshot of the dying king. Nor was the post-
ponement of Edward's return for nearly two years quite as irresponsible
as it appears. Thought had been given to the possibility of Henry's death
before he left. A large number of castles had been handed over for a
period of five years and placed in the hands of his own men. Control of
his lands was vested in trustworthy hands, principally those of his uncle
Richard, earl of Cornwall. Unfortunately both Richard and his son
Henry 'of Almain', whom Edward had sent back to England to attend
to royal affairs, predeceased the king. Indeed, Henry 'of Almain' was
assassinated en route while at Mass in Viterbo by the sons of Simon de
Montfort, in dramatic revenge for his abandonment of the Montfortian
cause and their father's death. Although unexpectedly deprived of his
surest supporters, the others in whom Edward had confided his trust,
including Robert Burnell, successfully ran the country during the inter-
regnum.[13]

The contingency plans enabled his accession to proceed smoothly, but
there were inevitably many who saw the absence of the king as a licence
for crime and extortion. Once re-established in England, Edward
devoted almost a decade to setting the realm to rights.[14] He arrived
back in August 1274 and by the end of September most of the sheriffs
and the escheators had been replaced. He also set in motion the first of
the major inquiries which characterized his reign. The extent to which
these and subsequent initiatives, together with the legislation arising
from them, achieved real retribution for past misdemeanours and a
lasting improvement in government is questionable.[15] It was, however,
a clear signal to his subjects that he did not intend to tolerate any abuse
of the authority that he conferred on his officials. It was also the last
sustained period that he was able to devote to the internal affairs of the
kingdom.

---

[13] Howell, *Eleanor of Provence*, 249–53; Prestwich, *Edward I*, 74; Maddicott, *Simon de
Montfort*, 370–1.
[14] Much of this chapter draws heavily on Prestwich, *Edward I*, the major modern study
of this monarch.
[15] See chapter 6.

If reform and legislation were one leitmotif of Edward I's reign, his campaigns in Wales and Scotland were another. In both cases warfare was the result of his claims to overlordship, but the circumstances and outcome in the two countries were very different. The Norman baronage had settled the southern coast and the Marches (the borders) of Wales in the eleventh and early twelfth centuries.[16] Their right to wage private warfare and the greater freedom of action they enjoyed in their Welsh lordships made them a major force in the politics of England and Wales alike under the two Edwards. However, little headway had been made either by them or the crown in the heart of Wales or the north until the mid-thirteenth century. Henry III then succeeded in conquering the area known as the Four *Cantrefi* (land units roughly similar to an English hundred) in the north and, following the death of Llywelyn the Great in 1240, was acknowledged suzerain by the remaining Welsh princes. Direct Welsh rule was reduced to Snowdonia and Anglesey. What this Plantagenet victory would mean in practical terms and whether it was to be of an enduring nature was for Edward I to determine.

The Four *Cantrefi*, a number of castles elsewhere and the honour of the Three Castles in south Wales formed part of the estates settled on the Lord Edward at the time of his marriage to Eleanor of Castile in 1254. It was not an easy endowment. Within two years the Welsh were in revolt, goaded by the insensitive administration of Geoffrey de Langley. Little might have come of this had Llywelyn ap Gruffudd not emerged as an effective leader of Welsh resistance. His initial success forced the crown to recognize him as Prince of Wales, supreme over other princes. Under the Treaty of Montgomery in 1267, Edward lost both lands and vassals. Henceforward other Welsh princes were to be subservient to Llywelyn who, in turn, would pay homage to the king of England as overlord of all. Failure to honour this obligation, together with Llywelyn's provocative plan to marry Simon de Montfort's daughter, led to the renewal of hostilities in 1276. This time Edward emerged the victor, capturing Anglesey, recovering his lost lands in the north and extending royal control significantly in central and west Wales.[17] Llywelyn was made liable for a huge £50,000 indemnity. Even though this payment was soon remitted, the settlement was not permanent. Insurrection led to war again in 1282. The English, unaccustomed to fighting in mountainous terrain in winter, adopted white tunics and stockings as camouflage against the snow. More important to their success, however, were the superior military resources that the crown could call upon. Llywelyn

---

[16] Davies, *Conquest*, pt 4, the most comprehensive recent study of the English in Wales.
[17] See map 6.

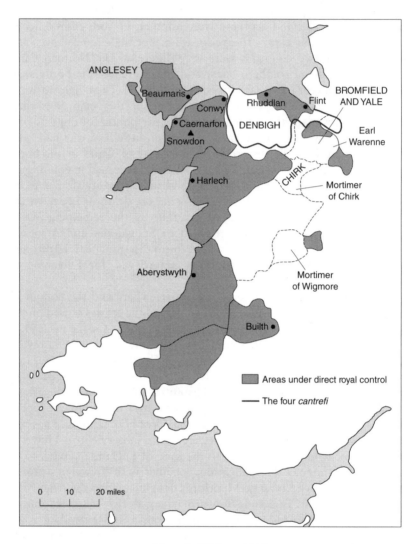

MAP 6   Wales *c*.1300

was killed in December 1282 and his younger brother Dafydd, on whom
leadership had devolved, was executed in a singularly unpleasant manner the following year. Edward was left in possession of Llywelyn's
treasure, including *Y Groes Naid*, a cherished fragment of the True
Cross, and his estates in Snowdonia and Anglesey. There were further
revolts in 1287, when Edward was absent in Gascony, and in 1294, but
in a contest between David and Goliath, Edward's Goliath once again

proved the winner. In 1294, Edward was able to divert the advanced preparations for a major French campaign to Wales, thereby finally achieving lasting conquest.

The fundamental issue throughout these struggles was how far Plantagenet rule was also to be English rule. The two countries had very different social structures, customs and laws, but unlike in Gascony, which had also been granted to Edward as part of his marriage endowment, the king was increasingly unwilling to work within the native tradition.[18] Instead, he imposed English institutions, often served by English officials, in areas under royal control and took steps to incorporate his vassals throughout the whole of Wales into the English judicial system. It was Llywelyn's experience in the king's courts in pursuit of his claim to the *cantref* of Arwystli that played the largest part in his disaffection and revolt in 1282. The Treaty of Aberconwy of 1277 had provided that disputes in areas under Welsh rule should be settled by Welsh law, and in the Marches according to Marcher law. This became the focus of dispute between monarch and prince. In practice, matters were not always as clear-cut as the terms of the treaty implied. Welsh law varied from place to place, the allegiance of lordships changed, and parties to litigation often belonged to different jurisdictions. It was unfortunate that there were political implications in reaching a judgement which led Edward to procrastinate. His motives in instituting inquiries into the nature of Welsh law and its application in the English courts as a preliminary to judgement have consequently been called into question. The collection of evidence and its subsequent use indeed appears somewhat selective. A suspiciously large number of witnesses claimed that they recalled pleas involving Welsh magnates heard before the king's justices 'because he is their superior', or even asserted that the king had the power to correct law and custom.[19] However, a genuine desire to ascertain the facts in order to promote better government is consonant with the king's activities elsewhere in his domains at this date. Certainly his policy towards Welsh law was revised after 1282. Under the Statute of Wales (sometimes known as the Statute of Rhuddlan) enacted in 1284, some Welsh laws were abolished, some allowed or 'corrected' and additions made where this was deemed necessary. English law was required in criminal cases, but Welsh law was permitted for civil cases, while at the same time making certain English writs available to those who wished to make use of them. Customs regarding land tenure were scarcely touched, other than to extend women's dower right to land as well as moveables and to allow them to inherit if the

---

[18] See chapter 8.
[19] *Cal Chancery Rolls Various, 1277–1326*, 190–210.

male line failed. The same statute provided for Wales to be 'wholly and entirely transferred under our proper dominion'. Less sweeping than it appears, this nevertheless heralded a new structure of English-style shires, with sheriffs and coroners in the royal lands in the north under the overall control of justiciars.[20]

English domination was not confined to alien laws and administration. Following the victory of 1277, Edward embarked on his famous programme of castle building. Aberystwyth, Builth, Flint and Rhuddlan belong to this period, followed by Conwy, Caernarfon and Harlech after the war of 1282–4 and Beaumaris after 1294–5. These huge projects were designed not only to ensure English supremacy, but to function as secure bases for merchants and royal officials. They also became a focus for new town plantation in a country largely unfamiliar with towns. Conscious attempts were made to attract non-Welsh settlers. These were a mixed bunch, English or sometimes from the Continent. Some were merchants, others had been recruited for the building works and chose to stay on. Some were attracted by the prospect of sizeable free tenements at a low rent, an all too rare commodity in the land-hungry late thirteenth century. Not all colonization was on virgin land. In some areas, the native Welsh were driven from the fertile lowlands with varying degrees of coercion. The king rewarded the earl of Lincoln, Earl Warenne, the younger Roger Mortimer and Reginald Grey with lordships carved out of the conquered territory, while they in their turn granted knights' fees to their followers in a way that was no longer possible in England. By such means, conquest was made permanent. Finally, in 1301, Prince Edward, who had been born amid the building works at Caernarfon in 1284, received the king's Welsh lands as an appanage, together with the title of Prince of Wales, thereby beginning the traditional association with the heir to the throne. Sadly there is no evidence for the tale that his father had offered the infant to the Welsh people as a prince who could speak no English, but the bond Edward II enjoyed with his Welsh subjects provided him with loyal, if not always well-conducted troops throughout his reign and it was towards Wales that he fled as its end.[21]

Arguably the resources devoted to bringing the Welsh under royal subjection greatly exceeded any advantage to the crown. The hugely expensive chain of Edwardian castles remains as a dramatic monument to the quality of medieval military architecture and royal ambition, but they cost large sums to garrison and maintain. In conception, they were among the most advanced in Europe. The work of the Savoyard James

[20] *Statutes of the Realm*, i, 55–68.
[21] Davies, 'Colonial Wales', 5–12; Tuck, *Crown and Nobility*, 18–26.

de St George, they were probably influenced by fortifications seen by the crusaders in the East and in Italy as well those of Savoy. Harlech took seven and a half years to build and cost something in the region of £9,500. At the height of its construction, some 950 workmen were committed to it. Even more were employed on the earlier projects. Many of them were skilled masons and smiths who had been assembled from all over the king's territory. Edward spent approximately £80,000 between 1277 and 1304 on castle building alone. His campaigns added substantially to this bill. It cost £55,000 to suppress the revolt of 1294–5.[22] This lavish outlay achieved the desired effect, but had Edward ruled with a lighter touch much of the Welsh resistance might have crumbled without resort to war. The lesser princes were not really united behind Llywelyn, who seems to have been only marginally less unpopular with them than with the king. As it was, the crown approached conquest and subjection with something of a blunt instrument and the ensuing cost added substantially to Edward's political troubles within England.

There were parallels between English involvement in Wales and Ireland, although the latter neither required nor received the same attention from the crown. The Anglo-Norman baronage had penetrated Ireland in a similar way, if somewhat later, bringing both English and Welsh settlers in their train. The county of Dublin and lordships of Leinster and Meath were more or less securely under English rule. Elsewhere control ebbed and flowed between cadet branches of the English nobility or ministerial families and the native princes over whom they claimed lordship. Unlike Wales, however, English governmental institutions and English Common Law were transferred wholesale to areas controlled by the English, leaving Irish law and custom unchallenged among the Irish. Although Irish politics were often turbulent, the absence of a leader of the calibre of Llywelyn ap Gruffudd able to rally unified resistance meant that Edward I was free to pay little attention to this part of his dominion. Whereas he spent more time in Wales than any of his predecessors, he never set foot in Ireland. It was no more central to Plantagenet concerns during his son's reign until, in the wake of English defeat at Bannockburn in 1314, the Scots under Edward Bruce invaded. The crisis was relatively short-lived, however, and by 1318 Bruce had been defeated and killed.[23]

Historians often use the term colonial to describe England's relationship with both Wales and Ireland at this date. Certainly it bore some of the classic hallmarks associated with nineteenth- and twentieth-century colonialism. Ireland was regarded primarily as a source of income and

[22] Prestwich, *Edward I*, 208–15.
[23] Frame, *Colonial Ireland*, chs. 2 and 5.

provisions. In his Welsh campaigns, Edward I drained away £53,000 or more in revenue, as well as shipping both timber and fighting men to Wales. When he was in extreme financial difficulty in 1299, he granted the profits of Ireland, excluding customs, to the Frescobaldi banking house in return for a loan of £11,000.[24] As in Wales, conquest offered an otherwise rare opportunity to loyal supporters such as Thomas de Clare, who was granted the lordship of Thomond in western Ireland in 1276.[25] Lack of respect for native culture and the imposition of alien institutions, both characteristic of colonial rule, were also evident. English attitudes to native law were a mixture of superiority and unease. Edward I believed that 'the laws which the Irish use are detestable to God', while Archbishop Pecham, having obtained a copy of Welsh law texts, declared them neither reasonable nor consonant with biblical teaching.[26] To interpret the relationship in colonial terms also acts as a corrective to the Anglocentricity which so long prevailed among English historians and to a continuing assumption that to be different means to be more primitive. However, to see a medieval society in terms of a debate about a very different world can also mislead and perhaps tells us more about modern nationalistic sensibilities than about the past.

England, no less than other parts of the British Isles, had been conquered and colonized by the same continental aristocracy. The native English, like the Welsh and Irish, were also ruled by kings and nobles speaking a different language and pursuing dynastic interests at their expense. Because this had begun earlier in England, the effects are less well documented, but the Anglo-Saxon chronicle makes it clear that the conquerors were no less resented. They were more easily assimilated in England because Anglo-Saxon government was taken over with very little change and there were already close cultural links with Normandy. Even so, it took several generations. Law played a much more prominent role in the jockeying between victor and vanquished in the thirteenth century because it had developed greatly in the interim. Appeals by the Welsh and Irish as if to a single immutable body of native law were often disingenuous. In every Plantagenet domain, law was a multi-layered, fluid and often inconsistent heritage of custom and practice. Welsh princes were already beginning to adopt English practices of their own volition, so when Edward introduced English law to Wales and Ireland, he might reasonably have been regarded as providing the best form of law currently available. His frequent appointment of native officials and his attempts to assert royal authority over the Marcher lords in the

---

[24] Prestwich, *Edward I*, 521–2; Frame, *Colonial Ireland*, 67.
[25] Frame, *Colonial Ireland*, 35–6.
[26] Ibid., 106–7; Davies, *Conquest*, 367.

1290s using the same judicial methods that he had earlier employed against his Welsh vassals, demonstrates that he was not hostile to the Welsh or Irish peoples as such. Edward I can thus be portrayed plausibly as a feudal ruler seeking to enforce his lordship and bring good government to his domains by the most effective means at his disposal, rather than using them as an instrument of deliberate English aggrandizement over subject races. However, in seeking to reach a balanced judgement on an emotive subject, it is worth remembering that the author of the *Vita Edwardi Secundi* expressed English lordship in Wales and Ireland as a 'yoke of slavery'.[27]

Despite certain parallels, Edward's relationship with Scotland was significantly different. Although initially settled in the same way by the Anglo-Norman baronage, the descendants of whom continued to hold either side of the border, Scotland was an established kingdom with well-developed governmental institutions of its own. The king of England claimed overlordship, however, and it was the implications of this that were to colour the relations between the two countries. Had there been a more stable political situation north of the border and a less autocratic monarch to the south, warfare might have been avoided.

The unexpected death of King Alexander III in 1286, leaving his three-year-old granddaughter Margaret of Norway as heir to the throne, opened the way to English intervention. The initial plan whereby Margaret was to marry Edward of Caernarfon foundered with her death *en route* to Scotland in 1290. This left Robert Bruce and John Balliol as rival claimants to the throne, looking to Edward I for arbitration. The opportunity to extend his powers that this represented proved irresistible. The special court convened at Berwick-upon-Tweed decided in favour of John Balliol, thereby leaving Scotland with a king temperamentally unsuited to resisting encroachments on his independence.

The uneasy relationship of two crowned heads who were yet vassal and lord in many ways mirrored the equally sensitive relationship between Edward and Philip IV of France.[28] Indeed, both King John and King Edward found themselves hauled before their overlord's court within a matter of months in 1293–4. On the principle that my enemy's enemy is my friend, Scotland inevitably became embroiled in Anglo-French disputes, giving birth in 1295 to the 'auld alliance' between England's historic foes. When some of the key Scottish nobles refused to serve in Edward's campaign against France, he determined to

---

[27] *Vita Edwardi Secundi*, 61.
[28] See chapter 8.

assert his overlordship by force. In a triumphant campaign in 1296, Berwick-upon-Tweed was sacked and its inhabitants massacred. Victory gained in the battle of Dunbar was followed by the capture of both Edinburgh and King John. The Stone of Destiny on which Scottish kings were inaugurated, along with the Scots crown and sceptre, was carried off to Westminster Abbey in a symbolic act of domination, reversed only in preparation for Scottish devolution 700 years later.

This was the high point of Edward's reign, with Scotland and Wales firmly under his control and reforms in place in England. Impressive as his record was, it was further enhanced by skilled promotion. From Anglo-Saxon times, when the cult of royal saints was harnessed to discourage the killing of kings, English monarchs had been expert manipulators of the image of kingship. Henry III had fostered the cult of Edward the Confessor, rebuilding Westminster Abbey at vast expense in the new Gothic style. Further adorned by Edward I, it gradually developed into a royal mausoleum to rival that of the French kings at St Denis.[29] The Eleanor crosses were yet another visible sign of royal majesty.[30] Touching for the king's evil (scrofula), a potent demonstration of the power to heal conferred on God's anointed, is first documented in England in 1276–7. In 1278 Edward and Queen Eleanor visited Glastonbury, where the supposed tombs of Arthur and Guinevere were opened. The Arthurian legend was subsequently evoked at 'round tables' (probably jousts) held at Nefyn in Wales in 1284 and Falkirk in 1302. An even more grandiose conceit was the linking of Caernarfon castle with the imperial Roman past, through its banded masonry and polygonal towers echoing the Theodosian walls at Constantinople.[31] Closer to home, the rebuilding of St Stephen's Chapel in the palace of Westminster, begun in 1292, was modelled on Louis IX's Ste-Chapelle in Paris. An obvious message was to be drawn from Edward's association with his saintly predecessor in the crusading movement. Even the opportunity presented by the knighting of Edward of Caernarfon in 1306 was fully exploited not only in the unprecedented grandeur of the occasion but also the way in which the oaths taken by the young knights were geared to the coming Scottish campaign.[32]

[29] There were, however, significant differences in the way in which the two were conceived. Binski, *Westminster Abbey*, 1, 91–3.

[30] See chapter 2.

[31] See plate 9. Rowlands, 'The Edwardian conquest', 52–5.

[32] Prestwich, *Edward I*, 512; Alexander and Binski, *Age of Chivalry*, 337–9. See chapter 5.

PLATE 9 The outer walls of Caernarfon Castle, 1283–92, showing the polygonal towers and banded masonry copied from the Theodosian walls of
Constantinople

Grand though occasions such as the 'round table' at Falkirk and the
Feast of Swans were, they could not mask the fact that the later years of
Edward's reign were played out in diminuendo. Although the Welsh
conquest proved permanent, that of Scotland did not. In 1297 the
Scots rebelled under William Wallace, who was victorious at the battle
of Stirling Bridge. Earl Warenne, the English commander, had overslept
and failed to deploy his forces effectively; and the Treasurer in Scotland,
who was killed in action, was flayed and his skin reputedly made into a
sword-belt for Wallace. In the following winter, the Scots ravaged the
English countryside as far south as Durham. Edward again mastered the
situation, although not without several campaigns and in the face of
uncertain support from his forces. Few carried their obstructiveness to
the lengths of Hugo Fitz Heyr, who, when summoned in 1300 to fulfil
his obligation to serve with a bow and arrow, turned up, fired his arrow
and went home again; but desertion was a serious problem among the

foot soldiers and even the earl marshall and constable withdrew at the
earliest opportunity.[33] Nonetheless, in 1298 Edward, by then present in
person, won the battle of Falkirk and by 1305 had gained the submission of all the leading rebels. Wallace himself was captured and executed
with the same savagery earlier meted out to Dafydd of Wales. Arrangements for the government of Scotland prepared in the spring and
autumn parliaments of 1305 placed Englishmen in the key offices of
state, although Scots were to serve alongside them in the king's Council
and to hold lesser offices. John of Brittany, the king's nephew, was
appointed his Lieutenant in Scotland. As in Wales, plans were made to
amend laws which were 'clearly displeasing to God and to reason'.[34]
Despite the involvement of Scottish representatives in drawing up the
new measures, this settlement crumbled as swiftly as that of 1296. The
decision to allow the rebels to buy back their confiscated estates,
while superficially conciliatory, won few friends in Scotland and alienated the English magnates to whom they had been granted in the mean
time. In 1306 the throne was seized by Robert Bruce, grandson of the
claimant of 1290 and a disappointed former ally of Edward I, leaving
Anglo-Scottish relations unresolved at the time of his death.

Even more ominously, by the 1290s, financial nemesis had caught up
with Edward. He had never been able to moderate his expenditure. As
early as 1255, he had borrowed extensively to defray the costs of his rule
in Gascony. His crusade probably cost around £100,000, much of which
he borrowed from the king of France and the Riccardi banking house. In
1286–9 he was again in debt to the Riccardi to the tune of £110,000. It
was an acute need for money which led to him selling the wardship of
Robert de Ferrers for 6,000 marks to his mother and her uncle Peter of
Savoy two years later, thereby initiating a grievance with unfortunate
political repercussions. When ordinary revenue, together with customs,
might amount to between £25,000 and £30,000, debts on this scale
inevitably threatened his freedom of action. More seriously, they led
him into conflict with his subjects, who alone could deliver him from the
consequences. His constant military campaigns would not have been
possible without an unprecedented level of taxation. This had been
borne with some patience until the clergy led the first serious protests
in 1294. Papal support for their protest was forthcoming in 1296, when
the increasingly heavy demands of secular rulers provoked the papal bull
Clericis laicos, which, for a brief period, forbade payment without papal
sanction.[35] Clerical protest was matched by that of the mercantile com-

[33] Prestwich, Edward I, 478–82, 484, 513–14.
[34] Ibid., 504.
[35] Ibid., 79–80, 237; Howell, Eleanor of Provence, 147. See chapter 4.

munity when wool belonging to both native and foreign merchants was
seized in 1297 so that the crown could raise money through its sale.
Meanwhile, the populace at large bitterly resented the prises needed to
supply the army. Their scale in 1296–7 caused severe hardship in the
areas affected and, amounting to additional taxation without consent,
they were considered an abuse of the king's ancient prerogative of
purveyance. The weightiest opposition came from the magnates, who
registered their displeasure by a refusal to serve abroad in the unpopular
Flanders campaign or to grant further taxes. In July 1297, Edward was
reduced to trying to collect an eighth, levied with the approval of what
the author of the *Flores Historiarum* described as 'those standing around
in his chamber' even though Parliament was in session and could have
been asked to give consent.[36] In August a list of grievances known as the
Remonstrances was orchestrated by the earl of Hereford and widely
circulated. Civil war appeared imminent when he and the earl of Norfolk took an armed force to the Exchequer to prevent the tax going
ahead. Only Wallace's rebellion in September 1297 and the mediation of
Archbishop Winchelsey averted the crisis. In October the royal Council,
led nominally by Prince Edward in his father's absence, issued the
Confirmatio Cartarum, a confirmation of the 1225 versions of Magna
Carta and the Charter of the Forest and an undertaking that future
taxation and prises would only take place 'with the common assent of
all the realm'.[37] This was reluctantly ratified by Edward in Ghent and,
on his return to England in 1298, he further responded with an inquiry
into all the abuses of his officials since the beginning of the war with
France. Much had changed, however, since the honeymoon years of his
accession. Complaints about evasiveness and equivocation, behaviour
more commonly associated with Henry III and, later, with Edward II,
were now voiced about the ageing monarch. In 1300 he was forced to
confirm Magna Carta, together with the far more detailed arrangements
to remedy his subjects' complaints known as the *Articuli super Cartas*,
in return for a sorely needed twentieth. That it was never collected bears
witness to the king's continuing resistance to complying with the conditions of its grant. The reluctance of the 1301 Lincoln parliament to grant
a tax without genuine redress of grievances meant that Edward tried to
manage without. The final years of his reign saw attempts to raise
money through every non-parliamentary means at his disposal. In this
context, it is interesting that in 1299 fines were charged for the first time
on licences to acquire land in mortmain.[38] Measures such as this were

---

[36] Taxes were assessed as fractions of the valuations of moveable goods. Tuck, *Crown
and Nobility*, 37; *Flores Historiarum*, iii, 295–6.
[37] *EHD*, *1189–1327*, 485–6.
[38] Raban, *Mortmain Legislation*, 55–60.

wholly inadequate to fund campaigns in 1300 and 1303–4, each costing anything between £40,000 and £80,000, and he ended his reign as he had begun it, accumulating debts and largely dependent on borrowed money.[39]

In striking contrast to the early years of his rule many of his leading magnates were now hostile. Longevity left him increasingly isolated. By 1297 almost all his earlier companions in arms were dead and their successors were less closely bound to him by ties of friendship. His policy in the Marches had alienated the earl of Hereford and explains why he became a leader of opposition. Edward's personal style was also perhaps less acceptable in old age than when he had been at the height of his powers. He is reputed to have told the earl of Norfolk, his other leading opponent, that he could either go to Gascony or hang.[40] He had always relied on forcefulness rather than persuasion to control the nobility, but advancing age and financial difficulties undermined his ability to dominate them. Never generous with grants, by the end of a long reign it was clear that loyalty would be unlikely to reap much in the way of material reward. Indeed, his attempts to claw back lands already held by the nobility trespassed on the bounds of the acceptable.[41] By the later 1290s he depended heavily on the leverage provided by the nobility's debts to the crown to ensure obedience.

Infirmity and the political frustrations of his last decade strained Edward's always choleric temper. Much as the nobility suffered, his principal victim was his eldest son and heir. Edward of Caernarfon was a late child, born to Edward and Eleanor of Castile in 1284 after more than thirty years of marriage. It was increasingly likely that he would assume the burden of kingship at an early age, and so unavoidably he became the focus for his father's impatient expectations. Even at his most genial, Edward had the bluff insensitivity of a man of action. It is not surprising, therefore, that he did not handle the situation well; some of the disasters of his son's reign can be attributed to the older man's inept response to a youth whose tastes and extreme emotions he deplored and whose confidence he undermined by his higher regard for the competence of his nephews John of Brittany and Thomas of Lancaster.

When Edward II inherited the throne at twenty-three, he had neither the maturity nor the experience to deal effectively with the problems he inherited. These were very pressing. Edward I died just as he was about to embark on a campaign against the Scots. The royal coffers were

---

[39] Prestwich, *Edward I*, 514.
[40] Tuck, *Crown and Nobility*, 36; *Guisborough*, 290.
[41] See p. 36.

empty and the crown in debt to the tune of £200,000. The magnates and realm could, however, have been expected to rally behind the king in tackling these problems. Just as Edward I had enjoyed the support of contemporaries, many of their heirs now surrounded his son. However, Edward II's initial popularity soon evaporated in the face of his deeply resented dependence on Piers Gaveston. Placed in the young prince's household in 1300 by Edward I as a suitable companion and role model, Gaveston had quickly become the object of Prince Edward's 'inordinate affection'. Whether the relationship was primarily homosexual or whether, as Pierre Chaplais has argued, it derived much of its intensity from Edward's formal adoption of Gaveston as his brother, it soon gave rise to serious concern.[42] This reputedly came to a head when Prince Edward sought to procure the county of Ponthieu for Gaveston. Guisborough's account of the king's furious reaction: 'You wretched bastard, do you want to give lands away now? You who have never gained any?', while tearing out fistfuls of his son's hair, is in keeping with Edward's character, but may owe more to a biblical exemplar.[43] True or not, Gaveston was exiled on the orders of Edward I in February 1307, only to be recalled less than two weeks after his death in July. The gifts and lands then showered upon him provoked alarm and jealousy in equal measure among the magnates. Offence was caused above all by his enfeoffment with the earldom of Cornwall, usually reserved for a member of the royal family and supposedly destined for one of Edward II's half-brothers.

How far Gaveston himself contributed to the ensuing political crisis is a matter of opinion. He revelled in his position as favourite, exercising a tight control over royal patronage. This was doubly resented, given the nobility's pent-up hopes of a new and more open-handed monarch. 'Haughty and puffed up', according to the *Vita Edwardi Secundi*, 'his arrogance was intolerable to the barons'.[44] He further trampled their feelings by playing a leading role in Edward's coronation, the sort of occasion which always gave rise to bickering over precedence. His robes of imperial purple trimmed with pearls instead of the cloth of gold worn by his peers were typical in their lack of tact. Yet more offence was given when he and his followers trounced the other earls at a tournament he organized at Wallingford to celebrate his earldom and marriage to Margaret de Clare, sister of the earl of Gloucester. The cruel nicknames, such as 'black dog' for the earl of Warwick and 'burst belly' for the venerable earl of Lincoln, subsequently attributed to him, also made

---

[42] Chaplais, *Piers Gaveston*, *passim*. The other recent biography is Hamilton, *Piers Gaveston*.

[43] *Guisborough*, 382–3; Chaplais, *Piers Gaveston*, 21.

[44] *Vita Edwardi Secundi*, 15–16.

gratuitous enemies.[45] When given a serious role in government, however, he comported himself with some restraint and competence. There were no apparent complaints when he was left in charge of the realm while Edward went to France for his marriage to Isabella, daughter of King Philip IV in 1307–8. His military record was respectable and he acquitted himself well as Lieutenant of Ireland in 1308–9, despite serious unrest. Although English chroniclers gave him scant credit for this, his rule was praised by those writing in Ireland. He made little use of the sweeping powers that Edward had conferred upon him, suggesting that the problem lay not so much with Gaveston himself as with the king.

Edward's overriding goal of recalling Gaveston from enforced exile in 1308–9 and again in 1311 distorted the political agenda and left his magnates with that most difficult of situations – a king whom they could not trust. Even then the situation might not have been irredeemable had Edward met with military success in Scotland. There, however, he conspicuously lacked the martial skill and inclinations of his father. He failed to live up to the promise of his first campaign in 1300. In 1306 he preferred not to linger in Scotland, and within eight weeks of Edward I's death in 1307 he had again returned south, not to return in person until 1310. Although in the interim he had issued summonses for military service, held Council meetings to discuss what to do about Robert Bruce and taken prises, he showed little desire to confront the enemy. An apparent preference for truces meant that there was little to be shown for the levies. When a campaign was eventually mounted in 1310, Bruce deliberately refused to engage with his more powerful opponent and instead relied on guerrilla tactics. By 1311 he was ravaging the north of England. Although the magnates were partly to blame for refusing to serve alongside Gaveston, Edward in failing to defeat the Scots had also failed in one of the most fundamental of kingly duties: to protect the realm.

As in Henry III's reign and again at the end of Edward I's, the magnates were driven to impose what they could not achieve by other means. Their first move was the Boulogne agreement of 1308 in which they asserted their desire to see the honour of the king and rights of the crown preserved. This was followed by a series of articles known as the Declaration of 1308, presented in Parliament in April of that year. The most determined effort to bring Edward under control was embodied in the texts compiled by the twenty-one earls, barons and prelates elected Ordainers in 1310. Known as the Ordinances, these were published in Parliament and throughout the realm in 1311. In all these documents, Edward's opponents were at pains to distinguish between

[45] Hamilton, *Piers Gaveston*, 75.

the person of the king and the office he held. Although the removal of Gaveston clearly loomed large in their aims, they also sought remedies for many of the grievances that had been at issue in earlier reigns. Time had transformed Simon de Montfort into a hero and contemporaries saw the Ordinances as belonging to the reforming tradition of the mid-thirteenth century. They echoed the Provisions of Oxford of 1258 in attempting to give the baronage control over patronage and the king's choice of officials. They went further, however, in seeking to give Parliament a voice in hitherto untrammelled royal activities, notably waging war and leaving the country without permission.[46] Like earlier attempts at reform, they crucially depended on the crown's co-operation for their effectiveness. This was not forthcoming. The problem of Gaveston was solved by his capture by the earl of Pembroke and brutal execution at the hands of Lancaster and Warwick in June 1312. The problem of the king defied resolution.

The next decade was dominated by Thomas of Lancaster's single-minded determination to see the terms of the Ordinances implemented.[47] A near contemporary and cousin to the king, he had grown up in royal favour. He was also pre-eminent among the magnates by virtue of the inheritance of five earldoms following the death of his father, Edmund, Henry III's second son, and father-in-law, Henry de Lacy, earl of Lincoln. A key figure in the reign, he is also something of an enigma. Despite exhaustive researches, his modern biographer John Maddicott remained unable to explain why Lancaster turned so strongly against the king in 1308 or why, even at the height of his influence, he showed such marked reluctance to spend time at court. Although he was far from commanding the consistent loyalty of his peers, he was at times seen as heir to Simon de Montfort and became the object of a popular cult within weeks of his death. Given his political role, it is all the more extraordinary that in the last five years of his life he rarely ventured outside his estate at Pontefract (Yorkshire).[48] Posterity has felt even more ambivalent about him than his contemporaries did. He appears to have combined genuine piety with a reprehensible personal life. As Higden's later fourteenth-century translator rather picturesquely put it, he 'defouled a greet multitude of wommen'.[49] Despite being the only magnate rich enough apparently to resist the lure of royal patronage, in accepting the Treaty of Leake in 1318 he seems to have put personal gain before defence of the Ordinances. It is this want of principle, rather

[46] Prestwich, 'The ordinances', 10–12.
[47] The following account of Thomas of Lancaster is drawn from Maddicott, *Thomas of Lancaster*.
[48] Ibid., 92–3, 331.
[49] *Polychronicon*, viii, 315.

than the rumours of his dealings with Robert Bruce in 1316, 1319 and again in 1321 that have damaged his reputation in modern eyes.

Lancaster rarely enjoyed the unswerving support of the other magnates for any length of time. Gilbert de Clare, Edward's nephew and brother-in-law of Gaveston, could usually be counted on to mediate rather than attempt anything more forceful. The earl of Pembroke parted company with the baronial cause after 1312 because his personal guarantee of safety to Gaveston on his surrender had been ignored; even the earl of Gloucester had told him unsympathetically that he should 'learn another time to negotiate more cautiously'.[50] With Gaveston removed, the inbred loyalty of other magnates began to re-emerge. Moreover, as the author of *Vita Edwardi Secundi* observed in something of an understatement, 'it is not safe to set oneself up against the king, because often the issue is wont to be unfortunate'.[51] In other respects, too, Edward's position strengthened at this time. The death of Archbishop Winchelsey in 1313 removed a long-standing opponent. Furthermore, Philip IV of France offered his support now that Gaveston, his daughter's rival for the king's affections, was dead. All appeared favourable for Edward until the political scene was once more transformed by the disastrous defeat at Bannockburn in 1314.

Not only did Edward flee humiliatingly from the field leaving Robert Bruce victorious and the English driven from Scotland, but the young earl of Gloucester was killed, leaving three sisters as his heirs as well as depriving the king of one of the few moderate voices. The irretrievable breakdown of relations between Edward and his mightiest subject as a result of Gaveston's death now proved to be a disaster for the country as well as the king. Edward needed Lancaster's military support if Robert Bruce was to be successfully opposed, but neither king nor earl seemed capable of decisive action; Lancaster's campaign of 1316 proved abortive, while Edward's attempt to recover Berwick in 1319 ended in failure, leaving truces as the only means of limiting Scottish raids. That the heaviest war taxation of the reign coincided with the Great Famine only added to the misery. The country could not afford war, but nor could it afford to abandon the north indefinitely to Scottish depredation. The gravity with which the political impasse was regarded in powerful circles at home and abroad can be seen by repeated attempts at mediation by papal and French envoys and by the native episcopate. Formal *rapprochements* between Lancaster and the king were negotiated in 1313 and 1314 as well as in the Treaty of Leake, but none enjoyed more than transient success. By 1317, however, much of Lancaster's support had

---

[50] *Vita Edwardi Secundi*, 26.
[51] Ibid., 44.

leaked away. Relations with his fellow magnates were not helped when Earl Warenne kidnapped his wife in April of that year in what appears to have been a purely personal quarrel.[52] That he gained a second opportunity to lead concerted opposition to the king was due to the emergence of a new coterie of royal favourites.

The two Despensers, father and son, came to dominate the court between 1317 and 1321. The family had a record of royal service reaching back to Henry III's reign and held considerable estates in the Midlands and southern England. From this solid foundation, they developed into key figures in Edward II's final years. The king's lavish grants to them, combined with the younger Despenser's ambitions in south Wales made possible by his wife's one-third share in the Gloucester inheritance, drove the earl of Hereford, Roger Mortimer of Wigmore, and other Marcher lords into open opposition. Even Pembroke and other moderate earls found their loyalty once more strained by the Despensers' outrageous disregard for the law. Between 1321 and 1322 anarchy shaded into civil war. Yet although Edward was forced to give way to demands for the exile of his latest favourites (during which the younger Despenser took to piracy), Lancaster failed to rally the baronage solidly behind him. His character had never been such as to keep friends, but a fatal blow to his reputation was struck by the latest tales of his dealings with Robert Bruce, always given some substance by the apparent immunity of his estates from Scottish raids. His defeat and capture at Boroughbridge in 1322 demonstrated that even the most unsatisfactory king would ultimately prove able to defeat the mightiest subject, providing the latter lacked allies.

The remaining years of the reign witnessed ever more graphically what could happen when the king's authority was unchecked. Either victory released a vein of savagery and miserliness in Edward II's character, or, more probably, he succumbed to the malign influence of the Despensers. This was the view of the author of the *Vita Edwardi Secundi*, who further wrote that the nobility were 'terrified by threats and the penalties inflicted on others'.[53] The Marcher rebels were for the most part imprisoned, but the garrison of Leeds Castle (Kent) was summarily executed on its surrender in 1321. This was followed by the slaughter of many of those captured after Boroughbridge, following trials under martial law which allowed them no opportunity to put their defence. Such extreme punishment for internal rebellion was unprecedented, although it was given a vestige of legitimacy by the accusation of treasonable dealings with the Scots. Less easy to justify was the way in

[52] Maddicott, *Thomas of Lancaster*, 197.
[53] *Vita Edwardi Secundi*, 136.

which the sentences were carried out. The hanging, drawing and quartering of all but the most illustrious prisoners and the deliberate decision to carry out the executions in the vicinity of their estates was new and intimidating. Equally vengeful was the imprisonment of the wives and children of the rebels, often on a harsh regime. Lancaster's widow was coerced into parting with some 175 knights' fees to the Despensers and she was not alone. Those who escaped with their lives were kept in a state of perpetual insecurity, unsure of the king's favour and owing large fines. More than £17,000 was demanded of the Contrariants, as they came to be called, following Boroughbridge.[54] The rule of law ceased to have meaning at any level of society and no one felt safe from royal arbitrariness or Despenser rapacity.

The king himself gained hugely from the confiscated estates of the Contrariants. Few were granted to any but the Despensers and, by 1324, the revenue from those remaining to him in England alone was valued at £12,500. Although Edward had been forced to borrow the huge sum of £140,000 from the Italian banker Antonio Pessagno between 1312 and 1319, and was still borrowing from other Italians in 1321, by 1322 he was in an unprecedented position to hoard reserves. In 1323, £27,000 had been transported in fifty-five barrels from York to the Tower of London, a saving made possible by the thirteen-year truce with the Scots after yet another futile campaign. In his last desperate flight westwards towards Wales, Edward carried at least £29,000 in cash and when he was finally captured his officials handed over nearly £62,000, more than a year's ordinary revenue.[55] This substantial sum was achieved not just at the expense of the Contrariants, but through petty economies such as the longer hours, shorter holidays and cuts in pay demanded of his Exchequer clerks.[56] Such wealth, combined with the Scottish truce, freed the monarchy for the first time in generations from the sort of restraint that a demoralized and depleted Parliament ventured to exert through continuing refusal to grant taxation.

Rule of this extreme nature could not endure. Too few of Edward's subjects had any interest in its continuance. Crucially, no lord could feel confident in his title to land, the very foundation of feudal society. It was Queen Isabella who was to prove the catalyst for her husband's removal. Her position had never been comfortable, her relationship with his favourites at best uneasy and somewhat humiliating. It became untenable when war broke out between England and France in 1324. As sister to the French king, Charles IV, her loyalty was called in question and her

[54] Buck, *Politics*, 174, 206.
[55] Ibid., 165; Fryde, *Tyranny*, 22, 88, 91, 94, 105.
[56] Fryde, *Tyranny*, 100.

estates confiscated. She was nonetheless despatched to France to negotiate between the two warring monarchs, a duty she undertook, according
to the *Vita Edwardi Secundi*, 'very joyfully'. While there, she mixed with
English exiles, notably Roger Mortimer of Wigmore, who had escaped
from the Tower in 1323 and who became her lover. In 1325, with
singular imprudence, Edward II allowed their son Prince Edward to
join the queen in France in order to render homage for Gascony. With
the heir to the throne in her custody, she had little to gain from returning
peaceably to an intolerable situation. The scene was thus set for the
invasion force which landed under her leadership in Suffolk in September 1326.[57] The king's disaffected subjects flocked to her support.

Edward was taken prisoner, but as long as he was alive there was a
real likelihood of his rescue and restoration. His death, announced in
September 1327, was therefore timely. He was burried with due cere-
mony in Gloucester Abbey, but his precise fate is a mystery. The traditional story of murder with a red hot poker emerged at an early date in
Higden's *Polychronicon*. In the words of his translator, 'he was sleyne
with a hoote broche [hot spit] putte thro the secrete place posterialle',
but there is no firm evidence for this. Other sources embellished the
story or claimed ignorance. There is even an account of his escape to end
his life as a hermit in Italy. The balance of probability must be murder,
even if the supposed means appears suspiciously symbolic in view of his
reputed homosexuality.[58]

For the first time a crowned monarch had been deposed, formally if
not very legally. A justification was put before what some contemporaries described as an assembly (not a parliament in the king's absence) in
January 1327 and Edward's 'consent' for his son to assume the throne
sought by a deputation of prelates, magnates and commons.[59] The
unthinkable had been done; God's anointed had been removed and
with him a powerful inhibition. Such a precedent made easier the subsequent deposition and murder of Richard II, Henry VI and the young,
uncrowned Edward V. It marked the first step along the road to the full
panoply of the trial and execution of Charles I 400 years later. It did not
solve the immediate problem of a ruler whose closest allies saw government as a synonym for plunder. Only when the young Edward III
mounted a coup against his mother and Mortimer in 1330 was some
vestige of stability and good lordship restored.

---

[57] Ibid., 146–8; Tuck, *Crown and Nobility*, 88–90; *Vita Edwardi Secundi*, 135.
[58] *Polychronicon*, viii, 325; Fryde, *Tyranny*, 204–5; Saaler, *Edward II*, 140–1.
[59] Fryde, *Tyranny*, 196.

8

England and the Wider World

Despite its separation from the Continent by sea and the loss by 1259 of most of the crown's possessions in France, England was far from isolated from the rest of Europe. Culturally the legacy of the Norman conquerors and the Angevin inheritance lived on in language and an enduring orientation of the court and aristocracy towards France. Marriage alliances with Spain as well as France and close relations with courts of Savoy and the Low Countries created a network of rulers who had more in common with each other than the people they ruled and who brought in their wake foreign kin and servants who often played a prominent role at home and overseas. This was particularly true of the Poitevin and Savoyard relatives of Henry III and his queen, whose presence caused so much trouble in the 1250s. It was wider dynastic interests, too, which more often than not lay behind the wars in which England became embroiled.

The English church, notwithstanding native idiosyncrasies such as those cathedrals staffed by monks rather than secular canons, was part of wider Christendom sharing common institutions and a leader based mainly in Rome or Avignon. A constant stream of clerics passed back and forth to the papal Curia as royal ambassadors or on routine business. The Hereford World Map, drawn c.1277–89, and similar maps of the period show Jerusalem at the centre. The Holy Land and its fate had been the preoccupation of Europe's rulers for three centuries, and by the later thirteenth century England was at the forefront of the crusading movement. Topographical exactitude was not the aim of such maps, indeed would not have been possible. They were statements about the world in its theological, mythological and historical context, a world in which England, even to Englishmen, belonged on the outer fringes. In this respect, cosmography had a measure of geographical truth. England was indeed located towards the periphery of the European trading nexus. It was nonetheless very much part of it; the Low Countries and

Italy depended on England for raw wool, while England in its turn thirsted for the wines of Bordeaux and an assortment of luxury goods and specialist commodities obtainable only as imports. All these factors tied England securely into the wider European scene and ensured a cosmopolitan outlook in many of the upper ranks of society.

Without Plantagenet family interests, links with the Continent would have been of a completely different order. The most English thing about Edward I was his birth in June 1239 at Westminster. By blood, mother tongue and culture he was almost entirely French, a heritage only leavened for Edward II by a Spanish mother. The abbey of Fontevrault in the Loire valley where Henry II and Richard I were buried continued to hold a secure place in royal affections, notwithstanding its location deep in French territory. Henry III's heart was sent there for interment, despite Westminster Abbey's emerging role as the family mausoleum, and alms were still being offered there by Edward III. From the mid-twelfth century, marriage had brought territories and alliances which set the agenda for England's relations with the rest of Europe for centuries to come.

In 1200, the Plantagenets were masters of Normandy and a swathe of western France from Anjou to the Pyrenees.[1] By 1272 most of this had been lost, leaving only Gascony, which Edward I held as duke of Aquitaine.[2] Circumstances surrounding this loss and the needs of the surviving duchy dominated Anglo-French politics. Concern for Gascony's southern borders and King Alphonso of Castiles's claim to the duchy was instrumental in bringing about Edward I's marriage to Alphonso's sister Eleanor, which in turn drew England into the affairs of the Iberian peninsula. Political connections brought important economic links in their wake and a certain amount of cultural cross-fertilization as people of all sorts moved from one to another of the domains associated with the royal family. It was in western rather than eastern Europe that Plantagenet interests really lay, but for a time it seemed as though England would also be drawn into German imperial politics. In 1257 Richard of Cornwall, brother of Henry III, had been elected King of the Romans (in effect Holy Roman Emperor, ruler of Germany). He was succeeded on his death in 1272 by Rudolph I of Hapsburg, leaving Edward I to retrieve the English connection by a marriage alliance between the two houses. However, Rudolph's son

---

[1] The principal sources for Gascony are Vale, *The Origins*, and Labarge, *Gascony*.

[2] Gascony and Aquitaine (or Guyenne in French) were referred to interchangeably at the time, although technically Gascony was a linguistic entity, denoting the area south of the River Garonne where a distinctive dialect of the *langue d'oc* was spoken, and Aquitaine was the wider administrative area ruled by the Plantagenet dukes. X. de Planhol, *An Historical Geography of France*, Cambridge, 1994, 124, 127. See map 7.

died before this could be accomplished and Edward's attention was soon diverted by more pressing concerns.

Although Gascony was the only French territory surviving to Edward I on his accession, it was soon augmented by lands elsewhere. In 1279 he became count of Ponthieu by virtue of Queen Eleanor's inheritance on the death of her mother. In the same year he finally gained the Agenais from the French crown under the terms of the Treaty of Paris, followed in 1286 by the southern Saintonge (see map 7). These transfers had been agreed by Henry III in 1259 in return for his formal renunciation of all claim to Normandy, Maine, Touraine, Poitou and Anjou. The most problematic aspect of a generally unsatisfactory treaty was the acceptance that Aquitaine would henceforward be held as a fief of the French crown. The performance of liege homage that this entailed was an inevitable source of friction between rulers who otherwise regarded themselves as monarchs of equal standing, especially when the English king procrastinated over it unreasonably as Edward II was doing in 1323. It also raised a number of practical questions as to how far the obligations of the duke of Aquitaine might be binding on the king of England. Another unfortunate consequence was the possibility of appeals from ducal justice to the higher court of the Parlement of Paris, an option enthusiastically embraced by the Gascon nobility when it suited them and obstructed wherever possible by the ducal administration. It is not surprising that these and other resentments boiled over into war in 1294–8 and again between 1324 and 1326.

What was clear to contemporaries, although sometimes less so to their more Anglocentric successors, was that neither Gascony nor Ponthieu were English colonies. Title was vested in the persons of the Plantagenets, not the crown of England. There was no question of the transfer of English institutions in the way that occurred in parts of Wales and Ireland. English administrative practices, so far as they obtained, were of a more superficial nature; Gascony had its own largely unwritten laws and customs and a very different social structure. This was dominated by a turbulent frequently impoverished nobility revelling in its cherished right to make private war. Despite the governmental challenge this posed, Edward I had a strong personal attachment to the duchy, having been granted it (though without the title) by his father in 1249 at the age of ten, and having cut his administrative teeth there in the 1250s and 1260s as well as the nineteen months he lingered there between 1272 and 1274 on his way back to England to assume the throne. He spent another extended period there between 1286 and 1289, instituting reforms in the characteristic style familiar to England. At the beginning of his reign, he was moved by the need to assert ducal authority over Gaston VII of Béarn and to put in place an administrative machine able

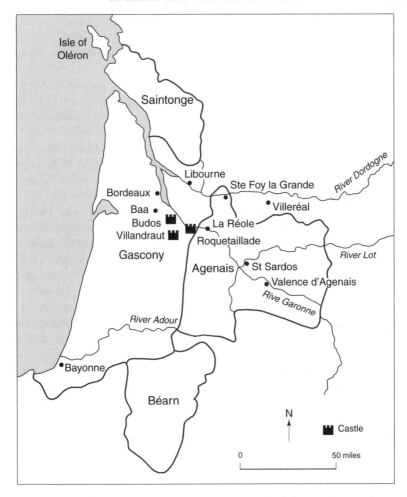

Isle of Oléron

Saintonge

Libourne

Bordeaux

Ste Foy la Grande

Baa

Villeréal

Budos

La Réole

Villandraut

Roquetaillade

Gascony

River Lot

Agenais

St Sardos

Valence d'Agenais

Rive Garonne

River Adour

Bayonne

Béarn

River Dordogne

N

Castle

0   50 miles

MAP 7   Plantagenet lands in south-west France in 1286

to function in his absence. So chaotic was the tenurial structure, that neither Edward nor his vassals had much idea of the terms on which their estates were held. This was remedied in a series of inquiries whose returns survive as the *Recogniciones Feodorum* of 1273–4. For the most part they recorded conventional military obligations, but there were some quirky exceptions. Should the duke of Aquitaine come to visit in person, the lords of Pommiers were required to serve him a meal of pork, beef, cabbages, mustard and hens, wearing red hose and gilded spurs as they waited on him. In similar vein, Vital de Miramont listed in meticulous detail arrangements governing the candle that he was obliged to hold in his hand should he in his turn have to wait at table.[3]

Not least of Edward I's problems in Gascony was that there was no equivalent of the extensive English royal demesne. He was more copiously endowed with vassals than with lands of his own. Accordingly, he lacked a core of tenants on whose loyalty he had first call. This he attempted to remedy through a vigorous policy of town plantation. In 1274 he commanded his seneschal Luke de Tany 'to erect towns or *bastides* in the king's name' wherever he thought fit, orders that were extended to the seneschal of the Agenais on its restoration in 1279. He founded thirteen *bastides* himself while he was present in Gascony between 1286 and 1289. This policy was continued by Edward II, leading to a second wave of plantations between 1308 and 1320. In many instances, foundation was achieved through partnership with local lords. When this happened, the lord provided the land and the duke the privileges which enabled the new community to attract settlers and prosper as a commercial centre. In this way, the Plantagenets created a constituency with a vested interest in their rule and also gained welcome extra revenue.[4] Their key supporters, however, were to be found in Bordeaux and Bayonne. As the last remaining major ports in Plantagenet hands, they enjoyed great prosperity. Bayonne's fortunes rested with the carrying trade, while Bordeaux fell heir to the entire wine trade between England and France. Wine was brought to England and carried in casks up the Thames for storage in warehouses bearing names such as la Réole (a port on the River Garonne), and Gascon vintners enjoyed a powerful and privileged position in London. More often than other aliens, they were allowed long periods of residence and were not obliged to lodge with natives. Some had permanent homes in London and were admitted as citizens. These trading links were the cement which bound the mercantile and maritime elites to their duke and England to Gascony. Bordeaux's brief and traumatic flirtation with the French crown between 1294 and 1303 demonstrated all too clearly where its real interests lay. Bayonne, which, by contrast, had not wavered in its loyalty, was rewarded by Edward I's full and unusual repayment of the loan granted him between 1296–8.

Once he had become king, Edward I could not easily make frequent visits to his duchy. Indeed he was the last crowned head to spend any time at all there. Edward II visited only fleetingly in

---

[3] They record the replies of the Gascon nobles to four questions: what did they hold from the duke; what obligations did such holding entail; had any of these holdings been alienated; and finally did they have any allodial land (land not subject to any lord)? Vale, *The Origins*, 65–6; *Receuil*, no. 23, 19–20.

[4] Beresford, *New Towns*, 10, 354–9.

1313.[5] For practical purposes, therefore, Gascon administration was partially integrated into the English system. By 1284 there was a keeper of the rolls on the English model. Important documents were issued in duplicate and one copy sent to England. This was just as well, since the Bordeaux archives, evacuated to England in 1294, were dumped with the white friars on the Isle of Oléron by sailors disgruntled with their unpaid wages and, but for one register, were lost to the French.[6] All letters leaving the English Chancery for Aquitaine were enrolled on separate Gascon Rolls and, after 1292, accounts were returned to the Exchequer at Westminster. More miscellaneous material was dealt with by the relevant departments in England and filed alongside other documents. This was efficient, but it was no substitute for a ruling presence, and so, just as justiciars were created to govern twelfth-century England during long royal absences, in similar circumstances Plantagenet dukes appointed seneschals and royal lieutenants to rule on their behalf in Gascony. The English or Savoyard seneschals who were principally responsible for administering justice were generally capable, their neutrality welcomed by a nobility suspicious of fellow Gascons. Financial affairs were normally dealt with by the constable of Bordeaux, although exceptional arrangements were made with the crown's bankers when Plantagenet finances made it necessary. By these means, whether present or absent, Edward I brought a measure of order and good government to Gascony.

Perhaps because he lacked his father's personal knowledge of the duchy, Edward II proved less adept. He managed to forfeit the loyalty of his vassals, most crucially the powerful Albret family. His seneschals were changed too frequently to promote stable government. Nor was his choice of men always wise. John de Ferrers, who was murdered in 1312 and whose appointment may have been a misconceived attempt to get him away from his enemy Walter Langton, lacked overseas experience. However, the administrative infrastructure remained in place and measures were taken to ensure that it continued to function effectively. In 1310 the bishop of Norwich and earl of Richmond were commissioned to inquire into the state of the duchy and to set up a public archive. Attempts were made to remedy problems arising from the wartime loss of records. In 1315, transcripts of missing documents were requested from London, where the copies were stored in sacks and coffers in the Tower. These were duly made in a series of registers and sent to Bordeaux, but the work was so shoddy that they were recalled for correction in 1318 and never returned.[7]

[5] E. M. Hallam, *The Itinerary of Edward II and his Household, 1307–1328*, List and Index Society, ccxi, 1984, 98–102.

[6] *Gascon Register*, i, xii–xiii.

[7] Ibid., xiii–xvi.

In financial terms, the duchy was an asset to the English crown most of the time. Its annual revenue, depending to a large extent on customs paid on goods trading through Bordeaux, fluctuated between about £12,000 and £17,000 per annum, more than that from all the English counties put together. This income was frequently harnessed to the king's more pressing needs at home. Gascon dues, like the more modest income from Ponthieu, allowed the English crown to raise loans from Italian merchant houses and the papacy. It was in order to recover these that the duchy's finances were administered, not by the constable of Bordeaux but by the Riccardi of Lucca after 1289 and papal agents between 1314 and 1317, while those of Ponthieu were in the hands of the Frescobaldi between 1299 and 1308.[8] Revenue was adequate to sustain the cost of ducal government except for the period when Edward I was resident between 1286 and 1289. Even then, he was only in financial difficulty because he distributed largesse on a royal rather than ducal scale. The costs of war, however, were a different matter. Although the conflict which broke out in 1294 was fought in Gascony, it cost Edward I approximately £400,000, the equivalent of the total revenue from all his domains. This financial burden played a large part in the political crisis in England and left debts which were still a charge on his son and grandson. The war of St Sardos between 1324 and 1326 was less expensive and Edward II was better able to afford it. Nevertheless, both wars were an added burden to an English ruler and a distraction from troubles in the kingdom.

In peacetime, the kingdom as well as the king derived benefits from the Gascon connection. England gained from the import of commodities it could not produce for itself. Wine was the most important. Although beer was the staple English beverage, there was a sizeable minority demand for wine among wealthier people whose forebears came from wine-drinking regions. Wine was produced in England, but then, as now, the climate made it an uncertain business. Imported wine was also not without its problems, subject as it was to severe buffeting *en voyage*. It was, however, generally deemed drinkable on arrival, although it was sometimes judged necessary to adulterate it with honey, egg white or other sweeteners to make it palatable. At the height of the trade in 1308–9, 102,000 tuns of wine left Bordeaux destined mainly for England. On average, some 6,000 to 8,000 tuns were imported into London each year. In return, England generally exported grain, along with cloth, herring and leather, but in 1315–17 some of this trade was reversed, bringing much needed corn to England, since

---

[8] Prestwich, *Edward I*, 307; Wright, *The Church*, 171; Johnstone, 'The county of Ponthieu', 435.

Gascony was not afflicted by the Great Famine.[9] Men as well as goods made the journey from Gascony to northern shores. Nobles were often willing to serve Edward I in the Scottish and Welsh campaigns, particularly when Aquitaine was in French hands between 1294 and 1303. During the Welsh revolt of 1282–3, there were 1,500 crossbowmen on the royal pay-roll and it was ships from Bayonne that brought supplies to the army.[10] Such support could not be assumed. Edward II's attempts to secure Gascon troops for Scotland met with resistance and his demands for assistance in his campaigns played a part in the alienation of the Agenais prior to 1324.

The most negative aspect of the crown's possessions in Gascony was undoubtedly the way in which England was dragged into domestic quarrels with the French king. Whenever relations between the two sovereigns broke down, the running sores created by the Treaty of Paris erupted into challenges to Plantagenet rule in the duchy. In 1259 too much had depended on the personal stature of Louis IX and his desire at all costs to achieve a permanent settlement of territorial disputes between kin; both he and Henry III had married daughters of Count Raymond-Berengar V of Provence. Henry's willingness to come to terms may have been influenced by his awareness of the impending contest with the reformers at home. At the time, critics on both sides had felt that the concessions were too great. Significantly, one of the most vocal opponents to the treaty had been the young Lord Edward, who presciently questioned the wisdom of acknowledging Aquitaine as a fief. There was a good case for arguing that it had never been subject to the French crown and this claim was revived as relations between the monarchs worsened in the 1290s.

One reason for this deterioration had been Edward I's inheritance of the mantle of Louis IX of France as the most respected ruler of his generation. His energy and reforming skills marked him out as exceptional, but he owed his moral authority to his record as a crusader. He cherished this image as arbiter among his royal peers. When he intervened in the French dispute with Aragon he was behaving in a manner wholly appropriate to such pretensions, but the young Philip IV did not appreciate the good offices of the man he regarded as his vassal.

A further twist to Anglo-French relations was given by the fortuitous election of two Gascon popes in succession, Clement V in 1305 and John XXII in 1316. Clement had even served Edward I as a clerk earlier in his career. He was strongly attached to his native land and, even after his elevation, spent time in Bordeaux, where he had been archbishop.

---

[9] James, *Studies*, 160–1; Vale, *The Origins*, 141, 143.
[10] Davies, *Conquest*, 349–50.

The expenses of his entourage were a headache for the seneschal and its consumption of wine caused a shortage in England. More seriously, such strong associations with a Plantagenet domain and its ruler inevitably hindered delicate negotiations with the French monarchy. Not only was his impartiality prejudiced, his advancement of his Gascon friends and relations was a scandal even by the standards of the day. He created thirteen Gascon cardinals including seven from his own family circle. Many others received lesser preferment. Major Gascon families rushed to make alliances with the new power in the land, the consequences of which were felt far outside the borders of Aquitaine. Although prejudiced, an Italian cardinal summed up contemporary sentiment when he complained that Clement wanted 'to reduce the church to a corner of Gascony'. Clement's decision to reside in France rather than Rome and centre his administration on Avignon further exacerbated the situation and left him vulnerable to French pressure.[11] Although an independent city, it was surrounded on all sides by French territory. If the Templars were a striking casualty of his need to balance all these considerations, so too was any pretence of acting as a neutral broker between the kings of England and France.

After a long period in which scholars on both sides of the Channel showed little interest in Plantagenet territories, there has been a revival of interest in Gascony. The same cannot be said for Ponthieu, where the standard works are two short articles, one of which was published in 1914.[12] The county was far smaller than Gascony and closer to England. It was also different in its social and economic structures, having more in common with Flanders than south-west France. Urban oligarchies rather than unruly vassals tended to be the cause of civil strife.[13] Unlike Gascony, the association of the English crown with Ponthieu gave rise to relatively few disputes with the French king. During Edward I's rule as count, relations between the two courts were cordial and the terms of his tenure were undisputed. There were nevertheless similarities with Gascony in the way in which the territory was administered. Indeed, acts of the count of Ponthieu were routinely enrolled on the Gascon rolls alongside those of the duke of Aquitaine.[14] As in Gascony, government was in the hands of a seneschal, usually an Englishman with proven experience. Thomas of Sandwich, seneschal between 1278 and 1288, typically had earlier served as sheriff of Essex and had been employed on diplomatic business in Flanders and Brabant. Like

[11] Wright, *The Church*, 168; Menache, *Clement V*, 23–34, 40–53.
[12] Johnstone, 'The county of Ponthieu', 435–52; Shealy, 'The persistence', 33–51.
[13] Shealy, 'The persistence', 35.
[14] *Gascon Rolls*, iv.

Gascony, Ponthieu also contributed in financial and practical ways to royal campaigns in Scotland and Wales. In 1282, Edward I borrowed money from burgesses in Abbeville and other major towns to finance his Welsh war. Ships also brought corn and other provisions to Scotland in 1301 in support of Prince Edward, who had succeeded his father as count on the death of Queen Eleanor in 1290.

Although Edward I spent only a few weeks altogether in the county, stopping for a mere eight days on his way out to Gascony in 1286 and six further days on his return in 1289, it is likely that there too he proved a more effective ruler than his son. Prince Edward was only six years old when he became count, but he did not grow up to be particularly conscientious, judging by complaints that he did not reply to letters sent from his seneschal. Failure to restore harmony by the seneschal following the revolt of the disenfranchized in Abbeville in 1307 created opportunities for the French crown, as overlord, to intervene. Not until Edward III became king was effective government restored.[15]

Although each of the Plantagenet territories had distinctive customs, rule by a single family resulted in a cosmopolitan cadre of officials who served wherever they were required. One of the most distinguished was Otto de Grandson, a Savoyard and knight by profession who, having accompanied the Lord Edward on crusade, subsequently served him on important diplomatic missions. He was involved in peace negotiations in Wales in 1277 and, along with Henry de Lacy, received back the confiscated duchy of Aquitaine from the king of France in 1303. In the meantime, he had been to Rome, back to Wales and then to Acre to prepare for Edward's prospective second crusade (a trip from which he was lucky to escape with his life since he was in Acre when it fell to the Muslims in 1291). Although he never held major office in England, he was granted the wardenship of the Channel Islands in 1275 and served as a largely absentee justiciar in Wales in 1284.[16]

Among the many English officials found abroad, Robert Burnell was the most prominent. First appearing in the service of the Lord Edward in Gascony in the 1260s, he contributed significantly to government there as well as in England. Together with Otto de Grandson, he negotiated the settlement with Gaston of Béarn in 1278 and at the same time took steps to repair the damage caused by Luke de Tany's over-zealous regime as seneschal. He was in Gascony again with the king between 1286 and 1289, when he was heavily involved with the administrative reforms which culminated in the ordinances of 1289. His service was intended to leave a permanent mark on the duchy through the foundation of Baa

[15] Shealy, 'The persistence', 40–1.
[16] Kingsford, 'Sir Otho de Grandison', 125–95.

(derived from Bath, representing his bishopic of Bath and Wells), a now vanished *bastide* to the south of Bordeaux. This was one of several *bastides* to bear the name of English servants of the duke. As events turned out, Libourne was to prove an altogether more enduring memorial to Roger de Leyburn, another of Edward's supporters from his earliest days and lieutenant in Gascony between 1269 and 1272.

The efforts of royal officials were supplemented at crucial times by members of the royal family and aristocracy. So it came about that Edmund, earl of Lancaster, having failed in his attempts to negotiate a secret treaty with the French king, died at Bayonne in 1296 while acting as his brother's lieutenant in the ensuing war. Henry de Lacy, earl of Lincoln, succeeded Edmund as lieutenant, an office he held until 1299 and again between 1303 and 1305. William de Valence, Poitevin half-brother to Henry III, conducted the negotiations for the return of the Agenais in 1279, where he too left his name on a *bastide*, Valence d'Agenais. If English officials and nobles were frequently to be found in the duke's service in Gascony, the traffic was not entirely one way. In 1286 there were forty Gascons at Edward's court, precursors of the ill-fated Piers Gaveston, who arrived in England to make his fortune in 1296.

Among Englishmen serving in Gascony who were not part of the close court circle, Thomas of Sandwich, after his spell as seneschal of Ponthieu, went on in the following year to become mayor of Bordeaux. After a somewhat stormy period in office there, he returned to England and a series of judicial appointments before he disappeared from the records in 1294.[17] Of such lesser men, Henry le Waleys is perhaps the most interesting. A merchant whose fortune had been made in the wine trade rather than a knight, he served as lord mayor of London in 1273–4 and mayor of Bordeaux in the following year. In a long career which saw two more terms as lord mayor of London, he was associated with new towns in Gascony as well as in England.[18]

Thomas of Sandwich and Henry le Waleys were men of rank. Less well documented were the English clerks serving in the Gascon administration. Their presence can be inferred from the surviving form of the *Recogniciones Feodorum*. The returns appear to have been transcribed, probably on the orders of royal officials, before war broke out in 1294. Work was distributed among copyists and checkers, each of whom signed his portion. Names such as Henry de Coventre and J. de Suthwelle are unambiguously English. Their English hands, the frequently inaccurate rendering of place-names and even worse transcrip-

---

[17] Johnstone, 'The county of Ponthieu', 443 n.
[18] See chapter 3.

tion of returns in Gascon dialect also point to English workmanship. Perhaps the exceptional nature of the project required outside assistance, but it is unlikely that they were the only English clerks employed in Gascony at that date.[19]

The similarities between England and Gascony did not arise wholly out of their common government. There were parallels with developments elsewhere in Europe. The incidence of new town plantation is one example. These ventures were a widespread phenomenon in the thirteenth century, part of the drive towards colonization fuelled by increasing population. In most areas, plantations had peaked by the 1260s. This was certainly true of those established in the Agenais and throughout his county of Toulouse by Alphonse de Poitiers from the mid-1240s until his death in 1271, and also those founded by a variety of local lords in England. Political conditions in Gascony discouraged such enterprise until the control of the duchy stabilized after 1259. The late surge in Gascon plantations was therefore no accident, but even though Edward I was active in Gascony, he was more committed still to another late flowering of new towns, those built on conquered or reconquered land in Wales. He even attempted to establish a victualling port in Scotland on the Solway Firth, although that project was defeated by successive floods. He was unusual in that his interest was not that of a mere policy maker. As well as his personal visits to sites in Wales and his residence at Caernarfon while work was in progress, he is recorded at Libourne, Villereal, Ste Foy la Grande and other Gascon *bastides* including Baa, where in 1287 he spent eight shillings on drinks for the inhabitants. At Berwick in 1286 he went so far as to wheel a token barrow of earth. Nor was he the only link between the new towns of his domain. Just as Gascons were to be found in the armies in Scotland and Wales and Englishmen served alongside Gascons and Catalans in Gascony, so English settlers were to be found in Gascon *bastides* and Gascons among the English and Flemings who were attracted to the new towns in Wales. Given the ubiquity and cross-connections between new towns, it is not surprising that the way in which plots were laid out in grid patterns and the form of their privileges showed common features in whichever country they were found. This was also true of castles. Those built by the minor nobility at Budos, Villandraut and Roquetaillade in Gascony in the early fourteenth century showed a distinct family resemblance to the great castles built by Edward I in Wales in the 1290s and which in their turn were the work of a Savoyard master mason.[20]

[19] *Receuil*, xv–xxi.

[20] Beresford, *New Towns*, 28–30, 35, 83, 181, 196–7; Vale, *The Origins*, 106. See chapters 3 and 7.

Common approaches to administration are also evident in many parts of western Europe as well as within the common confines of Plantagenet rule. A recent French scholar has commented on 'une veritable fureur' of inquiries undertaken by rulers throughout Europe from the 1230s. The hundred roll and *Quo warranto* proceedings in England, the extents of conquered land in Wales, the *Recogniciones Feodorum* of 1273–4 of Gascony and the *per quod warrantum* investigations held there after its restoration in 1303 following the war, all belong to this broader context. Returns from other inquiries dating from the 1240s to the early fourteenth century survive from France, Flanders, the papal court at Avignon, Naples and Bologna as well as England. They encompass surveys of lands, rights and revenues and assorted census material. In 1240 Frederick II investigated the conduct of imperial tax collectors in Sicily. Seven years later, Louis IX wanted to know about general maladministration before embarking on his crusade. His brother, Alphonse de Poitiers, intended to set in place a fairer tax system in Languedoc.[21] The Lord Edward urged Henry III to authorize an inquiry into ducal rights in Gascony in 1259, although nothing was done. Plantagenet inquiries into the obligations of tenants, the alienation of seignorial rights and the corruption of officials may have been frequent and ambitious, but they were not unusual. Nor were their legislative concerns. If the Statute of Mortmain of 1279 was brought into being in response to long-standing English anxiety about the seemingly unending expansion of ecclesiastical landholdings, the problem was not unique to England. The ways in which governments attempted to find solutions differed from one country to another, reflecting local tenurial arrangements. Nevertheless, whether in England, Italy, France or the Low Countries, the objective was the same even as the means varied.[22]

It is also worth noting that attitudes to the Jews transcended territorial boundaries. Often arising from a common response to papal urgings, persecution was frequent throughout Europe. Edward's legislation of 1269 and 1275 echoed the measures introduced by his father-in-law Alphonso of Castile in 1265. Expulsion from England, when it came in 1290, had been preceded and possibly influenced by expulsion from Gascony in 1287. Charles of Anjou expelled the Jews from Anjou and Maine in 1289. French royal policy showed the shift found in England from conversion under Louis IX to expulsion in the 1290s, although it differed in its implementation. Philip IV began with a series of regional and selective exclusions, followed by a wholesale, if temporary, expulsion in 1306.[23]

[21] Glenisson, 'Les Enquêtes administratives', 17–25.
[22] Raban, *Mortmain Legislation*, 22–3. See chapter 4.
[23] Mundill, *England's Jewish Solution*, 276–84.

Religion was as important as high politics in drawing England into the wider European scene. The great religious orders spread across Christendom irrespective of secular boundaries. Most were continental in origin and English houses often owed allegiance to a parent house abroad. The Cistercians had a strongly hierarchical structure in which political borders played no part and which required regular visitation of daughter houses. Thus, Fountains Abbey in Yorkshire was visited by monks from Clairvaux in Burgundy, while those from Fountains might visit Lyse near Bergen in Norway. Heads of houses were also summoned together to General Chapters, where matters of importance to the whole order were dealt with. All this necessitated travel overseas. Moreover, the presence of foreign religious in English houses or English religious abroad was by no means unusual. The dual loyalties generated by these external links did not pass without criticism. In 1307 the Statute of Carlisle forbade financial contributions to parent institutions where these were overseas and in the following year Cistercian abbots were prevented from attending the General Chapter at Cîteaux. Alien houses, chiefly those founded in the aftermath of the Norman Conquest as daughter houses of great Norman abbeys such as Bec, were a source of anxiety, particularly in time of war. In 1295 and again during the war of St Sardos of 1324–6, the property of alien priories was seized and bishops were ordered to remove alien monks from the coast and navigable rivers to secure places far inland where they could not act as spies.[24] The international nature of the military orders was even more marked. The Street of Knights in Rhodes, where the Hospitallers established their base in 1309, saw knights of the English 'Tongue' living alongside those of France, Italy, Germany and Castile, each in their own house. The whole way in which their affairs were organized reflected their focus on the eastern Mediterranean. Small numbers of knights maintained the English preceptories (houses) and the bulk of their revenues were transmitted overseas. The chain of preceptories stretching from England to the Near East had a signal advantage for the medieval traveller. Funds deposited at one Templar house might be realized on arrival at another, thereby obviating the need to carry large quantities of coin, with all its attendant danger and inconvenience. The constant outflow of liquid wealth was a matter of concern to rulers, however, and no doubt contributed to the ultimate dissolution of the order.

The strongest thread linking the disparate parts of Christendom, with overarching authority, was the papacy. People from every country thronged the papal court as litigants, suppliants or emissaries. The English were no exception. Most came to Rome or Avignon for a

[24] Wright, *The Church*, 236–7.

specific purpose. A few were resident, serving the Pope as officials or servicing the needs of those who required professional representation. Although the majority of the *curiales* (officials at the court) under the Avignon Popes were French, Englishmen wielded influence out of proportion to their numbers. Several rose to be judges of the highest papal court, soon to be known as the *Rota*. One such was William Bateman, who grew up in Norwich in the early years of the fourteenth century. To this day, the college he established at Cambridge treasures as its Founder's Cup a silver gilt chalice bearing an Avignon silver mark.[25] Others, such as William of York in the time of Edward I, acted as proctors (attorneys) on behalf of those who were unable or unwilling to make the journey to Rome or Avignon themselves. It was characteristic of the universal atmosphere pervading the papal court that one of the most successful proctors, employed by senior churchmen in England, Scotland, Wales and Ireland, was Andreas Sapiti, a native of Florence. Expatriates at a more humble and non-clerical level have escaped the records, but the English stonemason at work on the cathedral in Avignon under John XXII was unlikely to have been the only one.[26]

Some proctors, such as the chronicler Adam Murimuth who was employed by the king, the university of Oxford and the archbishop and monks of Canterbury in the early fourteenth century, were not based at the papal court but travelled from England when the occasion demanded. This was also true of diplomats at the highest level. The English crown despatched twenty-five embassies between 1305 and 1334. Papal missions also came to England, where they often dealt with cases referred to the papal court under delegated powers. Cardinal Peter of Spain came in 1306, to be followed by further nuncios in 1312–13 and 1317–18. Although it was comparatively rare, Englishmen were from time to time elevated to the college of cardinals. Archbishop Kilwardby in 1278 was followed by three more Dominicans, the last of whom, Thomas Jorz, died in 1310. For Kilwardby, it spelt the end of his career as primate of England.[27]

It is not easy to assess the extent to which papal justice impinged on English life. Ecclesiastical jurisdiction covered matters as diverse as matrimony, excommunication, testamentary issues and heresy, as well as more specifically clerical questions arising from disputed benefices, visitation rights, defects of orders or apostasy. At first glance, this seems wide enough to generate substantial traffic between England and the

[25] Ibid., 101–6; E. Taburet-Delahaye, 'L'Orfevrerie au poinçon d'Avignon au xive siècle', *Revue de l'art*, 108 (1995), 15–16.
[26] Wright, *The Church*, 107, 109–13.
[27] Ibid., 48, 113–17, 125.

Continent, even though English monarchs, jealous of their legal jurisdiction, from time to time exercised their right to prevent cases leaving the country. In practice, the well-established procedures for cases to be heard in England by papal nuncios or specially appointed judges delegate, or the possibility of using proctors to act as representatives at the Curia, limited the number of litigants who needed to travel abroad. Fewer than eighty cases seem to have been heard before the papal court itself between 1305 and 1334.[28] As was so often the case in relations between the medieval church and state, a working accommodation had been reached which more or less satisfied all parties, including the actual litigants.

If it is not always clear how often papal justice involved journeys to the papal court, it is more difficult still to gauge the significance of the Pope's right under certain circumstances to provide to vacant benefices in England. Provision to episcopal and archiepiscopal office had long been a papal preserve. By the early fourteenth century this right had been extended considerably. Vacancies caused by anyone dying at, or within two days' journey of, the papal court, or whose office had been secured by translation, exchange or resignation under the auspices of the Pope, were drawn into the net. John XXII is known to have made 782 provisions to England alone in a pontificate lasting eighteen years.[29] But raw numbers would be deceptive. Some provisions never took effect. A much higher proportion were made at the behest of the crown or other powerful figure, giving the Pope very little practical influence over the choice of candidate. Of course there were instances of unsuitable papal provision. How else would an unordained member of the Albret family have become archdeacon of Canterbury under Clement V?[30] However, it has long been recognized that the intrusion of such foreigners was the exception rather than the rule.

Against the background of what one might loosely call clerical business traffic, there were overseas journeys more overtly religious in character, as both rulers and the population at large felt moved to take the cross or undertake pilgrimages. Although the days were long past when undisciplined hordes flocked to the east in the wake of leaders such as Peter the Hermit, the notion of a crusade still carried a powerful charge. England had become prominent in the crusading movement when the death of Louis IX fortuitously left the Lord Edward to assume leadership of the expedition setting out from Aigues Mortes in 1270. Aside from the status it conferred on him, the crusade had more

[28] Ibid., 139.
[29] Ibid., 6–35, table D, 279.
[30] Vale, *The Origins*, 97.

personal implications for Edward as well as for his English followers. Like many young nobles, he had already travelled abroad, participating in tournaments and mixing with his continental peers. Opportunities to visit France readily presented themselves, but even in youth his experience was not confined to France alone; he had received his knighthood in Burgos at the hands of King Alphonso of Castile on the occasion of his marriage. The crusade broadened his horizons yet further. Apart from Palestine and North Africa, the journey to and from the Holy Land enabled him to visit Rome and many of the leading courts of Europe. As well as providing the chance to meet the Pope, then at Orvieto, and other rulers, his travels gave him a taste for the Italian architectural and decorative work that he subsequently commissioned for Westminster Abbey.[31] As the sole ruler with crusading experience, the papacy thereafter looked to him to assume leadership whenever a new crusade was mooted. Although he never embarked on a second crusading expedition, Edward responded with a renewed vow in 1287 and the presence of Otto de Grandson in Acre in 1291 indicates that it was not just a token gesture.

Although probably motivated in part by a sense of adventure, Edward was almost certainly driven to fulfil his crusading vow by a sense of conventional piety. It was not a convenient time to leave England and he was not encouraged to do so by either his father or the Pope.[32] It is more difficult to assess the motives of his followers. Nearly three hundred knights and their men are known to have joined his forces and those of his brother Edmund. Many no doubt were bound by ties of lordship and the formal contracts under which they were obliged to serve. Some may have been compelled by the church to take the cross in expiation of their sins or sought to escape from problems at home, but it would be unduly cynical to deny to them any spontaneous religious commitment. The relatively small number of clergy known to have participated suggests that most travelled in someone's retinue, imbued more with a sense of duty to their patron than any independent crusading zeal, but again it is easy to underrate what cannot in the nature of things be documented. Even more elusive, is the number, identity and motivation of the camp followers who must surely have accompanied the fighting forces. Only Queen Eleanor was important enough to excite comment.[33]

By the later thirteenth century, crusading was a serious military enterprise. Pilgrimages, by contrast, could be undertaken by ordinary people, individuals as well as groups. One of the most enduring images of the

[31] Binski, *Westminster Abbey*, 103; Vale, *The Origins*, 34; Prestwich, *Edward I*, ch. 3.
[32] Prestwich, *Edward I*, 68.
[33] Lloyd, *English Society and the Crusade*, 126, app. 4.

Middle Ages is the solitary pilgrim complete with staff and distinctive broad-brimmed hat on which were pinned the small lead badges sold at every shrine. Although many English pilgrims settled for their nearest shrine or perhaps that of Thomas Becket at Canterbury, others chose to travel long distances. The ultimate destination was Jerusalem. Long after it fell into Muslim hands, well-organized trips were run by the Venetians.[34] These were exceedingly uncomfortable for all but the wealthy. Those of slender means were better advised to go elsewhere on foot, relying on alms and seeking shelter in hospices founded at the bleakest and most hazardous points on their journey. The introduction of the jubilee in 1300 enhanced the attractions of Rome for pilgrims of all rank, but one of the most popular shrines for English pilgrims was that of Santiago de Compostela, as witnessed by the number of its cockleshell badges found in England. The journey was long and dangerous. Regular shipping links with Gascony meant that many took ship to Bordeaux and then struggled overland across the marshes of the Landes before finally crossing the Pyrenees and picking up the main pilgrim road across northern Spain to Santiago. A twelfth-century *Pilgrims' Guide* gives a graphic picture of the discomforts this entailed. The Landes especially were 'a God-forsaken region with very few stopping places', where travellers were harried by great swarms of 'giant flies'.[35] To the natural hazards facing pilgrims were added theft and violence. Venetian seamen were required to take an oath not to steal more than five shillings from their passengers. On other routes, Englishmen were among the predators. In 1318, John of London was accused of robbing pilgrims as they slept in a Spanish hospice. A year later English bandits were captured at Pamplona.[36] Although one cannot set a figure on those who embarked on trips to overseas shrines or assume that their motives were entirely pious, they clearly comprised a steady stream of men, women and children from all walks of life, each of whom sought a destination tailored to their means and their needs.

The other reason for ordinary people to voyage abroad was the pursuit of trade. Political links fostered commercial opportunities, as the importance of trade with Bordeaux demonstrated. Trade with Castile also flourished until the death of Queen Eleanor in 1290 and the preference of King Alphonso's successor for a French alliance. Only when peace was restored between England and France in 1303 did things improve again.[37] The damaging effects of the Anglo-French

---

[34] Sumption, *Pilgrimage*, 185–190.
[35] Ohler, *The Medieval Traveller*, 191.
[36] Sumption, *Pilgrimage*, 180, 189.
[37] Childs, *Anglo-Castilian Trade*, 11, 15.

conflict of 1294–1303 were also evident on England's trade with Flanders. Overseas ventures were at best a chancy business. At sea, bad weather, piracy or enemy shipping could spell complete disaster. Nor were overland routes always safer. Whether in transit or selling their goods in a foreign land, alien merchants needed the security of peace between their trading partners and royal protection from dishonesty or worse.[38]

Political conditions could promote or hinder trade, but they did not wholly define it. Long before the later thirteenth century, a complex network of trading had grown up stretching from Scandinavia in the north, Russia in the east and outwards from the Mediterranean to Africa and Asia in the south. Wherever there was a market, merchants could be found to supply it. Ships were chartered irrespective of country of origin and those ships carried goods and crews from many countries. English merchants and seamen were certainly part of this myriad activity, but it is unclear how prominently they featured.

Customs records do not exist before the late thirteenth century and even then they are problematic to use. Apart from endemic evasion, aliens alone were subject to customs, leaving English mercantile activity unrecorded. This explains why the traditional picture of England's trading relations with the wider world shows foreigners coming to England rather than Englishmen trading abroad. There is little doubt that Italian merchants and shipping dominated Mediterranean trade, just as their bankers led the rest of Europe in sophisticated financial techniques. Equally it is known that, on the northern trading routes, Hanseatic cities were beginning to exclude merchants from elsewhere; English merchants who had traded in Bergen earlier in the thirteenth century were increasingly replaced by those of Lübeck.[39] Where evidence does exist, however, it shows extensive English involvement, especially in the markets most important to England. The Bordeaux customs accounts of 1303–4 reveal the presence of ships not just from London and the major ports, but also from lesser ports around the entire coast. Numbers were often small, one each from Ilfracombe, Chepstow, Wareham, Orwell, Dunwich and Hartlepool for example, but together they constituted a significant share in the carrying trade. In 1307–8, 316 of the 624 ships at Bordeaux were English. As the century wore on, English merchants as well as English shipping came to play a larger role in Flemish and Gascon markets, where their freedom from customs gave them a commercial advantage over aliens. In the 1320s they achieved dominance in

---

[38] See chapter 3.
[39] *Handbook to the Cultural History of the Middle Ages, Supplementary to the Displays and Exhibits in Bryggens Museum*, Bergen, 1978, 23.

the wine trade, while their hold on the wool trade had grown from around a third in the late thirteenth century to more than two-thirds in the early fourteenth century.[40] English merchants were well established in Antwerp by the end of the thirteenth century, with their own courts and assemblies. By the early years of the following century they were allowed to elect their own mayor and enjoyed the same privileges as Hanseatic and Genoese merchants.[41] Some merchants were ambitious enough to engage in triangular trade. In 1319, Bristol merchant Thomas Mustard was to be found in Ireland, whence he exported wool to Flanders. The money gained from its sale was then employed to purchase wine in Bordeaux, which was in turn shipped to Waterford, completing the triangle.[42]

Notwithstanding such occasional glimpses of enterprise, the fact remains that England lay towards the outer limits of the richest trade routes and its merchants are most commonly seen, where they can be seen at all, engaged in trade to and from England. The days when England and the Netherlands would vie to master the world's carrying trade and their trading companies would rule as virtual monarchs in East Asia still lay a long way in the future. Whereas seventeenth-century English and Dutch merchants ventured abroad in search of exotic imports, in the thirteenth and fourteenth centuries this role fell naturally to the Italians. Routes to the east had been opened up with the establishment of the crusader kingdom of Jerusalem. Before long, silks, spices, dyes, scented wood and porcelain were transported overland from Persia, through Damascus to Acre from where they were shipped to Europe. Marco Polo, who left Venice in 1271 to spend more than twenty years in China, followed his father and uncle in making his fortune in eastern trade.[43] Nor was this an isolated family venture. By the end of Edward II's reign western traders were quite common in China. Pegolotti, whose handbook is so informative about English wool producers, also offered practical advice on trade with the east, some of which was gleaned from his personal experience in the service of the Bardi banking house in the Crimea.[44] England provided a ready market for the goods of these merchants, but the English themselves are not known to have played any part in their activities. Nor were they to be found among the Franciscan missionaries at work in India and China from the mid-thirteenth century. Such contact as there was with the east arose through Edward I's

[40] Childs, 'The English export trade', 133. I am also most grateful to Dr Childs for making unpublished data available to me.
[41] Nightingale, *Medieval Mercantile Community*, 90.
[42] James, *Studies*, 167.
[43] Burman, *The World*, 48–53, 87–103.
[44] Ibid., 104–6. See chapter 3.

diplomatic links with the Mongol Khan from the mid-1270s in connection with a possible crusade. It was the English king's personal prestige that made Bordeaux, where he was then resident, an obvious destination when the Khan's ambassador toured Europe to raise support in 1287. In 1292, Edward himself initiated contact with the east. He sent Geoffrey de Langley to Persia on what turned out to be an abortive mission, yielding only a leopard needing to be fed on live mutton, to show for a long and hazardous journey and the expenditure of well over £3,000.[45]

Medieval England was in many ways tied more securely into continental Europe than its modern counterpart, notwithstanding present-day membership of the European Community. Although obstacles of all sorts faced foreigners, whether aliens in England or the English abroad, this did not prevent a stream of people leaving and entering the country for one reason or another. The medieval English were also linguistically better equipped for travel than their descendants.[46] One should not forget, however, that all these outward looking connections were balanced by countless peasants who never left their native community and who lived a life of isolation barely imaginable in the days of modern communications and media.

[45] Lloyd, *English Society and the Crusade*, app. 1 and 2; Prestwich, *Edward I*, 313–14; Cuttino, *English Diplomatic Administration*, 175–6.
[46] See chapter 5.

Conclusion

Edward I and Edward II have been differently served both by their contemporaries and by historians. One is hailed as a great king, 'England's Justinian', 'Hammer of the Scots'; the other as an ignominious failure, declared insufficient to rule at the time of his deposition, and subsequently characterized as dishonourable and incompetent.[1] These black and white judgements imply that there was a sharper demarcation between the character of the two reigns than was in fact the case. Something less clear-cut is closer to the truth, at least as this generation might see it. It is not to devalue Edward I's achievements or to forget Edward II's failings to set them in context. In youth, Edward I was prone to the same weaknesses as his son. Impetuous generosity encouraged both to make injudicious grants to their followers, even if the Lord Edward's favour did not concentrate so exclusively on single individuals. Nor can Edward I's reign be seen as a complete triumph. Arguably the real descent into misrule occurred in the 1290s rather than with his son's accession. By contrast, institutional reform of a high order continued unabated under Edward II, notwithstanding that it was largely directed towards increasing his income.

Despite Edward I's inquiry into administrative abuses in 1298, the initiative for addressing such grievances, firmly in his own hands at the beginning of the reign, was already passing from the crown to the magnates. Their attempts to exercise control over the monarch, which so dominated events under Edward II, were prefigured in the *Confirmatio Cartarum* and the *Articuli super Cartas*. To a modern eye, Edward I's greatest achievement was the energy with which he tackled misgovernment in the 1270s and 1280s and caused the series of great reforming statutes to be enacted. This ended in the face of revolt in Wales and threats to Plantagenet interests in Scotland and Gascony. No medieval

[1] Fryde, *Tyranny*, 198; Tuck, *Crown and Nobility*, 50; Barrow, *Robert Bruce*, 250.

monarch could hope to avoid all such challenges to his rule, but Edward's readiness to use force where others might have opted for less aggressive methods carried a heavy penalty. Modern commentators are apt to be less impressed by military prowess than their medieval forebears. Contemporaries valued the glory of conquest and the protection from invasion that victory conferred, whereas we more cautiously assess the political consequences and count the financial cost. Without doubt it was the need to resource his campaigns that caused the breakdown of Edward I's relations with his subjects. However, it is hard to judge Edward II's reluctance to fight the Scots more favourably. The author of the *Vita Edwardi Secundi* appears just in blaming him for leaving the English 'a leaderless people'.[2] Peace and solvency, while laudable in the abstract, were no adequate answer to the sufferings of his northern subjects and the Scottish threat to the integrity of the realm.

It has been suggested that rebellion by its Welsh and Scottish vassals had a brutalizing effect on the English monarchy.[3] This is hard to assess. The treatment of Simon de Montfort's corpse following his death at the battle of Evesham shows that savagery never lay far below the surface; his hands, feet and testicles were hacked off. Even so, he died in battle and was not mutilated alive with due judicial process as happened during the following reigns.[4] Edward I appears to have reserved a special harshness for those who broke their oath of fealty to him. Dafydd ap Gruffudd was dragged to the scaffold, hanged alive, cut down and disembowelled so that his intestines could be burned before his eyes and, after death, was quartered. William Wallace suffered the same fate. The imprisonment of Robert Bruce's sister and the countess of Buchan in cages in 1306 also went beyond punishments customary for women.[5] The reign of terror unleashed on the Contrariants following the battle of Boroughbridge seems quantitatively different even from this and qualitatively different from the punishment of the Disinherited in the 1260s. The latter endured confiscation and crippling fines, but they were not hanged, drawn and quartered. Whether the escalation in political violence which so concerned the author of the *Vita Edwardi Secundi* was entirely due to Edward I's autocratic temperament and Edward II's progressive detachment from reality, or whether closer definition of treason with its draconian penalties also played a part is a matter of judgement, but it seems to have happened.[6]

---

[2] *Vita Edwardi Secundi*, 61.
[3] Fryde, *Tyranny*, 60.
[4] Maddicott, *Simon de Montfort*, 342.
[5] Prestwich, *Edward I*, 202, 508.
[6] Childs, 'Resistance and Treason', 180ff.

The political nation was very small, but given the nature of medieval society disruption at the top had unfortunate consequences for everyone, especially in the countryside. Corruption and abuse of authority were endemic, but a strong monarch such as Edward I could keep it in check, at least until his financial needs became paramount. Edward II's inability to uphold the rule of law was as fundamental a failing in a monarch as his inability to protect his subjects from Scottish raids.

How far the increased frequency of warfare under the two Edwards had a brutalizing effect on the populace at large is another open question. In the northern counties, there can be little doubt of its impact. To the destructiveness of the Scots was added the marauding of the king's Welsh and Irish troops, but one can only guess at the implications for the social fabric within traumatized settlements. Counties further south escaped the remorseless raids, but life had always been a grim experience for ordinary people, and it grew nastier still during the early fourteenth century, when the vagaries of the climate, famine and disease coincided with near anarchy. The unusually large armies put into the field against the Scots and the conditions suffered by ordinary foot soldiers added a further element of brutality. The chivalric code was not for the infantry; their lives were expendable. Quite apart from the horrors of battle, they sometimes faced starvation when supplies failed to arrive. Unfortunately we know almost nothing personal about those who served. Recruited from the shires by commissioners of array, and probably selected within their own communities, some may have welcomed the opportunity to escape poverty. However, failure to muster the full numbers ordered by the king and the very high rate of desertion suggest otherwise.[7] Military service must have been a rude shock to men who had little experience of the world beyond their fields, and as the survivors made their way home following demobilization, new habits of looting and violence were disseminated throughout the realm.

Yet, desperate though life undoubtedly was for a population confronted by exceptional crises and often poised on the brink of subsistence, it was played out against a background of striking achievements. For all its shortcomings, the administrative infrastructure was remarkable and sturdy enough to bear the strain of misgovernment. In the arts and architecture, this was the time when some of the finest and most ornate work of the Middle Ages was created. In a host of ways – law, language, constitutional precedent – far-reaching developments were

---

[7] Prestwich, *War, Politics and Finance*, ch. 4; *idem, Edward I*, 480; Fryde, *Tyranny*, 124, 129–30.

Appendix 1
'Seletive Family Trees'

178

Selective family tree showing links by marriage between the English and other ruling houses

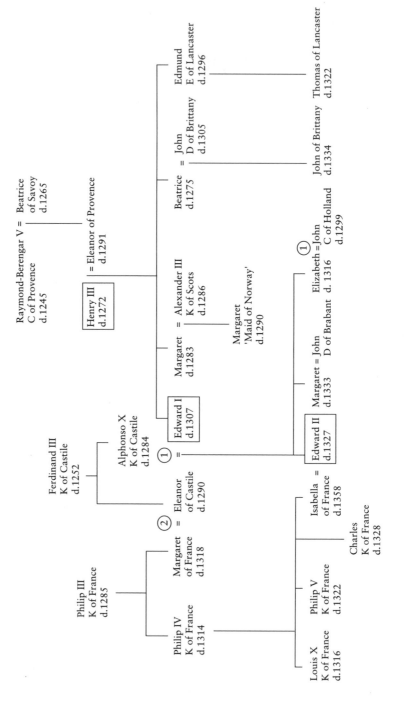

Selective family tree showing links by marriage between the crown and nobility

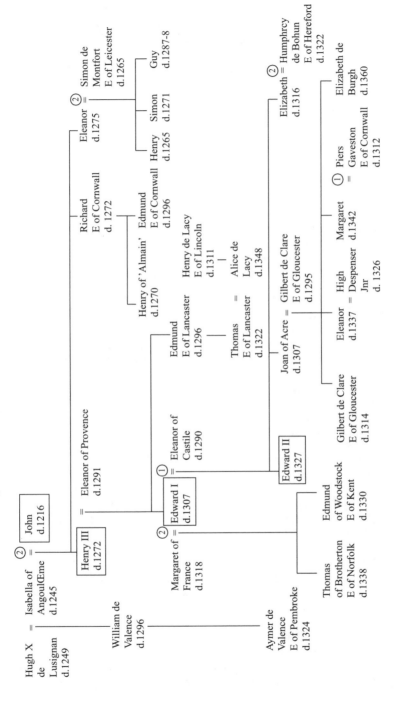

Appendix 2
Chronology

1259	Provisions of Westminster
1261–2	Lord Edward in Gascony
1264	Mise of Amiens; Battle of Lewes
1265	Reform Parliament; Battle of Evesham
1266	Dictum of Kenilworth
1267	Statute of Marlborough; Treaty of Montgomery
1270	Lord Edward on crusade
1272	Death of Henry III and accession of Edward I
1273–4	Edward I in Gascony
1274	Replacement of escheators and sheriffs
1274–5	Hundred roll inquiry
1275	Statute of Westminster I; Statutes of Exchequer; Statute of Jewry
1276–7	First Welsh War
1277	Treaty of Aberconwy
1278	Statute of Gloucester
1278–94	*Quo warranto* proceedings
1279	Statute of Mortmain
1279–80	Hundred roll inquiry
1282–4	Second Welsh War
1283	Statute of Acton Burnell
1284	Statute of Wales; birth of Edward II
1285	Statute of Westminster II; Statute of Winchester; Kirkby's Quest
1286	Bull *Circumspecte agatis*; death of Alexander III of Scotland
1286–9	Edward I in Gascony
1287	Statute of Gloucester
1289	Dismissal of judges
1290	Statutes *De quo warranto* and *Quia emptores*; expulsion of the Jews; death of Queen Eleanor of Castile
1291	*Taxatio*
1294	Seizure of Gascony by French crown
1294–5	Welsh rebellion and conquest
1294–8	War with France
1296	Sack of Berwick-upon-Tweed; Battle of Dunbar; Bull *Clericis laicos*
1297	Battle of Stirling Bridge; Remonstrances; *Confirmatio Cartarum*

1297–8	Edward I in Flanders
1298	Battle of Falkirk
1300	*Articuli super Cartas*
1301	Wales granted to Edward of Caernarfon
1303	Gascony restored to Plantagenet rule
1304	Siege of Stirling
1305	Ordinance for the government of Scotland; execution of Wallace
1306	Robert Bruce seizes Scottish throne
1307	Gaveston's first exile; death of Edward I and accession of Edward II
1308	Boulogne Agreement; Declaration
1308–9	Gaveston's second exile
1311	Ordinances; Gaveston's third exile
1312	Gaveston executed; birth of Edward III
1314	Battle of Bannockburn
1315–17	Great Famine
1316	Lancaster's abortive Scottish campaign
1319	Edward II's campaign to recapture Berwick
1321–2	Civil War
1322	Scottish campaign; Battle of Boroughbridge; Lancaster executed
1323	Thirteen-year truce with Scotland
1324–6	War of St Sardos with France
1326	Invasion of Queen Isabella, Prince Edward and Roger Mortimer
1327	Deposition and death of Edward II

Bibliography

A Sources

This section is arranged alphabetically by the abbreviated forms that are used in the footnotes.

Unprinted

BL (British Library)
    Add. MS 35296   Spalding Priory register
    Add. MS 42130   Luttrell Psalter
    Cott. Otho B xiv.   Pipewell Abbey manuscript
    Cott. Vesp. E xxii.   Peterborough Abbey register

CUL (Cambridge University Library)
    Add. MS 3020–1   Thorney Abbey cartulary

PRO (Public Record Office, London)
    E32/12   Essex forest roll, 1277
    E401/1565   Norwich tally roll, 1233

Printed

Annales Monastici, ed. H. R. Luard, 5 vols, Rolls Series, London, 1864–9.
British Borough Charters: British Borough Charters, 1042–1307, ed. A. Ballard and J. Tait, 2 vols, Cambridge, 1913–23.
Cal Chancery Rolls Various, 1277–1326, London, 1914.
Cal Close: Calendar of Close Rolls, 1272–1509, 47 vols, London, 1900–63.
Cal Lib: Calendar of Liberate Rolls, 1226–72, 6 vols, London, 1916–64.
Cal Pat: Calendar of Patent Rolls, 1232–1582, 71 vols, London, 1906–86.
Chron Majora: Matthaei Parisiensis, Chronica Majora, ed. H. R. Luard, 7 vols, Rolls Series, London, 1872–84.
Close Rolls: Close Rolls, 1227–72, 14 vols, London, 1902–38.

Documents of the Baronial Movement: *Documents of the Baronial Movement of Reform and Rebellion, 1258–67*, ed. R. F. Treharne and I. J. Sanders, Oxford, 1973.

Early trailbaston proceedings: 'Early trailbaston proceedings from the Lincoln roll of 1305', ed. A. Harding, in R. F. Hunnisett and J. B. Post (eds), *Medieval Legal Records Edited in Memory of C. A. F. Meekings*, London, 1978, 143–68.

EHD, 1189–1327: *English Historical Documents, 1189–1327*, ed. H. Rothwell, London, 1975.

Feudal Aids: *Feudal Aids, 1284–1431*, 6 vols, London, 1899–1920.

Flores Historiarum, ed. H. R. Ward, 3 vols, Rolls Series, London, 1890.

Gascon Register: *Gascon Register A*, ed. G. P. Cuttino, 3 vols, British Academy, 1975.

Gascon Rolls: *Gascon Rolls Preserved in the Public Record Office, 1307–17*, ed. Y. Renouard, London, 1962.

Gervase of Canterbury: *The Historical Works of Gervase of Canterbury*, ed. W. Stubbs, 2 vols, Rolls Series, London, 1879–80.

Guisborough: *The Chronicle of Walter of Guisborough*, ed. H. Rothwell, Camden Society, 3rd ser., lxxxix, 1957.

Henry de Bray: *The Estate Book of Henry de Bray*, ed. D. Willis, Camden Society, 3rd ser., xxvii, 1916.

Hotot estate book: 'Estate Records of the Hotot Family', in E. King (ed.), *A Northamptonshire Miscellany*, Northamptonshire Record Society, xxxii, 1983.

Life of Aelred: *The Life of Aelred of Rievaulx by Walter Daniel*, ed. and trans. F. M. Powicke, London, 1950.

Political Songs: *Thomas Wright's Political Songs of England from the Reign of John to that of Edward II*, ed. P. R. Coss, Cambridge, 1996.

Polychronicon: *Polychronicon Ranulphi Higden Monachi Cestrensis*, ed. C. Babington and J. R. Lumby, 9 vols, Rolls series, London, 1865–86.

Receuil: *Receuil d'actes relatifs à l'Administration des rois d'Angleterre en Guyenne au XIIIe siécle (Recogniciones Feodorum in Aquitania)*, ed. C. Bémont, Paris, 1914.

Records of the City of Norwich: *The Records of the City of Norwich*, ed. W. Hudson and J. C. Tingey, 2 vols, Norwich, 1906–10.

Register of Walter Giffard: *The Register of Walter Giffard*, ed. W. Brown, Surtees Society, cix, 1904.

RH: *Rotuli Hundredorum*, 2 vols, Record Commission, London, 1812–18.

Rot Litt Claus: *Rotuli Litterarum Clausarum in Turri Londinensi Asservati*, ed. T. D. Hardy, 2 vols, Record Commission, London, 1833–44.

Rymes of Robyn Hood: *Rymes of Robyn Hood: An Introduction to the English Outlaw*, ed. R. B. Dobson and J. Taylor, Gloucester, 1989.

Select Cases Concerning the Law Merchant, AD 1270–1638, ed. C. Cross, Selden Society, xxiii, 1908.

Select Cases in the Court of King's Bench: *Select Cases in the Court of King's Bench under Edward I*, ed. G. O. Sayles, 7 vols, Selden Society, 1936–71.

Select Pleas: *Select Pleas in Manorial and other Seignorial Courts*, ed. F. W. Maitland, Selden Society, ii, 1889.

Statutes of the Realm: *Statutes of the Realm (1101–1713)*, 11 vols, Record Commission, London, 1810–28.

Trokelowe: *Chronica Monasterii S. Albani: Johannis de Trokelowe et Henrici de Blaneforde*, iii, ed. H. T. Riley, Rolls Series, 7 vols, London, 1863–76.

Vita Edwardi Secundi: *The Life of Edward II, Vita Edwardi Secundi*, ed. and trans. N. Denholm-Young, London, 1957.

Walter of Henley: *Walter of Henley and other Treatises on Estate Management and Accounting*, ed. D. Oschinsky, Oxford, 1971.

Women in England: *Women in England c.1275–1525*, ed. and trans. P. J. P. Goldberg, Manchester, 1995.

Women of the English Nobility and Gentry: *Women of the English Nobility and Gentry, 1066–1500*, ed. and trans. J. Ward, Manchester, 1995.

York Memorandum Book (1376–1493), ed. M. Sellers and J. W. Percy, 2 vols, Surtees Society, cxx and cxxv, 1912–15.

Yorkshire Hundred and Quo Warranto Rolls: *Yorkshire Hundred and Quo Warranto Rolls, 1274–1294*, ed. B. English, Yorkshire, Archaeological Society, xli, 1996.

B   General and narrative works

This section includes the abbreviations used in the footnotes and chapter bibliographies for journal titles.

AgHR: *Agricultural History Review*.

Alexander, J. and Binski, P. (eds), *Age of Chivalry: Art in Plantagenet England, 1200–1400*, London, 1987.

Beresford, M., *New Towns of the Middle Ages: Town Plantation in England, Wales and Gascony*, 2nd edn, Gloucester, 1988.

Bristol and Gloucs Arch Soc Trans: *Transactions of the Bristol and Gloucestershire Archaeological Society*.

Britnell, R. H., *The Commercialisation of English Society, 1000–1500*, Cambridge, 1993.

Clanchy, M. T., *England and its Rulers, 1066–1272: Foreign Lordship and National Identity*, Glasgow, 1983.

Clanchy, M. T., *From Memory to Written Record: England, 1066–1307*, 2nd edn, Oxford, 1993.

EcHR: *The Economic History Review*.

EHR: *The English Historical Review*.

Giuseppi, M. S., *Guide to the Contents of the Public Record Office*, 3 vols, London, 1963–8.

Gransden, A., *Historical Writing in England*, 2 vols, London, 1974–82.

Handbook of British Chronology, ed. E. B. Fryde, D. E. Greenway, S. Porter and I. Roy, 3rd edn, London, 1986.

Harding, A., *England in the Thirteenth Century*, Cambridge, 1993.

Heath, P., *Church and Realm 1272–1461: Conflict and Collaboration in an Age of Crises*, London, 1988.

Jordan, W. C., *The Great Famine: Northern Europe in the Early Fourteenth Century*, New Jersey, 1996.

Kershaw, I., 'The Great Famine and agrarian crisis in England, 1315–22', in R. H. Hilton (ed.), *Peasants, Knights and Heretics: Studies in Medieval English Social History*, Cambridge, 1976, 85–132.

Knowles, D., *The Religious Orders in England*, 3 vols, Cambridge, 1960–74.

Knowles, D., *The Monastic Order in England*, 2nd edn, Cambridge, 1966.

Knowles, D. and Hadcock, R. N., *Medieval Religious Houses: England and Wales*, 2nd edn, London, 1971.

Lamb, H. H., *Climate History and the Modern World*, London, 1982.

Leyser, H., *Medieval Women: A Social History of Women in England, 450–1500*, London, 1995.

Miller, E. and Hatcher, J., *Medieval England: Towns, Commerce and Crafts, 1086–1348*, Harlow, 1995.

Nightingale, P., *A Medieval Mercantile Community: the Grocers' Company and the Politics and Trade of London, 1000–1485*, New Haven and London, 1995.

Parry, M. L., *Climatic Change, Agriculture and Settlement*, Folkestone, 1978.

Platt, C., *The English Medieval Town*, London, 1976.

Postan, M. M., *The Medieval Economy and Society*, London, 1972.

Prestwich, M., *Edward I*, 2nd edn, New Haven and London, 1997.

Prestwich, M., *War, Politics and Finance under Edward I*, London, 1972.

Raban, S., *Mortmain Legislation and the English Church, 1279–1500*, Cambridge, 1982.

Rackham, O., *The History of the Countryside*, London, 1986.

Taylor, C., *Village and Farmstead: A History of Rural Settlement in England*, London, 1983.

TRHS: Transactions of the Royal Historical Society.

Tuck, A., *Crown and Nobility 1272–1461: Political Conflict in Late Medieval England*, Oxford, 1985.

VCH: Victoria County History.

VCH Cheshire, ed. C. R. Elrington, 3 vols, Oxford, 1979–87.

VCH Oxfordshire, ed. C. R. Elrington et al., 13 rols, Oxford, 1907–96.

VCH Suffolk, ed. W. Page, 2 vols, London, 1907–11.

Ward, J. C., *English Noblewomen in the Later Middle Ages*, Harlow, 1992.

C   Chapter bibliographies

This section lists a selection of titles cited in the footnotes. Details of references not included in the bibliography for a chapter are given at the first citation in that chapter, unless they occur in sections A or B. For the abbreviations of journal titles, see section B.

Introduction

Campbell, B. M. S., 'Measuring the commercialisation of seigneurial agriculture *c.*1300', in Britnell, R. H. and Campbell, B. M. S. (eds), *A Commercialising Economy: England, 1086 to c. 1300*, Manchester, 1995, 132–98.

Hindle, B. P., *Medieval Roads*, Princes Risborough, 1982.

Taylor, J., *The Universal Chronicle of Ranulf Higden*, Oxford, 1966.

Chapter 1: The Land

Bailey, M., 'The concept of the margin in the medieval English economy', *EcHR*, xlii (1989), 1–17.

Bailey, M., '*Per impetum maris*, natural disaster and economic decline in eastern England, 1275–1350', in Campbell, *Before the Black Death*, 184–208.

Baker, A. R. H., 'Evidence in the *Nonarum Inquisitiones* of contracting arable lands in England during the early fourteenth century', *EcHR*, 2nd ser, xix (1966), 518–32.

Campbell, B. M. S., 'Agricultural progress in Medieval England: some evidence from Norfolk', *EcHR*, xliii (1983), 379–404.

Campbell, B. M. S. (ed.), *Before the Black Death: A Study of Social and Agrarian Conditions*, Manchester, 1991.

Campbell, B. M. S., 'Measuring the commercialisation of seigneurial agriculture *c.*1300', in Britnell, R. H. and Campbell, B. M. S. (eds), *A Commercialising Economy: England 1086 to c.1300*, Manchester, 1995, 132–98.

Hoskins, W. G., *The Making of the English Landscape*, London, 1955.

Lennard, R., *Rural England, 1086–1135*, Oxford, 1959.

McNamee, C., *The Wars of the Bruces: Scotland, England and Ireland, 1306–1328*, East Linton, 1997.

Maddicott, J. M., 'The English peasantry and the demands of the crown, 1294–1341', *Past and Present*, suppl. 1, 1975.

Mate, M., 'The agrarian economy of south-east England before the Black Death: depressed or buoyant?', in Campbell, *Before the Black Death*, 78–109.

Mate, M., 'Medieval agrarian practices: the determining factors?', *AgHR*, xxxiii (1985), 22–31.

Mate, M., 'Profit and productivity on the estates of Isabella de Forz (1260–92)', *EcHR*, xxxiii (1980), 326–34.

Poos, L. R., 'The rural population of Essex in the late Middle Ages', *EcHR*, 2nd ser., xxxviii (1985), 515–30.

Postan, M. M. and Titow, J., 'Heriots and prices on Winchester manors', in M. M. Postan, *Essays on Medieval Agriculture and General Problems of the Medieval Economy*, Cambridge, 1973, 150–85.

Razi, Z., *Life, Marriage and Death in a Medieval Parish: Economy, Society and Demography in Halesowen, 1270–1400*, Cambridge, 1980.

Smith, R. M. (ed.), *Land, Kinship and Life Cycle*, Cambridge, 1984.

Stephenson, M. J., 'Wool yields in the medieval economy', *EcHR*, xli (1988), 368–91.

Titow, J. Z., *English Rural Society, 1200–1350*, London, 1969.

Chapter 2: The People: Rural Society

Camille, M., *Mirror in Parchment: The Luttrell Psalter and the Making of Medieval England*, London, 1998.

Coss, P. R., 'Sir Geoffrey de Langley and the crisis of the knightly class in thirteenth-century England', in T. H. Aston (ed.), *Landlords, Peasants and Politics in Medieval England*, Cambridge, 1987, 166–202.

Hatcher, J., 'English serfdom and villeinage: towards a reassessment', *Past and Present*, xc (1981), 3–39.

Hilton, R. H., *A Medieval Society: The West Midlands at the End of the Thirteenth Century*, London, 1966.

Hilton, R. H., 'Peasant movements in England before 1381', in E. M. Carus-Wilson (ed.), *Essays in Economic History*, 3 vols, London, 1954–62, ii, 73–90.

Holmes, G. A., *The Estates of the Higher Nobility in Fourteenth-Century England*, Cambridge, 1957.

Howell, M., *Eleanor of Province: Queenship in Thirteenth-Century England*, Oxford, 1998.

Kershaw, I., *Bolton Priory: The Economy of a Northern Monastery, 1286–1325*, Oxford, 1973.

King, E., *Peterborough Abbey, 1086–1310: A Study in the Land Market*, Cambridge, 1973.

Knowles, C. H., 'The resettlement of England after the Barons' War, 1264–7', *TRHS*, 5th ser., xxxii (1982), 25–41.

McFarlane, K. B., *The Nobility of Later Medieval England*, Oxford, 1973.

McNulty, J., 'Henry de Lacy, Earl of Lincoln (1251–1311)', *Transactions of the Lancashire and Cheshire Antiquarian Society*, li (1936), 19–43.

Mate, M., 'Profit and productivity on the estates of Isabella de Forz (1260–92)', *EcHR*, xxxiii (1980), 326–34.

Page, F. M., '*Bidentes Hoylandie: a medieval sheep-farm*', *Economic Journal, Economic History suppl. 1*, 1929, 603–13.

Parsons, D. (ed.), *Eleanor of Castile, 1290–1990: Essays to Commemorate the 700th Anniversary of her Death on 28 November 1290*, Stamford 1991.

Parsons, J. C., *Eleanor of Castile: Queen and Society in Thirteenth-Century England*, New York, 1995.

Raban, S., 'The land market and the aristocracy in the thirteenth century', in D. Greenway, C. Holdsworth and J. Sayers (eds), *Tradition and Change: Essays in Honour of Marjorie Chibnall*, Cambridge, 1985, 239–61.

Raban, S., 'Landlord return on villein rents in North Huntingdonshire in the thirteenth century', *Historical Research*, lxvi (1993), 21–34.

Razi, Z., *Life, Marriage and Death in a Medieval Parish: Economy, Society and Demography in Halesowen, 1270–1400*, Cambridge, 1980.

Razi, Z. and Smith, R. (eds), *Medieval Society and the Manor Court*, Oxford, 1996.

Schofield, R., 'Did mothers really die? Three centuries of maternal mortality in "The World We Have Lost"', in L. Bonfield, R. Smith and K. Wrightson (eds), *The World We Have Gained: Histories of Population and Social Structure:*

Essays presented to Peter Laslett on his Seventieth Birthday, Oxford, 1986, 231–60.

Smith, R. A. L., *Canterbury Cathedral Priory: A Study in Monastic Administration*, Cambridge, 1943.

Ward, J. C., 'Elizabeth de Burgh, Lady of Clare (d. 1360)', in C. M. Barron and A. F. Sutton (eds), *Medieval London Widows, 1300–1500*, London, 1994, 29–45.

Wretts Smith, M., 'Organisation of farming at Croyland Abbey, 1257–1321', *Journal of Economic and Business History*, xli (1931–2), 168–92.

Chapter 3: The People: Towns and Traders

Barron, C. M. and Sutton, A. F. (eds), *Medieval London Widows, 1350–1500*, London, 1994.

Black, A., *Guilds and Civil Society in European Political Thought from the Twelfth Century to the Present*, London, 1984.

Bridbury, A. R., *Medieval English Clothmaking: An Economic Survey*, London, 1982.

Britnell, R. H., *Growth and Decline in Colchester, 1300–1525*, Cambridge, 1986.

Britnell, R. H., 'The proliferation of markets in England, 1200–1349', *EcHR*, 2nd ser., xxxiv (1981), 209–21.

Britnell, R. H. and Campbell, B. M. S. (eds), *A Commercialising Economy: England 1086 to c.1300*, Manchester, 1995.

Carus-Wilson, E. M., *Medieval Merchant Venturers*, 2nd edn, London, 1967.

Childs, W., 'The English export trade in cloth in the fourteenth century', in R. Britnell and J. Hatcher (eds), *Progress and Problems in Medieval England: Essays in Honour of Edward Miller*, Cambridge, 1996, 121–47.

Harvey, B., *Living and Dying in England, 1100–1540: The Monastic Experience*, Oxford, 1993.

Hatcher, J., 'Mortality in the fifteenth century: some new evidence', *EcHR*, 2nd ser., xxxix (1986), 19–38.

Hilton, R. H., *The Economic Development of some Leicestershire Estates in the Fourteenth and Fifteenth Centuries*, London, 1947.

Hilton, R. H., 'Lords, burgesses and hucksters', *Past and Present*, xcvii (1982), 3–15.

Keene, D., 'A new study of London before the Great Fire', *Urban History Yearbook*, 1984, 11–21.

Lloyd, T. H., *Alien Merchants in England in the High Middle Ages*, Brighton, 1982.

Lopez, R. S. and Raymond, I. W., *Medieval Trade in the Mediterranean World*, London, 1955.

Moore, E. W., *The Fairs of Medieval England: An Introductory Study*, Toronto, 1985.

Nightingale, P., 'The growth of London in the medieval English economy', in Britnell and Hatcher, *Progress and Problems*, 89–106.

Penn, S., 'The origins of Bristol migrants in the early fourteenth century: the surname evidence', *Bristol and Gloucs Arch Soc Trans*, ci (1983), 123–30.

Platt, C., *Medieval Southampton: The Port and Trading Community*, A D *1000–1600*, London, 1973.

Rosser, G., 'Crafts, guilds and the negotiation of work in the medieval town', *Past and Present*, cliv (1997), 3–31.

Westlake, H. F., *The Parish Gilds of Medieval England*, London, 1919.

Williams, G. A., *Medieval London: From Commune to Capital*, London, 1963.

Chapter 4: The Church

Barber, M., *The New Knighthood: A History of the Order of the Temple*, Cambridge, 1994.

Barber, M., *The Trial of the Templars*, Cambridge, 1978.

Burton, J., *Monastic and Religious Orders in Britain, 1000–1300*, Cambridge, 1994.

Camille, M., *The Gothic Idol: Ideology and Image-Making in Medieval Art*, Cambridge, 1989.

Camille, M., *Mirror in Parchment: The Luttrell Psalter and the Making of Medieval England*, London, 1998.

Crosby, A. W., *The Measure of Reality: Quantification and Western Society, 1250–1600*, Cambridge, 1997.

Denholm-Young, N., *Seignorial Administration in England*, London, 1937, new imp. 1963.

Dobson, R. B., *Durham Priory, 1400–1450*, Cambridge, 1973.

Duffy, E., *The Stripping of the Altars: Traditional Religion in England c.1400–c.1580*, New Haven and London, 1992.

Elkins, S. K., *Holy Women of Twelfth-Century England*, Chapel Hill and London, 1988.

Frankis, J., 'The social context of vernacular writing in thirteenth-century England', in P. R. Coss and S. D. Lloyd (eds), *Thirteenth-Century England*, Woodbridge, 1986, 175–84.

Golding, B., *Gilbert of Sempringham and the Gilbertine Order c.1130–c.1300*, Oxford, 1995.

Kershaw, I., *Bolton Priory: The Economy of a Northern Monastery, 1286–1325*, Oxford, 1973.

King, E., *Peterborough Abbey, 1086–1310: A Study in the Land Market*, Cambridge, 1973.

Kosminsky, E. A., *Studies in the Agrarian History of England in the Thirteenth Century*, Oxford, 1956.

McHardy, A. K., '*De heretico comburendo*, 1401', in M. Aston and C. Richmond (eds), *Lollardy and the Gentry in the Later Middle Ages*, Stroud, 1997, 112–26.

Manguel, A., *A History of Reading*, London, 1997.

Menache, S., *Clement V*, Cambridge, 1998.

Pantin, W. A., *The English Church in the Fourteenth Century*, Cambridge, 1955; repr. Toronto, 1980.

Partner, P., *The Murdered Magicians: The Templars and their Myth*, Oxford, 1982.

Platts, G., 'Robert Mannyng of Bourne's "Handlying Synne" and South Lincolnshire Society', *Lincolnshire History and Archaeology*, xiv (1979), 23–9.

Raban, S., *Mortmain Legislation and the English Church, 1279–1500*, Cambridge, 1982.

Rouse, E. C., *Medieval Wall Paintings*, 4th edn, Princes Risborough, 1991.

Rubin, M., *Corpus Christi: The Eucharist in Late Medieval Culture*, Cambridge, 1991.

Stephenson, M. J., 'Wool yields in the medieval economy', *EcHR*, xli (1988), 368–91.

Taylor, J., *The Universal Chronicle of Ranulf Higden*, Oxford, 1966.

Thompson, S., *Women Religious: The Founding of English Nunneries after the Norman Conquest*, Oxford, 1991.

Warren, A. K., *Anchorites and their Patrons in Medieval England*, Berkeley and London, 1985.

Wright, J. R., *The Church and the English Crown 1305–34: A Study Based on the Register of Archbishop Walter Reynolds*, Toronto, 1980.

Chapter 5: Culture

Blake, N. (ed.), *The Cambridge History of the English Language*, ii, 6 vols (general editor: R. M. Hogg), Cambridge, 1992– .

Brand, P., *The Origins of the English Legal Profession*, Oxford, 1992.

Burke, P., *Popular Culture in Early Modern Europe*, London, 1978.

Camille, M., *The Gothic Idol: Ideology and Image-Making in Medieval Art*, Cambridge, 1989.

Camille, M., *Image on the Edge: The Margins of Medieval Art*, London, 1992.

Camille, M., 'The language of images in medieval England, 1200–1400', in Alexander and Binski, *Age of Chivalry*, 33–40.

Camille, M., *Mirror in Parchment: The Luttrell Psalter and the Making of Medieval England*, London, 1998.

Childs, W. R., '"Welcome, My Brother": Edward II, John of Powderham and the Chronicles of 1318', in I. N. Wood and G. A. Loud (eds), *Church and Chronicle in the Middle Ages: Essays Presented to J. Taylor*, London, 1991, 149–63.

Coleman, J., *Public Reading and the Reading Public in Late Medieval England and France*, Cambridge, 1996.

Coss, P., *The Knight in Medieval England, 1000–1400*, Stroud, 1993.

Crane, S., *Insular Romance: Politics, Faith, and Culture in Anglo-Norman and Middle English Literature*, Berkeley and London, 1986.

Gage, J., *Colour and Culture: Practice and Meaning from Antiquity to Abstraction*, London, 1993.

Gage, J., 'Colour in history: relative and absolute', *Art History*, i (1978), 104–30.

Hilton, R. H. (ed.), *Peasants, Knights and Heretics: Studies in Medieval English Social History*, Cambridge, 1976.

Holt, J. C., *Robin Hood*, London, 1982.

Hyams, P., 'The Jewish minority in medieval England, 1066–1290', *Journal of Jewish Studies*, xxv (1974), 270–93.

Mundill, R. R., *England's Jewish Solution: Experiment and Expulsion, 1262–1290*, Cambridge, 1998.

Orme, N., *English Schools in the Middle Ages*, London, 1973.

Plucknett, T. F. T., *Statutes and their Interpretation in the First Half of the Fourteenth Century*, Cambridge, 1922.

Rokeah, Z. E., 'Drawings of Jewish interest in some thirteenth-century English public records', *Scriptorium*, xxvi (1972), 55–62.

Rose, M. and Hedgecoe, J., *Stories in Stone: The Medieval Roof Carvings of Norwich Cathedral*, London, 1997.

Roth, C., 'Portraits and caricatures of medieval English Jews', *The Jewish Monthly*, iv (1950), i–viii.

Rothwell, W., 'The teaching of French in medieval England', *The Modern Language Review*, xiii (1968), 37–46.

Stone, E., 'Profit and loss accountancy at Norwich Cathedral Priory', *TRHS*, 5th ser., xii (1962), 25–48.

Taylor, J., *The Universal Chronicle of Ranulf Higden*, Oxford, 1966.

Turville-Petre, T., *England the Nation: Language, Literature and National Identity, 1290–1340*, Oxford, 1996.

Wickham, C., 'Gossip and resistance among the medieval peasantry', *Past and Present*, clx (1998), 3–24.

Wilkins, N., *Music in the Age of Chaucer*, 2nd edn, Woodbridge, 1995.

Chapter 6: Government and Administration

Brand, P., *The Making of the Common Law*, London, 1992.

Buck, M., *Politics, Finance and the Church in the Reign of Edward II: Walter Stapledon Treasurer of England*, Cambridge, 1983.

Cam, H. M., *The Hundred and the Hundred Rolls: An Outline of Local Government in England*, London, 1930.

Chaplais, P., *Piers Gaveston: Edward II's Adoptive Brother*, Oxford, 1994.

Clanchy, M. T., 'Law and love in the Middle Ages', in J. Bossy (ed.), *Disputes and Settlements*, Cambridge, 1983, 47–67.

Coss, P., 'Sir Geoffrey de Langley and the crisis of the knightly class in thirteenth-century England', in T. H. Aston (ed.), *Landlords, Peasants and Politics in Medieval England*, Cambridge, 1987, 166–202.

Cuttino, G. P., *English Diplomatic Administration, 1259–1339*, 2nd edn, Oxford, 1971.

Denholm-Young, N., *Seignorial Administration in England*, London, 1937, new imp. 1963.

Fryde, N., *The Tyranny and Fall of Edward II, 1321–1326*, Cambridge, 1979.

Hallam, E. M., *Domesday Book through Nine Centuries*, London, 1986.

Hammer, C. I., 'Patterns of homicide in a medieval university town: fourteenth-century Oxford', *Past and Present*, lxxviii (1978), 3–23.

Hanawalt, B. A., *Crime and Conflict in English Communities, 1300–1348*, Cambridge, Mass., 1979.

Harriss, G. L., *King, Parliament, and Public Finance in Medieval England to 1369*, Oxford, 1975.

Maddicott, J. R., 'Law and lordship: royal justices as retainers in thirteenth- and fourteenth-century England', *Past and Present*, suppl. 4, 1978.

Musson, A. and Ormrod, W. M., *The Evolution of English Justice: Law, Politics and Society in the Fourteenth Century*, London, 1999.

Ormrod W. M. (ed.), *England in the Fourteenth Century*, Woodbridge, 1986.

Plucknett, T. F. T., *Legislation of Edward I*, Oxford, 1949.

Post, J. B., 'Crime in later medieval England: some historiographical limitations', *Continuity and Change*, ii (1987), 211–24.

Powell, E., 'Arbitration and the law in England in the late Middle Ages', *TRHS*, 5th ser. xxxiii (1983), 49–67.

Prestwich, M., 'English government records, 1250–1330', in R. Britnell (ed.), *Pragmatic Literacy, East and West, 1200–1330*, Woodbridge, 1997, 95–106.

Raban, S., 'The making of the 1279–80 hundred rolls', *Historical Research*, lxx (1997), 123–45.

Scales, L. E., 'The Cambridgeshire Ragman Rolls', *EHR*, cxiii (1998), 553–79.

Sutherland, D. W., *Quo Warranto Proceedings in the Reign of Edward I, 1278–94*, Oxford, 1963.

Chapter 7: Politics

Binski, P., *Westminster Abbey and the Plantagenets: Kingship and the Representation of Power, 1200–1400*, New Haven and London, 1995.

Buck, M., *Politics, Finance and the Church in the Reign of Edward II: Walter Stapledon, Treasurer of England*, Cambridge, 1983.

Carpenter, D. A., *The Reign of Henry III*, London, 1996.

Childs, W. R., '"Welcome, My Brother": Edward II, John of Powderham and the Chronicles of 1318', in I. N. Wood and G. A. Loud (eds), *Church and Chronicle in the Middle Ages: Essays Presented to J. Taylor*, London, 1991, 149–63.

Chaplais, P., *Piers Gaveston: Edward II's Adoptive Brother*, Oxford, 1994.

Davies, R. R., 'Colonial Wales', *Past and Present*, lxv (1974), 3–23.

Davies, R. R., *Conquest, Coexistence and Change: Wales, 1063–1415*, Oxford, 1987.

Frame, R., *Colonial Ireland, 1169–1369*, Dublin, 1981.

Fryde, N., *The Tyranny and Fall of Edward II, 1321–1326*, Cambridge, 1979.

Hamilton, J. S., *Piers Gaveston Earl of Cornwall, 1307–1312: Politics and Patronage in the Reign of Edward II*, Detroit and London, 1988.

Howell, M., *Eleanor of Provence: Queenship in Thirteenth-Century England*, Oxford, 1998.

Johnstone, H., *Edward of Carnarvon, 1284–1307*, Manchester, 1946.

Maddicott, J. R., *Simon de Montfort*, Cambridge, 1994.

Maddicott, J. R., *Thomas of Lancaster, 1307–22: A Study in the Reign of Edward II*, Oxford, 1970.

Prestwich, M., 'The ordinances of 1311 and the politics of the early fourteenth century', in J. Taylor and W. Childs (eds), *Politics and Crisis in Fourteenth-Century England*, Gloucester, 1990, 1–18.

Rowlands, I., 'The Edwardian conquest and its military consolidation', in T. Herbert and G. E. Jones (eds), *Edward I and Wales*, Cardiff, 1988, 41–72.

Saaler, M., *Edward II, 1307–1327*, London, 1997.

Chapter 8: England and the Wider World

Binski, P., *Westminster Abbey and the Plantagenets: Kingship and the Representation of Power, 1200–1400*, New Haven and London, 1995.

Burman, E., *The World before Columbus, 1100–1492*, London, 1989.

Childs, W. R., *Anglo-Castilian Trade in the Later Middle Ages*, Manchester, 1978.

Childs, W., 'The English export trade in cloth in the fourteenth century', in R. Britnell and J. Hatcher (eds), *Progress and Problems in Medieval England: Essays in Honour of Edward Miller*, Cambridge, 1996, 121–47.

Cuttino, G. P., *English Diplomatic Administration, 1259–1339*, 2nd edn, Oxford, 1971.

Davies, R. R., *Conquest, Coexistence and Change: Wales, 1063–1415*, Oxford, 1987.

Glenisson, J., 'Les Enquêtes administratives en Europe occidentale aux XIIIe et XIVe siècles', in W. Paravicini and K. F. Werner (eds), *Histoire comparée de l'administration*, Munich, 1980, 17–25.

James, M. K., *Studies in the Medieval Wine Trade*, Oxford, 1971.

Johnstone, H., 'The county of Ponthieu, 1279–1307', *EHR*, xxix (1914), 435–52.

Kingsford, C. L., 'Sir Otho de Grandison (1238?–1328)', *TRHS*, 3rd ser., iii (1909), 125–95.

Labarge, M. Wade, *Gascony, England's First Colony*, London, 1980.

Lloyd, S., *English Society and the Crusade, 1216–1307*, Oxford, 1988.

Menache, S., *Clement V*, Cambridge, 1998.

Mundill, R. R., *England's Jewish Solution: Experiment and Expulsion, 1262–1290*, Cambridge, 1998.

Ohler, N., *The Medieval Traveller*, Woodbridge, 1989.

Shealy, E. H., 'The persistence of particularism: the county of Ponthieu in the thirteenth and fourteenth centuries', in J. S. Hamilton and P. J. Bradley (eds), *Documenting the Past: Essays in Medieval History Presented to George Peddy Cuttino*, Woodbridge, 1989, 33–51.

Sumption, J., *Pilgrimage: An Image of Medieval Religion*, London, 1975.

Vale, M., *The Origins of the Hundred Years War: The Angevin Legacy, 1250–1340*, Oxford, 1996.

Wright, J. R., *The Church and the English Crown, 1305–34*, Toronto, 1980.

Conclusion

Barrow, G. W. S., *Robert Bruce and the Community of the Realm of Scotland*, Edinburgh, 1988.

Childs, W., 'Resistance and treason in the *Vita Edwardi Secundi*' in M. Prestwich, R. H. Britnell and R. Frame (eds), *Thirteenth-Century England*, vi, Woodbridge, 1997, 177–91.

Fryde, N., *The Tyranny and Fall of Edward II, 1321–1326*, Cambridge, 1979.

Maddicott, J. R., *Simon de Montfort*, Cambridge, 1994.

Prestwich, M., *War, Politics and Finance under Edward I*, London, 1972.

Index

Places in England and Wales are located by current counties in the index and by medieval counties in the text.